Can Ho~

THE HISTORICAL SERIES OF THE REFORMED CHURCH IN AMERICA, NO. 47

Can Hope Endure?

A HISTORICAL CASE STUDY IN CHRISTIAN HIGHER EDUCATION

James C. Kennedy & Caroline J. Simon

WILLIAM B. EERDMANS PUBLISHING COMPANY
GRAND RAPIDS, MICHIGAN / CAMBRIDGE, U.K.

Wm. B. Eerdmans Publishing Co.

255 Jefferson Ave. S.E., Grand Rapids, Michigan 49503 /
P.O. Box 163, Cambridge CB3 9PU U.K.

www.eerdmans.com

Printed in the United States of America

10 09 08 07 06 05   7 6 5 4 3 2 1

Library of Congress Cataloging-in-Publication Data

ISBN 0-8028-2858-2

The Historical Series of the Reformed Church in America

The series was inaugurated in 1968 by the General Synod of the Reformed Church in America acting through the Commission on History to communicate the church's heritage and collective memory and to reflect on our identity and mission, encouraging historical scholarship which informs both church and academy.

General Editor
  The Reverend Donald J. Bruggink, Ph.D.
  Western Theological Seminary

Commission on History
  James Hart Brumm, M.Div., Blooming Grove, New York
  Lynn Japinga, Ph.D., Hope College, Holland, Michigan
  Mary L. Kansfield, M.A., New Brunswick, New Jersey
  Scott M. Manetsch, Ph.D., Trinity Seminary, Deerfield, Illinois
  Melody Meeter, M.Div., Brooklyn, New York
  Jesus Serrano, B.A., Norwalk, California

Contents

CONTENTS

Preface

Can Hope Endure? is a collaboration born of shared curiosity and concerns. When we began our research for this project, we suspected that Hope College is, if not unique, at least a rare institutional type in the landscape of American higher education. Our investigations into Hope's past, together with what we know about the nature and history of religiously affiliated colleges and universities, have borne this out. As is widely believed, the common pattern of colleges founded by church bodies is a weakening of the connection with their roots — often culminating in what historian George Marsden calls "established nonbelief." One main strand of Hope College's oral tradition makes the college look exceptional, depicting Hope as following the predictable trajectory, yet subsequently changing course. We were curious to verify whether this was so and, if it was, to investigate why and how Hope College moved toward "reestablishment" of the role of religion in its institutional life. We write out of a deep concern that Hope College, and other church-related institutions, continue to cultivate the means through which they remain faithful, in practice as well as words, to living out a Christian identity. Because of the rarity of reestablishment, the results of our investigation yield important lessons for all those who care about the future of church-related higher education. Furthermore, we discovered that Hope has lived out a complex "Middle Way" — a valuable variation on more standard models among denominational, evangelical, and mainline Christian colleges.

Can Hope Endure? is enriched by the "binocular vision" resulting from a professional historian and a professional philosopher examining the same body of data.[1] In addition to the depth perception fostered by interdisciplinary cooperation, our vision has been binocular in other ways as well. *Can Hope Endure?* was written by two people who had vivid but differing points of view at the time of the occurrence of the events described in Chapter Seven of this book. We are aware of the complications of being not just narrators but actors in the drama and try to face those complications in four ways: first, by talking through our differing earlier views and striving for mutual correction by challenging one another's initial interpretations of the data; second, by listening carefully and reading carefully new data from interviews and documents; third, by praying for the grace to have what twentieth-century moral philosopher Iris Murdoch called a "just and loving gaze"[2] for all the people whose stories make up the history that we are recounting; fourth, by acknowledging that our efforts to transcend any distorting personal biases are likely at times to fall short. With full awareness of our limitations, we have done our best to look squarely at Hope College in all its periods and say as much of the truth as we thought we could see and responsibly tell. As we worked, it became clear that though our vision is binocular, it converged on a univocal story that we can jointly tell.

Part of the reason that we were able to come to a shared understanding of Hope College's story is because we have been looking at

1. The differences in training between the authors have resulted in a differentially shared burden. As a historian, Professor Kennedy executed and oversaw most of the initial sifting of archival materials, conducted most of the interviews, and wrote the first draft of almost all of the historical narrative of the book. As a philosopher, Professor Simon's role has been three-fold. First, on the basis of her reading of the growing body of literature of church-related higher education, she framed many of the questions that shaped Kennedy's archival work. Second, she read a substantial amount of the archival material that had made the "first cut" for potential relevance to our investigation and supplemented (and at times disputed) his initial construction of the story. Lastly, she was the initial drafter of the more "reflective" or "philosophical" portions of the manuscript. In all cases, we passed drafts back and forth and revised one another's material; the book as a whole has become a joint product throughout.

2. Iris Murdoch, *The Sovereignty of Good* (New York: Ark, 1985), 66-72.

the same data, but a more important source of our agreement is theological. Despite our differences, we both see the rhythms of all history as the interplay of guilt and grace and — where grace has abounded and borne fruit — gratitude that God works despite human brokenness. In the end, we see Hope College's story through this lens, and this leads us to be unsurprised by the fact that there is much to admire about the story's protagonists, but also elements of Hope's history to wince at and regret.

It is with this in mind that we set before you the story of a very ordinary, though distinctive, college with very ordinary struggles. The saga that we have written reveals a college meeting challenges — at some times more successfully than others — and responding to external pressures and internal tensions that might have undermined its Christian identity. The resources Hope College called on lay in its own complex nature and heritage.

Can Hope Endure? does not pretend to be a comprehensive history of the college, in the manner attempted by the two existing histories of the college, Preston Stegenga's *Anchor of Hope* (1954) and Wynand Wichers's *Century of Hope* (1968). These accounts both offer a wider view of the college's past than is the case here, where our focus is on the religious nature of the school. Nor is the focus of this book even on religion, or Christianity, in the broadest sense of either term. The central historical question of this book is: How did Hope develop and sustain a Middle Way that differentiated it from both typically mainline and evangelical Protestant institutions?[3] Obviously, the quality of religious life at Hope College, from the activities of the religion department to Bible studies and social activism, is deeply relevant to

---

3. Historians of American Christianity who see mainline and evangelical Christians as having more in common with one another than with those (such as confessional Lutherans, Catholics, and Reformed) who stress more objectively churchly aspects of faith might doubt that negotiating a middle way between evangelicalism and mainline ecumenism is an especially interesting feat. (D. G. Hart, correspondence with the authors, February 5, 2004.) Yet the attempt to follow such a middle way is important to this particular history because it shaped Hope College's self-conception throughout so much of its life. Moreover, many current discussions, not just of church-related higher education but of internal and external denominational politics, assume that the divide between evangelicals and mainline Protestants is bridged only with difficulty. Thus, assessing the extent of Hope's success in bridging this divide has broad relevance.

that question. But the point of the study is not to catalog all the ways Hope College was (or was not) religious, but to account for the chief reasons why Hope College seems to have taken a path not frequently taken in American higher education.

Such a focus has determined both the research interests and the nature of documentation used in this book. On the one hand, we have tried to offer a wide sampling of religious expression as manifested at Hope College — students, faculty, trustees, administrators and alumni. Without making soundings of the religious culture at Hope College at various levels, we cannot aspire to make our history of the school comprehensible. For that reason, we have tried to listen to a range of voices throughout the length of Hope's history. On the other hand, the institutional direction of the college was often steered, at least in the largest contours, by the presidents of the colleges, and, at various points in the college's history, by the Board of Trustees. For that reason, we have made extensive use of revealing archival materials from presidential papers and Board materials — most of it never before published.[4] For that reason, the presidents of Hope College in particular loom large in our study.

Similarly, not all issues of religious identity have been given equal weight. For example, we have concentrated, especially for the period since the 1960s, on the hiring policy, and more specifically on the debate concerning whether only Christians ought to be hired. Given the pivotal role of the faculty in the Christian ethos of the school, this struck us as quite important — and it receives more emphasis than, say, the percentage of students attending church on a given Sunday — an interesting but less direct indicator of the school's religious character.

In sum, this is a history that is essentially *institutional* in its orientation — that is, it is concerned with the religious identity of Hope Col-

---

4. Hope College's Presidential and Board of Trustee archives, normally sealed for thirty years, were made available to us up through 1987 through the gracious permission of President Emeritus Gordon Van Wylen, President James Bultman, and Board of Trustees chair Kermit Campbell. For understandable reasons, access to any more recent materials from sealed archives has been impossible. Consequently the account of Hope's story from 1988-1999 is based only on accessible official archive materials, personal materials from various sources, and interviews. Moreover, time constraints severely restricted the number of relevant parties interviewed.

lege as an institution. At the same time, we have consciously tried to avoid the trap of conventional institutional history, in which the less pleasant aspects of history are tactfully avoided and the positive constantly accentuated. We have not touched Hope College up, though we have made choices about levels of disclosure out of sensitivity to the reputations of persons both living and dead. We have constantly distanced ourselves from writing a celebratory history of Hope College, yet the story written here is not in any way intended as a lamentation or a narrative of decline. We believe Hope's religious history shows too much historical complexity and moral ambiguity to make such a case. At the same time, we have consciously constructed a cautionary tale, a reminder that if communities like Hope College do not collectively come to a shared sense of Christian purpose that is at once broad and deep, the cultural forces around them — most of them not very friendly to Christianity — will make their choices for them. We hope that readers may gain some inspiration from our story, but that inspiration must come through an open and sometimes painfully honest appraisal of the school's past.

Our writing has consciously participated in an ongoing dialogue on the nature and sustainability of church-related higher education. Chapter One places Hope College in the context of the varied array of institutions founded by Christian bodies and examines the forces that test the durability of those institutions' religious identities. "Hope and Durability" frames the thesis questions that drive our inquiry: How did Hope College come to be the complex hybrid it was in the mid- and late twentieth century? And how durable is this hybrid?

Chapters Two and Three focus on Hope College's founding and the forces that shaped its early history. These chapters examine how Hope's early conception of its mission was formed by a set of complex tensions that made it natural for the college to pursue what we call the Middle Way. In Hope's first seventy-five years it was at once deeply Christian and focused on producing graduates who would be agents of transformation by serving the wider world. Its ethos was at once pious, practical, and progressive.

No human institution is static, and Chapter Four shows Hope College, even before the mid-twentieth century, feeling tugs and tensions that might lead it away from its early mission of producing messengers of hope who would elevate humanity. From 1925 onward

Hope had to face hard questions: Could it remain faithfully and fervently religious while remaining financially viable and, increasingly, academically ambitious?

As Chapter Five shows, as this question became urgent in the 1960s a positive answer to it seemed more doubtful. Would the acceleration of social change in the surrounding culture pull Hope College further and further from its religious roots? Or, alternatively, would Hope turn inward and become defensive in order to preserve its religious identity? As the title of this chapter indicates, this seemed at the time to many to be a period of crisis for Hope's Middle Way, a period that could have led to a weakening of Hope's Christian character.

If the 1960s can be read as a period of disestablishment, the 1970s, 1980s, and 1990s can be read as an extended period of reestablishment of Hope's Christian mission. Chapter Six examines how a Neo-Middle Way was negotiated that seemed, at least to many at the college, to re-center Hope, allowing it to remain faithful to its mission without being defensive or reactive. Chapter Seven, which deals with the period from 1987-1999, shows that historical trajectories can be both unpredictable and ambiguous. For some the overt religious fervor that filled Hope College's voluntary chapel services to capacity in the late 1990s were the fruition of the reestablishment of Hope's religious identity begun in the mid-1970s. For others, the 1990s were another vivid test of Hope College's Middle Way. Seen in this light, the 1960s tested the Middle Way by subjecting it to the forces of religious liberalism and (some would say) religious indifference; the late-1990s were a mirror image of this pattern — a time when the forces of religious conservatism were openly hostile to a *via media*.

But these broad summaries are by their very nature distorting — leaving out the historical complexity and moral ambiguity that truthful narrative requires and which Chapters Two through Seven aspire to supply. Chapter Eight seeks to reflect back on the larger picture that emerges from Hope's history, which is at once a winding path and a remarkably durable pattern of re-centering in the face of forces that push and pull at the college over time. As a liberal arts college Hope is heir to the classical tradition that took "know thyself" as a maxim for the cultivation of wisdom. As a Christian college Hope is heir to the exhortation of the epistle of James to not be like the absent-minded and foolish who look at themselves in a mirror and immediately forget what they see. *Can Hope Endure?* holds up the mirror of Hope College's history; its final chapter examines what that mirror can reveal about the steps that not just Hope College but any college that cherishes its Christian mission must take to sustain a Christian identity in the twenty-first century.

Acknowledgments

This work grew out of an earlier essay, "A Contested Past: The Role of Religion in Hope College's History, 1945-1987." Several dozen of our Hope College colleagues participated in a stimulating discussion of that essay. Many of them also sent us comments and suggestions, which have been incorporated into this expanded narrative.[5]

We are deeply grateful to the Rhodes Regional Consultation on the Future of Church-Related Higher Education and the Hope College Office of the Provost for grants that funded work on this project. Tim Cupery, Michael Douma, Melissa LaBarge, Paul Simon, and Michael Van Beek, Hope College students who assisted in the archival work for the project, were of significant help in early stages of our research. Geoffrey Reynolds and Lori Trethewey, of the Joint Archives of Holland, gave us deft and patient service. Many people generously gave of their time for interviews and shared materials with us from their personal archives. We would also like to thank D. G. Hart, Jeffery Tyler, Jacob Nyenhuis, James Boelkins, William Reynolds, E. W. Kennedy, and Anthony Perovich for the extremely helpful comments they made on drafts of the work and Elton Bruins of Hope College's A. C. Van Raalte Institute for constructing the biographical notes contained in Appendix Two.

Lived experience is denser than even the most thorough historical narrative can convey. We owe a debt of gratitude to many, many people who have poured out some portion of their lives for Hope College and made it a better place. This debt has made decisions of whom

---

5. In examining the question about disestablishment and reestablishment of elements of Hope's religious identity in the 1960s through the 1980s, we initially investigated the period from 1945 to 1987. Readers of the resulting essay urged us to expand the project from Hope's founding to 1999.

to name — whose work to take explicit note of and to place in the fore-
ground — painful at times, most especially in the part of Hope's history that we lived through. We could not write a book long enough to
acknowledge by name all the vital work of our colleagues, nor that of
those from Hope's past whose lives we have glimpsed through doing
this project. Their labors made Hope College and our lives better in
ways to which, regrettably, we cannot do full justice within these
pages.

1 Hope and Durability

- Can Christian Colleges Long Endure?
- Forces Testing Endurance
- Tensile Strength or Shapelessness?

On April 6, 1999, odd things were happening in Winants Auditorium at Hope College. Several dozen people were spread throughout the considerable expanse of the room, but what on earth were they doing? Although everyone faced the front of the room, there was no speaker or media presentation. People sat in silence; from time to time someone would silently get up to leave or someone new would silently enter. The earliest participants had arrived at 3:00 p.m. At 4:00 one of them stood up and thanked people for coming, at which point people quietly left.

This was not some piece of cutting-edge performance art, nor was it a psychological or sociological study of people's responses to group silence. Those among the faculty and staff of Hope College who came and went that day were responding to an invitation from a colleague to wait together. As the invitation said, "When a person waits alone, it is sometimes hard to tell waiting from indecision and dithering. But when the community waits together with openness and hope, especially when it is divided about the alternatives, that waiting can be empowering. In my view, waiting is not a passive process, but an active search."[1] Many of those who came — perhaps especially those

---

1. April 2, 1999, e-mail from Prof. Don Cronkite, personal archives of Ben Patterson.

who came the next week and the next to repeat the same exercise — found this an appropriate and useful way of being together at a time when their differences seemed to have turned speech into a rancorous cacophony. President Jacobson and his wife Jeanne were among the participants, as were faculty on various sides of issues that had been hotly debated in the 1990s (and earlier) at Hope College: the role of Christian commitment in the hiring policy for faculty; the practical consequences that the college's "context of the historic Christian faith" should have on campus-wide academic discussion and on college policy (especially regarding socially contested issues such as sexuality); how and whether it was possible for those with very different interpretations of the Christian tradition to move forward in a common direction. Most recently, these differences had coalesced into fierce loyalties to and strong aversions toward Hope College's innovative chapel program, headed by Dean of the Chapel Ben Patterson.

To some this might seem to be a low point for the life of this institution, and for most it was certainly a painful one. The pain for those at Hope College in 1999 was intensified by how much *niceness* had been a hallmark of Hope's ethos. Indeed, external experts brought in to evaluate the divisional and department structure of Hope in the fall of 1992 cautioned that "the enormous warmth and kindness people have for one another" might inhibit needed frank discussion about allocation of resources. They advised "that people may owe one another a bit more courage in their exploration of difficult issues."[2] Reaching a point where silence seemed the only way of being together without increasing pain must have made many present feel that the times were indeed out of joint.

Seen in another way, however, it is striking that Prof. Donald Cronkite, a member of the Biology Department, had issued an invitation to the faculty and staff of the Hope College community to wait together, and it is surprising that so many responded. Hope College was calling on spiritual resources at its core to live through troubled times. Hope College in the 1990s described itself as Reformed and ecumeni-

2. December 15, 1992, report of the External Divisional Review Team, Div/Dept Review Dec. 7-9, 1992, file, Joint Archives of Holland (hereafter JAH). The point of this review was to assess the effectiveness of the academic administrative structure comprised of three deans, each reporting to the provost, with responsibility for four divisions.

cal, and Cronkite was both a member of a Reformed church and deeply appreciative of Quaker practice. The fact that liberals and conservatives, Catholic and Protestant, faculty and administrators, could find some joint comfort in this practice of waiting "with openness and hope" shows that many at the college were unwilling to settle for either bitterness or permanent enmity. They were also unwilling to pretend that their disagreements were unimportant — a sign of courage and conviction.

This silent waiting was indeed out of the ordinary. But the roots of the deep divisions that led to its need, and the resources that made "openness and hope" a natural and not irrational response to those divisions, lie in Hope College's history. Moreover, though Hope College's history is particular, the story of the formation and travails of Hope's religious identity yields transferable lessons about the challenging enterprise of Christian liberal arts education.

Can Christian Colleges Long Endure?

To many who knew Hope College intimately in the late 1990s, the college seemed to be engaged in rhetorical and ideological civil war. Many of those who loved Hope College considered it special because it pursued a Middle Way: neither sectarian nor indifferent to its Reformed Christian identity; not creedal in its requirements of prospective faculty yet caring about whether they had a Christian faith; nurturing students' faith but mandating neither Christian affirmation for admission nor Christian practices after matriculation; neither wholly mainline nor wholly evangelical. With apologies to Abraham Lincoln, one might say that the 1990s tested whether Hope College, or any college, so conceived and so dedicated could long endure. And this is perhaps the most pressing question facing any church-related college or university — whether the sort of place it has become has a sustainable future. In the last several decades, many have asked that question about Christian higher education across the board. *Is* there hope for Christian liberal arts institutions? How *can* they endure in an age in which the divide between the church and the academy appears so wide and deep?

Like many who have written on this topic, we think that answers

3

to questions about the durability of Christian higher education are found in historical evidence. We join an ongoing conversation with a growing number of participants — a conversation worth having in no small part because its participants differ over their readings of the history of Christian higher education and in their degree of optimism about durability. Since its publication in 1994, Notre Dame historian George M. Marsden's widely cited *The Soul of the American University: From Protestant Establishment to Established Nonbelief*[3] has become a touchstone for discussion and debate.[4]

The leading question addressed by *The Soul of the American University* concerns two facts that seem, when taken together, somewhat surprising. First, almost all institutions of higher education established before the early twentieth century in the United States were founded with explicitly Christian aspirations. Second, by the late twentieth century many of these same institutions shared a widespread assumption that specifically Christian concerns were irrelevant or prejudicial intrusions in relation to the highest academic pursuits. Given that Marsden concentrates on Protestant colleges and universities, another way of framing Marsden's question is, as his subtitle indicates, How did higher education in America move from Protestant establishmentarianism to established nonbelief?

Marsden observes that virtually all the private colleges in the United States were founded by religious groups. Moreover, by as late as 1870 the vast majority of colleges in the United States had clergymen-presidents who taught courses defending biblical Christianity and who were concerned that Christianity be a living presence on campus. Yet, by the early twentieth century the evangelical Protestantism of many of these "old-time colleges" had been effectively excluded from the classrooms of the leading universities into which they had evolved. Marsden's exploration of how this came about is rich in specific accounts of individual institutional sagas, including careful examinations of the

3. George Marsden, *The Soul of the American University: From Protestant Establishment to Established Nonbelief* (New York: Oxford University Press, 1994).

4. Examples of valuable book-length discussions that we will not have space to treat here are Arthur J. De Jong, *Reclaiming and Mission: New Directions for Church-Related Colleges* (Grand Rapids: Eerdmans, 1990); Arthur F. Holmes, *The Idea of a Christian College* (Grand Rapids: Eerdmans, 1975, 1987); and Page Smith, *Killing the Spirit: Higher Education in America* (New York: Viking, 1990).

histories of Harvard, Yale, Princeton, Columbia, and the University of Chicago, as well as many leading state research universities.

Both fans and critics of Marsden often misinterpret his telling of the history of the American academy as a story of almost inevitable spiritual decline. The expression "slippery slope to secularism" is often used as a short formula for what Marsden has been assumed to reveal. That this oversimplifies and distorts his view is brought out quite clearly in a passage from an essay that slightly predates *The Soul of the American University*. In this essay by the same name, Marsden says,

> It is important to underscore that criticizing American higher education as it is typically defined today is far different from arguing that there was a lost golden age to which we should return. The contrast with former eras does highlight some features of the situation today; but that does not imply that one should return to former practices. Those practices themselves were often faulty and in need of correction and have thus led to over-correction that helped to set the current patterns. For instance, the old colleges and their predecessors were part of a Christian establishment that provided Christianity with an unjustly privileged social and political position and attempted to promote the faith by associating it with power and coercion. Although these institutions had many good features as well, they needed to be disestablished. Moreover, the nineteenth-century American colleges also simply needed to be improved academically.[5]

Though Marsden recognizes that the factors leading religiously affiliated colleges and universities to be assimilated to a homogeneous secular academy are formidable, he does not see this as inevitable nor, as indicated above, does he equate all aspects of secularization with decline.

The slogan "slippery slope to secularism" does, however, aptly characterize the reading of the history of the academy given by James Tunstead Burtchaell in his book *The Dying of the Light: The Disengagement*

---

5. George Marsden, "The Soul of the American University," in Marsden and Bradley J. Longfield, eds., *The Secularization of the Academy* (New York: Oxford University Press, 1992), 10.

of Colleges and Universities from Their Christian Churches.[6] Burtchaell's massive work examines the stories of dozens of schools founded by Congregationalists, Presbyterians, Baptists, Methodists, Lutherans, and Catholics. His conclusions are stated in terms of slippery slopes. Faculty at such colleges would, early on, be active participants in the religious identity of their college, but over the years a distinct trend would emerge. Faculty who once led chapel became passive attendees; eventually even attendance was viewed as a burden to be avoided. "The identity [of the college] would slide from [for example] Methodist to evangelical, to Christian, to religious, to wholesome, to 'the goals of the college' which by then were stated in intangible terms."[7] It is easy to see why Burtchaell called his book *The Dying of the Light.*

Yet in some ways this title is misleading, for there are indications that Burtchaell, like Marsden, also doubts that there was a past golden age. He doubts, in fact, that the connection between the colleges he examines and their founding denominations was ever very vital or significant: "It is fair to say that while every one of the colleges was from the start identified with a specific church, denomination, or movement, there was no manifest intensity in that identification, no very express concern to confirm or to be intellectually confirmed or critical within the particular faith of their communions."[8] This raises doubts about whether there was ever much light to die out.

Yet, compelling as some have found the Marsden thesis and its bleaker Burtchaellian version, there are optimists who see the matter at least somewhat differently. *The Sacred and the Secular University*[9] by Jon H. Roberts and James Turner, to take an example, is optimistic because its authors see the story of secularization as a kind of coming-of-age story. While they agree with Marsden and Burtchaell that there are powerful forces that erode the religious affiliations of church-related colleges and universities, they are almost uniformly pleased with the outcome.

Roberts and Turner's telling of the history of Christian higher ed-

6. James Tunstead Burtchaell, *The Dying of the Light: The Disengagement of Colleges and Universities from Their Christian Churches* (Grand Rapids: Eerdmans, 1998).

7. Burtchaell, *The Dying of the Light,* 829-30.

8. Burtchaell, *The Dying of the Light,* 823.

9. Jon H. Roberts and James Turner, *The Sacred and the Secular University* (Princeton, N.J.: Princeton University Press, 2000).

ucation is in some ways a more detailed account of what Marsden notes under the label of professionalization and methodological secularism (factors about which we will have more to say in the next section). They are more optimistic than Marsden and Burtchaell because they see secularization as having salutary effects. Specialization and methodological naturalism have been phenomenally successful, according to Roberts and Turner, in producing new knowledge. They emphasize that the de-centering of religious concerns is a natural outgrowth of specialization rather than the product of intentional efforts to disengage from founding churches. An introduction to the book, written by John F. Wilson, emphasizes the positive aspects of Roberts and Turner's telling of the history of American higher education. The decline of ecclesiastical control over higher education has made the modern university "freer to attend to the manifold religions of our society, and of the world at large, acknowledging their variety and responding to their vitality."[10] Moreover, the universities' independence from all particular religious groups allows for a critical distance and freedom to ask hard questions about abuse of power by the Church. Thus, Roberts and Turner indicate that it is a natural and good thing for "knowledge to shed its Christian chrysalis."[11]

Richard T. Hughes and William B. Adrian's *Models for Christian Higher Education: Strategies for Success in the Twenty-First Century*[12] and Robert Benne's *Quality with Soul: How Six Premier Colleges and Universities Keep Faith with Their Religious Traditions*[13] are optimistic for different reasons. These authors think that many institutions are counterexamples to prognostications of secularization. They believe many Christian colleges and universities have endured — remaining identifiably Christian and fully committed to (indeed improving their provision of) liberal arts education. They are convinced that the odds of future durability are increased by grasping the explanations of these specific instances of successes and replicating them.

Hughes and Adrian's approach is denominational and historical;

---

10. Roberts and Turner, *The Sacred and the Secular University*, 14.

11. Roberts and Turner, *The Sacred and the Secular University*, 122.

12. Richard T. Hughes and William B. Adrian, eds., *Models for Christian Higher Education: Strategies for Success in the Twenty-First Century* (Grand Rapids: Eerdmans, 1997).

13. Robert Benne, *Quality with Soul: How Six Premier Colleges and Universities Keep Faith with Their Religious Traditions* (Grand Rapids: Eerdmans, 2001).

Models of Christian Higher Education examines pairs of institutions affiliated with Roman Catholic, Lutheran, Reformed, Mennonite, Evangelical, and Baptist/Restorationist groups. Their concern is in exploring how "denominational distinctives and particularistic theological perspectives" shape Christian institutions of higher learning.[14] In his closing summary essay, William Adrian notes that while all of the institutions in *Models* have broadened and become more accommodating to their surrounding culture, "one countercultural element remains in common to all of the schools — a commitment to the validity and transcendence of the Christian faith."[15]

Robert Benne looks at six particular institutions that he sees as both successfully pursuing academic excellence and preserving their traditions. He attempts to discern from them general features that are markers of health for church-related colleges and universities. Benne's positive outlook leads him to list factors contributing to preservation of religious identity. Among those are (1) a founding tradition that produces enough intellectually capable individuals who see the relevance of faith to higher education to provide a healthy pool of future faculty and administrators, (2) good two-way communication between the college and its denomination, (3) seats on the board of trustees designated for members of the founding denomination, (4) leadership that provides effective vision linked to the founding tradition, (5) attention to the religious commitments of faculty when hiring and to those of students when recruiting, and (6) resources that provide institutional support to a well-attended chapel program and religious co-curricular activities. Benne also points out that at pivotal points in the life of an institution, one person can make a considerable difference: "all of the six schools surveyed had at one time or another real 'giants' who by force of personality and vision provided charismatic leadership."[16]

Given these conflicting viewpoints, how durable *is* Christian higher education? And — more fundamentally — is the history of higher education in America a developmental story, a coming-of-age story, or a tale of loss of soul or dying of the light? Even this brief sur-

14. Hughes and Adrian, *Models for Christian Higher Education*, 4.
15. Hughes and Adrian, *Models for Christian Higher Education*, 449.
16. Benne, *Quality with Soul*, 189.

vey of pessimists and optimists has revealed that disagreements come from at least two sources.

One source of disagreement involves variations in the sort of evidence examined and how that evidence is weighed. It is quite clear, for example, that Burtchaell and Benne take a very different attitude toward institutional self-ascriptions. Burtchaell often treats them with skepticism, while Benne gives them considerably more credence.

The second source of variation is more crucial: divergences concerning what counts as "good news" or success for church-related institutions. And here there are a myriad of questions. How *much* accommodation to the surrounding culture is compatible with living out of a robust sense of particularity as an institution shaped by a Christian tradition? The cultural ethos in the twenty-first-century United States is, in many places, at least vaguely religious and in some places much more than that; does it really count as "countercultural" in such an environment to have a broadly Christian commitment? And when does broadness become so broad as to be indistinguishable from diffuse spirituality or generically humanist[17] sentiment? *Can* an institution maintain a distinctive Christian identity without closing itself off from the demands of truth and justice? Is it indeed possible to reform the practices that Marsden reveals as shaped by Protestant establishmentarianism without undermining religious identity? Are institutions that consider themselves successful at pulling off the preservation of "quality with soul" simply adept at positive self-talk even as they unknowingly slide down the slippery slope to secularism? Over these matters, pessimists and optimists of various sorts will obviously differ.

Yet at the heart of all the matters over which pessimists and optimists disagree is a fundamental agreement: there *are* indeed powerful forces afoot that can and will test the endurance of any college that cares about preserving an active tie to its Christian foundation and vision. And these forces bring pressure to bear on actual academic communities: faculty, administrators, and students. To a more careful examination of these forces we now turn.

---

17. "Humanist," as we use the term, refers to one who is concerned with the study and welfare of human beings. "Humanism," though used by some as a negative term, is a positive thing. Our point here is just that, while there certainly are many Christian humanists, being a humanist is not in itself a Christian distinctive.

Forces Testing Endurance

Canvassing both the pessimists and the optimists yields an extensive list of forces that test endurance. The factors that Marsden identifies as contributing to the disestablishment of Protestant Christianity and the establishment of nonbelief are complex, but one key factor was a widespread desire to avoid "sectarianism." Although the early colleges in the United States were all founded by specific religious groups, it was generally agreed soon after their founding that these colleges should be "nonsectarian." This nonsectarianism arose, in part, from student concerns. Protestant students who were not members of the founding tradition of the college (say, Methodist students at a Presbyterian college) objected to required participation in a form of worship that made them feel excluded. They also did not want to take required theology classes that implied that their religious views were inappropriate. As this concern for "nonsectarianism" began to be applied to faculty, it meant that, for example, faculty should not be at threat of losing their jobs on the basis of taking a stand on issues that were a matter of "in-house" debate among Protestants. This "nonsectarianism" was, however, "exclusivist Protestant" in that it was assumed that Catholics, Jews, or "free thinkers" would not be suitable faculty members (and in most cases that they would not be suitable students). This Protestant exclusivism, which flavored the atmosphere at both private Protestant colleges and public universities, gave a strong motivation (though, of course, not the sole motivation) to Catholics and Jews to found their own institutions of higher learning.[18]

By the end of the nineteenth century, nonsectarianism was beginning to be defined more broadly:

> Exclusivist Protestant aspects of the outlook were becoming an embarrassment in a more diverse society. State schools felt the pressures first, but very soon so did any schools, especially prestigious schools, that hoped to serve the whole society. In the decades from the 1880's until the First World War, such schools rapidly moved away from most of their substantive connections with their church or religious heritages, dropping courses with explicit theo-

18. Marsden, *The Soul of the American University*, 55-59, 76.

logical or biblical references and laicizing their boards, faculties, and administrations.[19]

This more broadly conceived nonsectarianism eventually resulted in "an 'inclusive' higher education that resolved all the problems of pluralism by virtually excluding all religious perspectives from the nation's highest academic life."[20]

As the significance of nonsectarianism was being reconceived, so was the role of the professoriate. As late as the mid-nineteenth century, most faculty members were expected to be generalists who could teach almost anything.[21] However, by the late nineteenth century the German research university model was having an increasing influence on American educators. Under this influence, research (the discovery or creation of new knowledge) was seen as the primary role of professors, especially at graduate universities, replacing the older model of the college teacher as a disseminator of received knowledge and a shaper of student character. The emphasis on research was accompanied by an assumption of specialization, for few were likely to make original contributions to multiple fields of study. This trend resulted in a growing assumption that a professor should refrain from holding forth on subjects outside his field of expertise. Whereas it might have been normal prior to the 1870s for someone teaching a science course to point out how the order of nature provides an occasion for praising the Creator, such theological pronouncements by non-theologians came, as the nineteenth century gave way to the twentieth, to be viewed by an increasing number of scholars as unprofessional.

The rise of a scientific-technological ideal of inquiry and its widening application to more and more fields of study led to what Marsden calls "methodological secularization" or what Douglas Sloan calls the "two realms" theory of knowledge.[22] The scientific method, and by extension scholarly methodology in general, was assumed to be value-neutral and devoid of theological assumptions:

---

19. Marsden, "The Soul of the American University," 26.

20. Marsden, *The Soul of the American University,* 5.

21. Marsden, *The Soul of the American University,* 81.

22. Douglas Sloan, *Faith and Knowledge: Mainline Protestantism and American Higher Education* (Louisville: Westminster John Knox Press, 1994).

. . . when entering the laboratory, pious Christians were expected to leave their religious beliefs at the door, even if they had prayed God to bless their work and came from their discoveries praising God for his work. Diversity of religious beliefs also made it particularly important for scholarly cooperation that their substance be kept out of the laboratories. Since the laboratory became a key metaphor and model for all advanced intellectual work, this ideal was extended throughout the university.[23]

Academic excellence, even at colleges and universities with explicitly Christian mission statements, came to be identified with the fruits of methodological secularization. As Sloan points out,

By the mid-twentieth century . . . "academic excellence" had become defined almost entirely in terms of the intellectual canons of the research university and its discursive, instrumentalist, and quantitative conception of knowledge. The basic assumptions of these canons meant, therefore, that now allegiance to academic excellence would, by definition, make increasingly marginal whatever distinctively religious orientation and commitments the college might have.[24]

In light of methodological secularization and the two-realms view of knowledge, the true scholar, whatever his or her religious commitments or lack thereof, was expected to apply the same religiously neutral procedures of inquiry to his or her field. To do anything else was to be seen as unscholarly and unprofessional.

One pervasively influential institutional embodiment of professionalization is *The 1940 Statement of Principles on Academic Freedom and Tenure*. This statement deserves extended attention, for its use has been crucial to shaping the American academy; moreover, the questions both the history of its original formulation and that of its interpretation raise about the linkage between professionalization and secularization are pivotal. The *1940 Statement* was co-authored by representatives of two national organizations, the American Association of University Professors (AAUP) and the Association of American Col-

23. Marsden, *The Soul of the American University*, 156.
24. Sloan, *Faith and Knowledge*, 204.

leges (AAC).[25] Historian Walter P. Metzger enriches Marsden's briefer treatment of the story, especially regarding the role of the AAC in the framing of the *1940 Statement*. Many of the institutions whose presidents were members of the AAC were church-related and were quite serious about their Christian identity and mission. Metzger attributes what he calls the "limitations clause" of the *1940 Statement* to the influence of the AAC, on the assumption that some AAC representatives were administrators of institutions concerned to preserve their religious identity. The limitations clause is the sentence that reads, "Limitations of academic freedom because of religious or other aims of the institution should be clearly stated in writing at the time of the appointment." The clause implies that limitations on academic freedom *are* in fact legitimate if promulgated in the right way. Metzger gives cogent historical reasons for thinking that this sentence would not have been in the *1940 Statement* if the AAUP, an organization whose ideals Marsden calls "the apotheosis of non-sectarianism," had been the sole author of the document and if the AAC had not included many church-related colleges who cared about their Christian identity.[26]

Though the framing of the *1940 Statement* involved secularists and "religionists," the term "limitations clause," quite often used in discussion of the *1940 Statement*, clearly signals the assumption that institutional neutrality is the "norm" of academic freedom. Subsequent controversies over the clause reinforced what Marsden calls the establishment of nonbelief. In the mid-1960s a special committee of the AAUP was formed to examine the issue of academic freedom at church-related colleges and universities. In a 1964 statement, the AAUP's Committee A on Academic Freedom and Tenure stated that church-related institutions should exercise wisdom and restraint in limiting academic freedom. They also maintained that "At some point in the scale of self-imposed restrictions a college or university that comes under them may, of course, cease to be an institution of higher education according to prevailing conceptions."[27] The Special Committee's assumption of institutional neutrality as a norm was embod-

25. Marsden, *The Soul of the American University*, 305-12.
26. Marsden, *The Soul of the American University*, 306.
27. Quoted in W. J. Kilgore, "Report of the Special Committee on Academic Freedom in Church-Related Colleges and Universities," *AAUP Bulletin*, Winter 1967, 369.

ied in its urging that "religious privilege not be employed to provide a sanctuary in which to avoid the full responsibilities of institutions of higher education" and encouragement to reconsider "any employment of this special clause."[28] Indeed, the current version of the AAUP statement includes an "interpretative" note saying that this clause may no longer be relevant, since many church-related institutions no longer think it necessary to limit academic freedom. Thus, recent AAUP discussions of the limitations clause imply that any exercise of it would put a church-related institution in jeopardy of no longer being a genuinely academic institution.

This illustrates what is perhaps one of the most vexing challenges facing Christian higher education. The history of *The 1940 Statement of Principles on Academic Freedom and Tenure,* whether looked at as a developmental story à la Roberts and Turner or as a slippery slope story à la Burtchaell, does look like a natural trajectory, for good or ill. Yet if concern about freedom of inquiry leads to secularization, indifference to academic freedom is no safe antidote. None who care about Christian higher education want to head down the slippery slope, yet rigidity and reactive fear of open inquiry hardly looks like a safe or sane alternative. As Richard Hughes laments, "many Christian colleges — and this is a story that Marsden and Burtchaell did not trace — cling so tightly to a particularistic, *a priori,* Christian worldview that they place limits on the search for truth, largely abandon the Enlightenment-based presuppositions of higher education, and thwart any possibility that they might eventually take their place in the larger American culture as serious colleges and universities of the highest order."[29] Indeed, it seems concerns of this sort were behind the AAUP motion that resulted in the formation of the Special Committee on Academic Freedom in Church-Related Colleges and Universities. This was not, in intent, a committee designed to foist a secularist agenda onto church-related schools, and if members at church-related schools had not suffered under what they perceived to be institutional rigidity, it is unlikely that the committee would have ever existed.[30]

28. Kilgore, "Report of the Special Committee," 369-70.

29. Hughes and Adrian, *Models for Christian Higher Education,* 1-2.

30. The motion for the committee's formation called for it to be "composed predominately of members from church-related institutions." The committee, in pursuing

But rigidity is not the only problematic stance for an institution to take, for some forms of flexibility amount to insipid shapelessness. Here Burtchaell's bracing skepticism may be a salutary reminder. As we indicated briefly above, Burtchaell's pessimism is fueled by his view that the rhetoric of his subject institutions is "more delusional than deceitful."[31] He thinks that

> the divorce between colleges and churches has been befogged by vision statements, goals statements, statements of purpose, covenants, bylaws, catalogue blurbs, reports from seminars and retreats, conversations, and other bilious prose which surge in greatest abundance just when the critical turn has been made, just when there is no longer any realistic possibility of restoration.[32]

While wholesale *a priori* skepticism about institutional self-descriptions is unwarranted, self-delusion (as a possibility rather than as a foregone conclusion) represents an additional potential obstacle to be acknowledged and guarded against by Christian colleges and universities that wish to maintain a robust religious identity.

In addition, Burtchaell adds what he calls the "subversive influence of Pietism"[33] to our growing list of forces that test endurance. Burtchaell's quarrel with pietism is that it tends to emphasize the spirit over the letter, individual commitment over institutional identity, and heart over head. Moreover, "pietists are inveterate simplifiers."[34] When pietism permeates a Christian academic institution, it will be unlikely that the Christian character of the college will reside in the classroom and much more likely that it will "live an eccentric existence in chapel, in volunteer service, and in clean living and all-around manhood."[35] Burtchaell sees pietism as affecting almost all of the institu-

---

its task, inquired into the actual policies on academic freedom of over two hundred church-related colleges; the results of this research shaped their recommendations. Moreover, the chair of the committee, W. J. Kilgore, was from Baylor University, a Baptist institution of a relatively conservative bent theologically.

31. Burtchaell, *The Dying of the Light*, 850.
32. Burtchaell, *The Dying of the Light*, 849.
33. Burtchaell, *The Dying of the Light*, 839.
34. Burtchaell, *The Dying of the Light*, 839.
35. Burtchaell, *The Dying of the Light*, 844.

tions that he examines, Protestant and Catholic alike, and affecting them for the worse.

Finally, economic forces also test the durability of Christian higher education, as Marsden and Adrian both acknowledge. Starting quite early in the history of church-affiliated institutions, colleges and universities sought to "market" themselves to broader populations of students. Few denominationally founded institutions could afford to cater only to students from their founding denomination. As colleges and universities sought to increase their academic reputation in order to compete, they were also less likely to hire through an "old boys' network" that allowed for discreetly prescreening faculty candidates for "acceptability" or "fit with the institution." Thus student bodies and faculties tended to become less and less religiously homogeneous. External accrediting agencies and funding sources often exerted pressure toward a nonsectarianism that amounted to secularism. The Carnegie Foundation, for example, offered attractive retirement programs for faculty members of colleges and universities, but only if the institutions were "nonsectarian."[36] Phi Beta Kappa has denied chapters to almost all Catholic and conservative evangelical colleges and universities on the grounds that their religious stance inhibits academic freedom.[37] More than one college dropped its former religiously explicit mission statement in response to such influences.[38]

Adrian underscores the more recent danger of having one's institutional agenda co-opted by the quest to attract "students and parents who are careful and demanding 'shoppers' in a consumer environment" by "responding to both the needs and whims of an activist clientele."[39] Institutions who are tempted to become all things to all "customers" obviously undermine distinctiveness, putting not only their religious identity but their nature as liberal arts institutions at risk.

The durability of Christian higher education thus will depend on

36. Marsden, *The Soul of the American University*, 281-82.

37. Marsden, *The Soul of the American University*, 437-38.

38. Marsden gives detailed accounts of how these factors affected Vanderbilt and Syracuse University, but notes that within the first four years of the Carnegie-funded retirement program that excluded "sectarian" institutions, twenty schools severed their denominational ties in order to qualify for participation (*The Soul of the American University*, 281-85).

39. Hughes and Adrian, *Models for Christian Higher Education*, 449.

adeptly meeting a complex array of challenges and striking salutary balances. Sectarian rigidity leads to a kind of living death by ossification for an academic institution, while unexamined accommodationism — whether market-driven adherence to the latest passing fad in the surrounding culture or status-driven acquiescence to the guild and the secular academy — leads to death by a thousand equivocations and compromises. Keeping all these forces that test endurance in mind, it is now time to descend from the rarified air of generality into which our brief survey of recent literature of Christian higher education has taken us. We now turn our attention to a particular case study in Christian higher education: Hope College in Holland, Michigan.

Tensile Strength or Shapelessness?

Seeing how uneasily Hope fits into the helpful typology of church-related colleges in Robert Benne's *Quality with Soul* helps to shed light on Hope College's peculiar nature. Benne groups institutions into four types: orthodox, critical-mass, intentionally pluralistic, and accidentally pluralistic. *Orthodox* institutions in Benne's classification see the relevance of their Christian vision as pervasive. They require a shared point of view upon matters that they view as fundamental to their faith tradition among their entire faculty and staff and, many times, among their students as well. *Critical-mass* institutions in Benne's classification give Christianity (and perhaps a specific Christian tradition) a privileged voice within the institution. They seek to have that voice embodied in a critical mass (a majority or a sizable minority) of their faculty and students. Religion courses will almost always be among the required courses at critical-mass institutions, but it would not necessarily be assumed that a "Christian perspective" would be taken in all courses throughout the curriculum. *Intentionally pluralist* schools are more likely to describe themselves as having a Christian heritage than to emphasize Christianity or a particular faith-tradition as part of their present identity. In such institutions, Christianity is one voice in the conversation, but it is not necessarily a privileged or even a very strong voice. Hiring policy at such institutions may weigh a candidate's identification with the institution's founding religious tradition as a positive but not decisive factor among many others. Finally, in *ac-*

cidentally pluralist institutions there is virtually no public acknowl-edgement of the institution's religious heritage. Benne sees a major di-vide between orthodox and critical-mass institutions on the one hand and intentionally and accidentally pluralist institutions on the other. In orthodox and critical-mass institutions, a Christian vision is the orga-nizing principle of the college or university. In pluralist institutions of both types, organizing principles have secular sources. As we will see, Hope College is difficult to categorize, even in a more complicated and refined revision of Benne's taxonomy. This reveals how complex Hope's present conception and practice of its religious nature is.

We prefer to substitute the term "comprehensive" for Benne's "orthodox," for not all institutions that seek to have their entire faculty be of a certain sort think of institutions that differ from them as hetero-dox.[40] Some colleges, for example, Abilene Christian University, seek to hire all of their faculty from their founding tradition. We will call these colleges and universities *comprehensively denominational* institu-tions. Other colleges, like Wheaton College, seek to hire only faculty members who can ascribe to a non-denominational or inter-denominational faith statement that is evangelical in content. We will call these schools *comprehensively evangelical* institutions. Other col-leges, like Whitworth, for example, might strive to hire all faculty members who are professing Christians but make only broad, ecu-menical stipulations about the nature of Christian faith and practice. We will call such colleges and universities *comprehensively ecumenical* institutions. As Marsden's history illustrates, yet another possible cat-egory would be that of *comprehensively Protestant,* the category initially exemplified by most of the institutions he examines.

In the same way that distinctions can be made among different types of comprehensive schools, critical-mass schools may be distin-guished in terms of what sort of critical mass they value. Some institu-tions (*denominational critical-mass* schools) might think it is important

40. In the earlier essay that contained the seeds of this book, we substituted the term "purist" for Benne's "orthodox" label and noted a variety of ways of being purist. Having found through discussion of that essay that "purist" (which we intended to be wholly descriptive) is almost impossible to strip of its evaluative overtones, we here em-ploy the term "comprehensive." The "purist" label is also used in Caroline J. Simon et al., *Mentoring for Mission: Nurturing New Faculty at Church-Related Colleges* (Grand Rapids: Eerdmans, 2003).

to have a critical mass of people who identify with the founding denomination of the college or university. Others (*ecumenical critical-mass schools*) value preserving a commitment to the Christian faith (as variously understood and practiced in many denominations) among a sizable portion of their faculty. Moreover, many nuances could be introduced into this taxonomy. An institution might, for example, be a hybrid of comprehensive ecumenical and critical-mass denominational, requiring all faculty to be Christians of some sort while also seeking to keep a critical mass of adherents of the college's founding denomination within its ecumenical mix.

Hope College is affiliated with the Reformed Church in America (RCA), a denomination that since the mid-nineteenth century has sought to be part of mainstream American Christianity,[41] albeit with regional differences in emphasis between the evangelical and mainline elements within its makeup. Founded officially as a four-year liberal arts college in 1866, in the first century of its existence Hope College primarily attracted students who were ethnically Dutch, doctrinally Reformed, and from the Midwest. However, Hope at present has many of the characteristics that Robert Benne attributes to critical-mass institutions. For example, Hope has voluntary rather than required chapel, and it is not owned by the RCA. With no substantial monetary support coming directly from the denomination and far less than half of its students being members of the RCA, Hope falls somewhere between critical-mass and intentionally pluralist classifications with regard to financial support and the composition of its student body. At the same time, Hope does seek to do what it can to recruit a "critical mass" of RCA students even in the face of declining numbers within its founding denomination. In the last several years, these efforts have resulted in about 20 percent of its students coming from its parent denomination.

However, despite these markers of a critical-mass or intentionally pluralist nature, Hope College's official hiring policy, for at least the last decade, has been interpreted (and probably implemented) by its administration as what we would call "comprehensively ecumenical."[42]

---

41. See Chapter Two.

42. The "probably" here stems from several complications, one being that since Hope encompasses a variety of opinions about what is central to the Christian faith,

One of the major controversies among the college's constituencies in the 1980s and 1990s was whether the policy, as stated in the faculty handbook, is a broadly Christian critical-mass policy or a comprehensive policy.[43] Hope strives to hire faculty who are committed Christians, but outside of the upper administration, it does not officially exercise a preference for Reformed Christians among its faculty. Hope College has no statement of faith to which faculty are asked to assent, though some candidates who consider themselves Christians would not pass muster with all of those responsible for evaluating their fit with Hope during the search process. That Hope College is serious in its striving for a comprehensively Christian faculty is evidenced by continuing institutional accountability on the issue of commitment to the Christian mission. Faculty members are asked to address how they see themselves contributing to the mission of the college as part of their evaluation for tenure and promotion to associate professor.

Even this brief sketch makes it clear why calling Hope College "comprehensive" — even when the term is combined with "ecumenical" — seems an uneasy fit for the college's present realities. Indeed, one might doubt that Hope's hybrid nature would allow it to be comprehensive about any part of its practice or self-conception. How did Hope College become the hybrid that it now is — combining comprehensive, critical-mass, and pluralist elements?

This book is, of course, largely a story of the historical forces that explain how Hope came to be such a hybrid. Despite its abiding ties to a Reformed denomination, and despite claims of being "rooted in the Reformed tradition," the college is a hybrid, not just structurally, but religiously. In fact the college, like its founding denomination, has stood at the crossroads of three related theological impulses. The first (if not in terms of present influence, then at least in length of pedigree) is Calvinism. Hope's founders had a deeply Calvinist vision for the college they saw as their "anchor of hope" for the future.[44] And indeed

---

those with a "broader" conception of Christianity may think that Hope's practice has been too restrictive to be ecumenical, while those with a "tighter" conception may think that some, perhaps numerous, exceptions have been made to the purportedly "comprehensive" policy.

43. See Chapters Six and Seven. The Hope College Faculty Handbook contains the official college policies regarding procedures and governance.

44. See Chapters Two and Three.

Hope College still exhibits sensibilities historically linked to Calvinism, such as acknowledging the "sacredness of secular work and study." One of the central ways the Reformed tradition has shaped colleges that call that tradition home is by taking seriously intellectual inquiry of all sorts. The Belgic Confession, one of the three standards of faith for Reformed Christians, cites knowledge of the "most excellent book" of natural creation as, along with the Bible, one of the two chief means we have of understanding God.[45] Calvinists have done at least their share in founding strong liberal arts colleges, in part to create an educated clergy, in part because they have taken seriously the importance of a broad curriculum for an educated laity. They value knowledge of God's creation because they wish to glorify God in all areas of life. In this respect, Hope College's educational vision still is clearly Reformed.

Yet other religious impulses have also profoundly shaped the college. Because the Reformed stand theologically in the middle of the Protestant spectrum, and because they have often shown strong affinities with wider American culture, it has been relatively easy for them to identify with broader currents in American Protestantism. Since its inception, Hope College has been strongly influenced by one such current: American evangelicalism. Evangelicalism, with its emphasis on "heart" religion, has been a second theological strand supplementing Calvinist influences. In contrast to more rationalistic strains of Calvinism, the religious culture at the college has tended to stress personal piety and character, with less emphasis placed on doctrine or on a systematic organization of a "distinctively" Reformed or Christian academic program. Stemming from this somewhat pietistic tradition, too, is a high commitment to the Christian ministry. In fact, Hope was founded as a place to train ministers, missionaries, and teachers for both the Western United States and the wider world. As a result, Hope has seen a very high percentage of its graduates serve in these callings.

This early emphasis on "heart" religion explains, at least in part, why what many consider another hallmark of Calvinist pedagogy — the intellectualist project of integrating faith and learning — is less evident at Hope than those familiar with other Reformed colleges might

---

45. The Belgic Confession, 1561 (revised 1619), Article II.

expect.[46] In contrast to some other Reformed colleges, Hope has never been particularly prescriptive about how Christian faith touches upon the academic endeavor; indeed, its academic community encompasses those with widely different stances on this issue, from faculty who systematically work out the implications of "a Christian world and life view" to those who ignore the issue altogether. Because of the college's non-prescriptive stance on this issue, and because of the religious diversity that this stance has engendered, some find it difficult to characterize Hope's educational vision as manifestly Reformed. Yet, as we will see,[47] its emphasis on shaping Christian character stemmed from the same Reformed impulse as its more intellectualist fellow Calvinist institutions — for at Hope the point of forming Christians was so that they could transform the world.

Hope's evangelical religious ethos, which was still evident in the immediate postwar period, became less pronounced during the 1960s, though many in the school's constituency — and some key officials in the administration — continued to identify with the evangelical view thereafter.[48] American evangelicalism found new vitality on campus in the course of the 1990s, in part because of what some would see as an influx of conservative Protestant students and what others would see as an emboldening of conservative students who had always been present in large proportions.[49] There is widespread agreement that Hope's religious climate shifted in the mid-1990s, in no small part because a Dean of the Chapel of decidedly evangelical conviction developed a popular, if controversial, student ministry and worship program. At the turn of the second millennium, the importance of

46. See Chapters Two and Three. While clearly evident at schools outside the Reformed tradition, the idea of integrating faith with learning — of attempting to bring one's faith to bear in the practice of one's scholarly efforts — has been for some time an explicit and guiding ideal at Christian Reformed colleges, for example, Calvin College and Dordt College. Christian scholars who are animated by this impulse often take their faith seriously in their academic endeavors by allowing their basic convictions to have a "governing interest" in the selection of topics for study. Moreover, for Reformed Christians, basic background religious beliefs characteristically function as "control beliefs" in the adjudication of competing truth claims. Reformed Christians hold that one appropriately accepts or rejects theories on account of their accordance with Christian beliefs.

47. See Chapter Three.

48. These changes and continuities will be addressed in Chapters Four and Five.

49. See Chapter Seven.

personal piety was again being underscored at Hope, in the filled-to-capacity chapel — if not in every classroom.

This evangelical emphasis relates uneasily to the third identifiable religious impulse at the college — the ecumenical Christian. Indeed, "uneasily" may be all too mild a term, given the painful conflicts that generated the "waiting" episode with which we began this chapter. When did the ecumenical impulse begin to manifest itself at Hope? Here there are no easy answers, for, a century ago, the difference between what we now call "mainline" and "evangelical" barely existed, and the term "ecumenical" was often used by Protestants to mean "inclusive of other Protestant groups not too dissimilar to ours." What can be said is that from the end of the nineteenth century Hope's leadership and faculty often consisted of men and women who considered themselves progressive-minded Protestants, eager for the Holland colony to shed its immigrant conservatism and engage the wider world. They did not go as far as A. J. Muste, a 1905 graduate who later became a leading American pacifist, but they held steadfastly to the "forward" look, more interested in (at least moderate) social progress than doctrinal purity. Academic excellence and the disinterested search for truth, free from "sectarian" inhibitions, were also central components of this mindset, and Hope's strong academic program, particularly in the natural sciences, was nurtured in no small part by it.

In the 1960s, this progressive Protestantism was transformed into a wider ecumenical vision that was willing to embrace other Christian traditions and, for some, other faiths or none at all as well.[50] Some would tie this ecumenical impulse back to Calvin, who they see not only as affirming that all truth is God's truth, but also that the discovery of that truth may come through the wisdom of those with other faith commitments.[51] Whatever the case, inspired by this ecumenism,

---

50. See Chapter Five.

51. In an unpublished essay ("Christian Higher Education: A Reformed Perspective"), Hope College professor of religion Steven Bouma-Prediger takes this view, quoting Calvin's *Institutes of Christian Religion* II.2.15: "Shall we deny that the truth shone upon the ancient jurists who established civic order and discipline with such great equity? Shall we say that the philosophers were blind in their fine observation and artful description of nature? Shall we say that these men were devoid of understanding who conceived the art of disputation and taught us to speak reasonably? Shall we say that they are insane who developed medicine, devoting their labor to our benefit? What shall

the college community has attempted to be hospitable to a wide range of belief and opinion. Indeed, many thought that Hope's ecumenism was becoming so broad and pervasive in the 1960s and early 1970s that a course correction was needed in order to prevent ecumenism from sliding into broad humanism and from there into secularism.[52] Yet despite those "checks" on the breadth and pervasiveness of Hope's ecumenical impulse, and despite what some would see as the ascendancy of evangelicalism in the late 1990s, Hope's faculty members still come from various branches of the Christian tradition, Roman Catholic, Orthodox, and Protestant. Officially, students of all faiths, or of no faith, are not only admitted but embraced as valued members of the college community. Furthermore, the ecumenical influences at the college have also given Hope graduates a strong impetus to engage in social witness, noticeable since the 1960s. This ecumenical Christian stance was particularly influential at the college in the 1960s and 1970s, though now too it is probably the vision with which the majority of faculty resonate most, and not a few alumni.

Hope's Reformed *cum* evangelical *cum* ecumenical hybrid explains, to a large extent, its mix of pluralist, critical-mass, and comprehensive features. The history unfolded in the central chapters of this book will make the details of these interconnections apparent.

But our goal is not just to understand how Hope College came to be a peculiar hybrid; it is to address the pressing question of its durability. Whether Hope's complex hybrid can endure is crucially dependent on whether it is a loose collection of disparate elements that constantly threaten to pull apart — to cannibalize, suppress, or exile one another — or whether its strands can be braided into a strong, flexible and mutually-correcting whole. Attempts have been made to state briefly what unites Hope's varied strands. The short mission statement developed in the late 1970s defines the college's purpose as offering "with recognized excellence academic programs in the liberal arts in the setting of a residential, undergraduate, coeducational college, and in the context of the historic Christian faith." A document meant

---

we say of all the mathematical sciences? . . . [W]e cannot read the writings of the ancients on these subjects without great admiration. . . . But shall we count anything praiseworthy or noble without recognizing at the same time that it comes from God?"

52. See Chapters Five and Six.

to function as an expansion of that brief statement, "A Vision of Hope," approved by the Board of Trustees in 1997, states that Hope is "a Christian college, ecumenical in character while rooted in the Reformed tradition." While there is wide verbal assent to these self-descriptions among Hope College's constituencies, the episode with which we opened this chapter — and more particularly the events leading up to it — call into question whether there is substantive consensus over Hope's nature and mission among and between its faculty and leadership. Even more crucially, the painful conflicts within the Hope College community during the 1990s throw into question whether Hope's complex hybrid possesses either coherence or a stabilizing center of gravity.[53] Those questions make this a vital time for Hope College to examine the history of its religious identity, for as contemporary philosopher Charles Taylor asserts, "We determine what we are by what we have become, by the story of how we got there."[54]

As this historical essay will make evident, Hope's history is open to both an optimistic and a pessimistic reading. As we will see in the coming chapters, Hope has indeed been shaped by the forces that test the durability of its Christian mission. An optimistic reading of Hope's story, in broad brush strokes, is that its early development of a hearty hybrid nature combining Reformed, evangelical, and ecumenical/progressive elements allowed it to develop a Middle Way that had tensile strength. While the forces of secularization *did* affect the college, its tensile strength allowed it to respond creatively to those forces — using them to hone its growing edges — while still maintaining a vivid but not rigid Christian identity. On this reading, the swerve toward secularization Hope appears to have taken in the 1960s and the raucous tug-of-war of the late 1990s were tests of Hope's endurance that it passed with flying colors — or at least with passing marks. A pessimistic reading of Hope's story, in equally broad strokes, is that Hope's sense that it was walking a Middle Way that combined its Reformed, evangelical, and ecumenical impulses has been, as Burtchaell might

53. Indeed, those more poetic than historically minded might, instead of being reminded of Lincoln's question and asking themselves whether Hope could long endure, have thought of W. B. Yeats and lamented (echoing his poem "The Second Coming"), "things fall apart; the center cannot hold."

54. Charles Taylor, *Sources of the Self* (Cambridge, Mass.: Harvard University Press, 1989), 48.

say, more delusional than deceitful. In its darkest version, pessimism would hold that the center never did hold; Hope's Middle Way has never been coherent or sustainable; the winds of the late 1990s cleared the fog of self-deception and revealed that Hope must make a choice. On this stark reading, Hope must decide to throw its weight in one of two directions, both of which have significant risks. Hope can move forward with an ecumenical vision that effectively excludes evangelicals and embrace the risk of attenuating its Reformed character into a shapeless, post-Christian spirituality or broadly humanist sentiment. Alternatively, Hope can risk rigidity by throwing its weight toward an evangelicalism that guards the purity of its Christian commitment in the usual way — faith statements to which faculty and students must subscribe; expectations about personal conduct meant to shape character into at least the appearance of Christian virtue; and checks on academic explorations that endanger theological self-definition.

The question of whether either wholesale optimism or wholesale pessimism, or some more nuanced assessment, is warranted cannot be adjudicated in an historical vacuum. We will return to these questions in due course in our final chapter after we have investigated what Hope College is at the turn of the second millennium by tracing how it got there.

2 The Roots of Hope College's Middle Way: Religious and Cultural Contours, 1866-1945

- Western Men, Eastern Money
- "Local Morality" and Churchly Vigilance
- Dutch Pilgrims and American Citizens

The roots of Hope College's Middle Way run deep in her history. Even prior to World War I, negotiating the tensions inherent in bridging diverse religious impulses, constituencies, and cultural influences had not only become habitual but was an explicit self-conception. The forces that held Hope to a "vital center" were multiple: the geography and culture of its Midwestern (then "Western") locale in Holland, Michigan, over against that of its early benefactors, the more sophisticated and wealthy power centers in the Eastern United States to which Hope College was a debtor financially and culturally; its Reformed and evangelical concern for the purity of the gospel and Christian propriety over against its abhorrence of schism and world-despising asceticism; its ethnic makeup heavily influenced by its Dutch immigrant origins over against its aspiration to be proudly American. Hope College's success depended on finding a middle way, as Edward Dimnent put it in 1918, between Iowa, on the one hand, which "found fault with one of our men because he was not Calvinistic and with another because he did not lead the chapel exercises" and the East, "which finds us all to[o] 'hide-bound'" on the other.[1] That the tensions of the Middle Way were not — are not — fully resolved goes a long way toward

1. Edward Dimnent, letter to Harry Hoffs, 20 November 1918, in "Correspondence from Dimnent, 1918-1919," in Dimnent Presidential Papers, JAH.

explaining why Hope College, even now, is situated along a boundary between more liberal and conservative theological currents in American life.

Western Men, Eastern Money

Hope College is the offspring of a single denomination, the Reformed Church in America. But it also owed its existence to the asymmetrical — and sometimes difficult — relationship between two quite different religious communities. The college's success depended upon the high degree of cooperation these two communities enjoyed with each other, yet some of its troubles would originate in the persistent differences between them.

By 1840, the Dutch Reformed Church had exerted a major presence in America for over two hundred years. The great majority of its congregations lay in New York and New Jersey, near the original communities of the first Dutch settlers. By the mid-nineteenth century, it was also wholly an English-speaking denomination, though by formal creeds and historical memory it retained a sense of kinship to the Netherlands. It was also, by American standards of the day, a relatively prosperous, educated, and — if then-President Martin Van Buren may serve as illustration — well-connected religious community, not the social and political equal of the Episcopal or Presbyterian churches, but close to it. To a very large extent, they were integrated into the mainstream American Protestantism of the nineteenth century: evangelical,[2] ecu-

2. As D. G. Hart has noted, in the late nineteenth century in the United States, "Although differences between liberal and conservative segments of the largest Protestant churches were beginning to surface, most members of these denominations considered themselves evangelical in the sense that they affirmed the deity of Christ, the authority of the Bible, the necessity of conversion, and the duty of holy living" (*That Old Time Religion in Modern America* [Chicago: Ivan R. Dee, 2002], 19). Hart goes on to state that "After the 1940s, an evangelical was someone who may have believed and practiced the same religion as nineteenth-century Protestants — a high regard for the Bible and its practicality, belief in the necessity of conversion and holy living, and zeal in seeking the conversion of others. But this form of faith no longer prevailed in America's oldest and largest denominations and their affiliated organizations" (20). Though Hart at points talks as if it is the surrounding culture and mainline Protestantism that changed while evangelicals held fast to pre-twentieth-century Protestant affirmations, a large part of

menically minded,[3] and increasingly less interested in doctrinal questions. What the Reformed lacked, however, were substantial numbers, either in terms of established Americans or new immigrants. As Congregationalists, Presbyterians, Baptists, and Methodists moved to establish institutions in the West, the Reformed Church did relatively little in the way of institution-building beyond their traditional base, despite the exhortations of the Rev. James Romeyn for the church to expand westwards with the country, and, as he put it in 1842, "train Western men for Western work on Western soil." It was Romeyn, in fact, who was one of the first in the denomination to see how the arrival of Dutch immigrants under Albertus Van Raalte to Western Michigan in the winter of 1847 played into this vision.[4]

Van Raalte and his fellow settlers — despite the fact that they shared the same Calvinist creeds with Romeyn and the Reformed in the Eastern United States — were cut from substantially different cloth. They spoke Dutch, of course, and were frequently of a lower economic and educational stratum. Their religious experience had been shaped in recent years by persecution in their land of origin after they had seceded from the established Reformed Church. The settlers' understanding of church, education, state, and society was molded by traditions and lessons learned in the Netherlands. In religious terms, though strong on Christian experience, they tended to be more doctrinal, less ecumenical, and (in the nineteenth century) less revivalist than the Americanized churches of the Eastern U.S. This did not preclude many of them from developing a willingness, even eagerness, to

---

the story that he tells concerns transformations within conservative Protestantism that resulted in post-World-War-II evangelicalism adding new elements to Protestant orthodoxy. These included, first, such a severe degree of pessimism about human nature that the trajectory of history was seen as inevitable decline that was accelerating and would end with the imminent return of Christ. Second, from the 1920s on, it involved grave suspicions about innovations in science, especially evolutionary biology, which in turn led to repugnance for most extra-Biblical higher learning. Third, it developed an interpretative scheme for the Bible that set out to accentuate its miraculous and supernatural nature.

3. As we have indicated in Chapter One and will see more clearly as this history unfolds, "ecumenical" shifts its meaning over time but during this period should be read as "nonsectarian Protestant."

4. See Henry Dosker's history of the college in *The Hope College Annual*, 1905, 103; Wynand Wichers, *A Century of Hope* (Grand Rapids: Eerdmans, 1968), 33.

learn the new ways of their adopted country, but it would be years, even decades, before the habits of mind instilled by the Old Country faded away.

Upon arrival in America, Van Raalte's group was financially befriended by key ministers in New York, and in this way found an ecclesiastical home in the Reformed Church, formally joining the denomination in 1850. Not all stayed — some came to distrust the "Eastern" church and formed the Christian Reformed Church in 1857 — but the theologically irenic Van Raalte and most of his followers did remain. The Union of 1850 that brought Van Raalte's group into the Reformed Church was a strategic partnership, offering the Eastern church a base in the West and in turn rendering the Western settlers badly-needed financial and institutional support. But the partnership was not one of equals. Not only did the Eastern church[5] possess much more wealth and control over the established denominational institutions, they were also much larger numerically. By the time of Van Raalte's death in 1876, the "Western" church did not quite constitute a fifth of Reformed Church in America (RCA) membership, though by this time it was growing rapidly from immigration and high birth rates. In the 1960s they finally surpassed the Eastern wing of the church in size.[6] But for the balance of the nineteenth century, institution-building in the Western RCA would depend not only on Western energy and Western vision, but on Eastern goodwill and Eastern pockets.

The advantages to the Reformed Church of creating and sustaining schools in the West were evident. The West needed Christian schools to instruct a regional leadership among the new settlers. This had been the vision of Romeyn, and as early as 1848 it was proposed that the settlers make possible "the academic preparation of schoolmasters, pastors and missionaries."[7] Training local students to meet local educational needs was certainly an important motivation, but the importance of missionaries in the early vision of the Michigan Hollanders is striking; the purpose of the Pioneer School, a precursor to Hope College founded in 1851, was "that our children be formed to

5. Defined here as anything east of Buffalo, New York.
6. "And Yet," *Christian Intelligencer*, 19 July 1877, 4.
7. This according to Van Raalte in Classis of Holland session; "Minutes of Classis Holland," 12 September 1872, 160.

spread the light of the Gospel in the dark places of the earth."[8] The educational ideal advanced by Van Raalte and other leaders in the "colonie" was at once local and universal, secular and religious; Eastern supporters of the Western churches were in complete agreement with this broad vision. All agreed that the West needed a Christian school of higher education, since the future of local Reformed congregations, and the denomination's general impact in the West, depended on creating educated Christian leaders there, both lay and clerical.

However, tensions arose between East and West over what *kind* of higher educational institution was needed to accomplish this purpose. For many Americanized Easterners, the answer was obvious: the liberal arts college, of the kind that already dotted the educational geography of the United States. The answer was, in short, an institution not unlike Rutgers College in New Brunswick, New Jersey, a school founded and sustained by the Reformed Church. Such a college would broadly train students to become scholarly, cultivated, and full of Christian character, whether they entered the ministry (as many did) or not. Philip Phelps, the first president of Hope College, would largely take his ideas of a liberal arts college from his own experience at Union College in New York, a school with strong, if informal, ties to the Reformed church. In this vision, Hope College would provide a liberal arts education to the best and brightest of the West — and send graduates who wanted to become ministers to the RCA's New Brunswick Theological Seminary in New Jersey.

But this was not Van Raalte's vision, however much he worked to maintain close ties with the East. Instead, his

> . . . goal was to make [Hope] a point of life for the whole Western Church, a Western New Brunswick.
>
> It would be an institution of general Scholarly development, but *for* and *above* all, preachers and missionaries would be prepared for their life's work. . . .
>
> It cannot be emphasized enough that Van Raalte's whole conception of the school crystallized around these last two things. For him, higher education did exist for the benefit of society; but *above*

8. "Dat onze kinderen gevormd zullen worden tot verspreiders van het licht des Evangelies in de duistere plaatsen der aarde," "Hope College in the Foreign Field," 1920 *Milestone*, 62.

everything else, for the Kingdom of God. Without the ultimate aim of preaching the Word, this School had little meaning for him.[9]

For Van Raalte and others in the Holland community, there was no reason why the college could not in fact be a theological seminary at the same time.[10] For them, the American liberal arts college was a foreign construction, for which they had no passionate interest. "Will a literary institution draw out more sympathy from the people of God?" asked Western pastor R. Pieters rhetorically in 1877, when the debate over Hope's direction was at its most animated.[11]

Because the Eastern-dominated General Synod[12] of the Reformed church was willing to listen to Western wishes, Hope College in 1866 became a college with a special theological department that could grant degrees to ministerial candidates. Phelps's grandiose and overwrought plans to create "Hope Haven University" in the 1870s stemmed largely from his desire to have Hope offer both an undergraduate liberal arts education *and* a bona fide graduate faculty of theology. Phelps's "both-and" strategy was the first effort in Hope's history to find a middle way between two constituencies. But it was a short-lived dream; poor financial management, reports of in-house bickering, and a distinct lack of Eastern enthusiasm to fund what seemed like a superfluous seminary in the West put an end to this neither-fish-nor-fowl construction in 1877, when the theological department was closed. Soon the remainder of the college was placed under trusteeship in order to restore financial order. In the wake of the closing, women were invited to enter the college in 1878 — perhaps in order to draw new students.[13] Most of the Western delegates to the de-

9. Henry E. Dosker, *Levensschets van Rev. A. C. van Raalte, D.D.* (Nijkerk: Callenbach, 1893), 207-8.

10. Calvin College, founded by Christian Reformed Dutch immigrants in 1876, in fact began as a seminary, and Rutgers itself separated seminary from college only in 1863, in line with an emerging representative American model of higher education.

11. R. Pieters. "Was it Wise?" *Christian Intelligencer,* 9 August 1877, 4.

12. The General Synod — an annual gathering of representative ministers and elders (lay leaders) — is the highest governing body of the RCA.

13. For a principled defense of allowing women to matriculate at the college, see H. Uiterwijk, "Toelating van Meisjes tot Onderwijs aan Hope College," *De Hope,* 5 September 1877, 1. In this Dutch-language article Uiterwijk, the pastor of Holland's Third Reformed Church, wrote, "For too long this weighty issue has been subordinate

nomination's annual Synod opposed closing the department; most of the Eastern delegates supported the move.[14] The closing of the department was met with anger in much of the Western RCA, and helped fuel distrust against the East at a time when other issues were causing a rift.[15] As a divisive issue, the question of whether theological or liberal arts education ought to serve as the college's reason for existence was relatively short-lived after the East agreed to establish a separate Western Theological Seminary in 1884.[16] But the episode illustrates the difference in vision of two vital constituencies of the college — the one that saw Hope first and foremost as an American (and Christian) liberal arts institution, the other which saw the college's chief (if not only) *raison d'être* as a "school of the prophets." The very direction of the college itself was swayed by the disagreements between these constituencies, and it is clear that Hope College was marked by a divergence in vision from its very foundation.

---

to other concerns. We have until now concerned ourselves exclusively with the education of young men . . . while we have treated quite without charity our daughters, who as women and mothers, and through their work in education and many other activities, have just as important a place in society. Is it not high time that we repent of our negligence in this respect, and follow a more noble course of action?" It might be added that Uiterwijk — known in Anglophone circles as Utterwick — stood at the progressive end of the social and theological spectrum in Holland, leaving the Reformed for the Congregationalists in the wake of the Masonic controversy and over opposition within his own congregation to the use of the English language in worship. See Elton J. Bruins, *The Americanization of a Congregation,* 2nd ed. (Grand Rapids: Eerdmans/RCA Historical Series, 1995), 13-42.

14. Minutes of the General Synod of the Reformed Church in America, 1877, 706-9; Editorial, *Christian Intelligencer,* 19 July 1877, 8-9.

15. One such issue was whether Freemasons — who were widely tolerated in Eastern churches but who were reviled as "Freethinkers" amongst the newer Dutch immigrants — could be members in good standing in the Reformed Church. There are some indications, for instance, that some of the immigrants distrusted the Rev. Giles Henry Mandeville, appointed provisional president of the college in the wake of its financial troubles. Mandeville was an Eastern clergyman thought to be a Freemason. Phelps, though also from the East, also opposed the presence of Masons in the church. In several crucial respects, Phelps took a position closer to the Western church than the Eastern, as in the case of theological education.

16. By 1884, enough money had been scraped together to found Western Theological Seminary, an institution closely related to but distinct from Hope College. For reasons of internal harmony and external growth, it served the whole denomination to establish a second, Western theological school.

But if Hope's existence depended on Eastern goodwill, it remained until the First World War, by virtue of its location, structure, and popular purpose, a school after Van Raalte's own heart. Until at least the 1920s Hope College very much identified itself as a regional, "Western" school of the Reformed Church in America. In the first decades of the college's existence, everyone understood that Hope's purpose was to serve Reformed congregations and mission enterprises in the West and abroad. The very organization of the Council of Hope College (renamed the Board of Trustees in the 1930s) indicates just how much the school was intended to be controlled by the Western church. From the beginning, the vast majority of its seats were reserved for ministers and elders of the Western classes.[17] This system would endure in modified form (with a modest increase in Eastern representation) until direct classical control of the college ended in 1968.

Similarly, Hope's student body was overwhelmingly Western in composition, coming as they did from Dutch Reformed communities in the Midwest.[18] In many years, students coming from Michigan would outnumber students from all other states combined, sometimes by better than two to one, until well after the Second World War. Students from New York were represented at Hope from the college's earliest years, but often few were in attendance at any given time before the First World War. Prominent Easterners may have been supportive of Hope

17. A "classis" (pl. classes — pronounced classees) is a local affiliation or collection of churches — it is the smallest regional governing body in Reformed church polity. In 1866, Western representation on the Board included Classis Michigan (whose representatives, from 1865 to 1869 included Speaker of the U.S. House of Representatives Schuyler Colfax, who in 1869 became Vice President of the United States under Ulysses Grant, resigning from office after the Crédit Mobilier corruption scandal of 1872), Classis Illinois, Classis Holland, and Classis Wisconsin, but many more would be added as the Western church rapidly increased in size. (See *Hope College Bulletin*, 1865-1866, 4-5.) Only a handful of trustees, whether from the denomination's Board of Education or elected by General Synod, came from the Eastern churches, since Hope College was regarded as an institution of the Western church.

18. In 1885, some twenty-five of the thirty-one students enrolled in the college were from Western Michigan, the balance made up of three students from Iowa and Wisconsin each. In 1892, there was a greater geographical diversity, at least regionally: Michigan was represented by twenty-three students, Illinois by fourteen, Iowa by eight, Kansas and Wisconsin by three each, Nebraska and South Dakota by two each, and Minnesota and New York by one each.

College, but that did not always mean that they wanted to send their children there. The Secretary of the RCA's Board of Education was forthright in articulating this sentiment to President Dimnent in 1928, while writing a letter of reference enabling his son to attend Hope College:

> I may as well say very frankly that I am not so pleased to hear of his decision to enter Hope. That feeling has nothing to do, of course, with the college as a college, for I am constantly recommending students to come there. But when it is one of my own, that is a different matter. If he should come and incur some of the displeasure that some students from this section [i.e., the East] have incurred as a result of relations with some members of the Faculty, it might not be conducive to the success of the close relationship which I am trying to maintain officially with Hope.[19]

The precise source of the "displeasure" Eastern students experienced is difficult to ascertain, though it may have been related to a renewed Western suspicion of the Eastern church stemming from the Fundamentalist-Modernist controversies of the 1920s.[20] It is clear, however, that Eastern students, at least by the early twentieth century, were regarded by the majority population as different. Barbara Timmer recalls of her time in the 1930s that skipping church on Sunday evenings and finding nothing objectionable to social dances were characteristics that marked Eastern students off from their Western peers.[21] Hope remained a school that in both numbers and ethos catered largely to Western students, overwhelmingly from West Michigan.

But Hope College's "Western" flavor was more spiritual than demographic, for it was certainly true to Van Raalte's vision that it become a "school of the prophets," that is, a training ground for ministers. Hope was exceptional in the number of students who became ministers, missionaries, mission school teachers, and ministers' wives.[22] At

19. Letter of W. D. Brown to Edward Dimnent, 27 August 1928, in "Correspondence to Dimnent, 1924-1929," in Dimnent Presidential Papers, JAH. The younger Brown apparently never did attend Hope.

20. See below, p. 39.

21. Conversation with Barbara Timmer, Holland, Michigan, 15 September 2001.

22. A 1929 estimate counted 335 ministers, 114 missionaries, and 49 wives of ministers among the 1,337 graduates of Hope College. The last category was new to

the beginning of the twentieth century, one source estimated that 63 percent of all Hope graduates had become ministers.[23] A tally of an alumni directory published in the *1930 Milestone* suggests that well over half of Hope's graduates had become ministers or gone on the mission field prior to the First World War. But with the graduating classes now becoming much larger and engaged in a variety of professions now demanded by society, it would become impossible to sustain the high percentages; the Class of 1914 was the last to render a majority to these ecclesiastical callings.[24] In the late 1920s, however, it was still estimated that around 40 percent of Hope graduates (including ministers' wives) had devoted their lives to these vocations — a remarkable percentage.[25] Moreover, in the decades after the 1920s, though the accounts are imprecise, the college evidently saw itself as continuing to provide a relatively high number of missionaries, ministers, and their spouses. Indeed, for at least some constituents in the Reformed Church, Hope's chief reason for being — and reason to support it financially — was that it provided ministers for the church. One student who graduated from Hope in the 1910s reported years later that President Ame Vennema (the last of Hope's clergymen-presidents) frowned upon all young men who did not aspire to enter the Christian ministry — and all women who did not aspire to become the wife of a minister.[26] And some professors, like the young Irwin Lubbers, worried in the 1920s that Hope's reputation was being damaged because it was still widely

the 1920s, when the number of women married to ministers was large enough, and considered spiritually important enough, to be included in the statistics; "Hope Memorirl [sic] Chapel Dedicated in Fine Style Last Friday Night," *The Anchor,* 12 June 1929.

23. John R. Mott, *The Future Leadership of the Church* (New York: Student Volunteer Movement of Foreign Missions, 1908), 112.

24. Drawn from the alumni directory of the *1930 Milestone,* 272-393.

25. "Hope Memorirl [sic] Chapel Dedicated in Fine Style Last Friday Night," *The Anchor,* 12 June 1929.

26. M. Jay Flipse, letter to Gordon Van Wylen, 20 November 1982, in "Vennema, Ame — Biographical," JAH. Flipse, who became a physician, wrote: "Vennema was disliked by the students. He thought there was only one purpose justifying Hope College['s] existence and that was to make preachers of all the men and preachers' wives of all the women. The study of scientific studies was taboo in his mind and he sought to penalize any student who sought to deviate from the Classical Course, which would prepare him for the ministry."

regarded in Midwestern circles as little more than a theological seminary.[27] Hope College remained in spirit, both among its students and Midwestern supporters, "a school of the prophets" long after other Christian liberal arts colleges had taken on a new, more broadly oriented view of their educational purposes. It was a vision that — though dissipated by the 1950s — continued to exert a strong mark on the college until the revolutionary changes of the 1960s.

To say that Hope College was primarily a Western institution is not, however, to deny that it remained an institution heavily dependent on Eastern benevolence — or that, over time, the Eastern churches came to think of Hope College as "their" school, too. In the first place, the faculty of the college in the nineteenth century[28] consisted largely of men (and only men) who had gained degrees from Rutgers College and New Brunswick Seminary, the RCA institutions of the East. Moreover, its first presidents were Easterners.[29] It was only at the very end of the nineteenth century that Hope could turn to its own graduates (and elsewhere) to fill a substantial number of teaching positions at the college.

The college's early dependence on Eastern money was even more pronounced. The impressive building program launched during the Gerrit Kollen years (1893-1911) was almost wholly financed from Eastern sources.[30] Indeed, two key buildings were financed by Easterners with no ties at all to the Reformed Church: Voorhees Hall and the Carnegie Gymnasium — the latter a testimony to Kollen's fund-raising skills, since Andrew Carnegie almost never gave money to denominational schools.[31] The Western church was too poor — and perhaps too

27. As told by Lubbers to Eugene Osterhaven, and related in an interview in Holland, Michigan, on 13 January 2003.

28. Starting with teacher John Van Vleck in the late 1850s.

29. Phelps, Giles Henry Mandeville (who served as interim president), and Charles Scott were all ministers from RCA churches in New York. W. H. S. Demarest, "The Men Who Built Hope," *Intelligencer-Leader,* 20 June 1941, 10-16.

30. These include Winants and Graves Halls and the Hoyt Observatory (no longer standing).

31. Demarest, "The Men Who Built Hope," 16; Wichers, *A Century of Hope,* 129-40. That Hope College was an exception within the pattern of Carnegie benevolence documented by Marsden and discussed in Chapter One does not seem to show anything significant about either. There is no evidence that Hope College cultivated the gift by trying to appear significantly more "nonsectarian" than it was at the time.

_al — to match this generosity even remotely, though giving improved under the presidency of Rev. Ame Vennema (1911-1918), who was especially tapped to increase church giving to Hope in both East and West.[32] But even as Western giving improved substantially in the years following the First World War, Eastern largesse remained an important base of support for the college.

In the long run, Eastern congregations often developed close ties to Hope College. Many Reformed clergymen posted in Eastern parishes carried degrees from Hope and probably served as boosters for their alma mater. The end of Rutgers as a denominational school in 1917 (when, after decades as serving as the state's land grant university, it formally became the State University of New Jersey) may have made Hope more appealing to some Eastern students as a church-related school, and its rising academic reputation may have served as additional reason to travel to Michigan for college. By the 1930s, it seems that roughly 10-15 percent of the Hope student body came from Eastern states, roughly proportional to those coming from Midwestern states outside of Michigan. This was a striking increase from the first several decades of the school, and Eastern student presence would remain strong until the 1970s.[33]

However much a Western school, Hope College owed a debt of gratitude to Eastern benefactors, and the institution was obliged to cultivate strong ties with both constituencies upon which it relied. This task fell primarily, though not exclusively, to the presidents of the college. After the series of Eastern clergymen-presidents, Hope was administered by a long line of alumni-presidents[34] lasting until 1970. All of them were of Dutch descent, born into the Western church (Michigan, Illinois, or Wisconsin). All were, by the standards of the day, well-traveled men who had seen something of the world. Kollen, following in Van Raalte's footsteps, made many extended trips to the East for money, and Vennema's pastorates had been exclusively in the East before being tapped as president in 1911. Edward Dimnent and Wynand Wichers, more than their predecessors, had scholarly ambitions and

32. Wichers, *A Century of Hope,* 146-48.

33. From a study of the origins of students, as listed in the *Hope College* annual, the *Milestone.*

34. Kollen, Vennema, Dimnent, Wichers, Lubbers, and Vander Werf.

had spent time in graduate school (though it would not be until after World War II that Hope would have presidents with Ph.D.s, starting with Irwin Lubbers and Calvin Vander Werf). Almost all of them followed their Eastern predecessors in attending Hope Church, Holland's earliest Anglophone Reformed church and the most self-consciously sophisticated and "Eastern" of the town's Reformed congregations.[35] All of these presidents were, in effect, mediators between East and West, intuitively acquainted with the sensitivities of the Western church from which they sprang while urbane enough to court and carry Eastern support.

The influence of both East and West on Hope College — and the college's attempts to mollify both groups — would have two profound effects on the school. The first is that the college suffered tensions whenever the Reformed Church underwent periodic bouts of irritation and suspicion between these two different sections. The debate over theological education and accompanying issues in the 1870s, the Fundamentalist-Modernist controversy of the late 1920s (fed in particular by Western concerns about heresy at New Brunswick Seminary), the rift over the direction and extent of ecumenism after the Second World War, and the turbulence of the 1960s — all of these impacted a denominational college that remained dependent on the goodwill of factions not always at peace with one another. But the second effect is perhaps even more important: the balancing act necessary for Hope's survival cultivated a centrist mindset at the college, at least in the upper echelons, which avoided clearly aligning itself with any camp that might seem too theologically conservative for a more liberal East or too liberal for a more theologically conservative West. From this root sprang Hope College's Middle Way — its rare and difficult path of steering between a "mainline"

---

35. The sole exception, Wynand Wichers, was active at Third Reformed Church, second only to Hope Church in catering to the town's professional class. Initially, after being founded in 1862 by Philip Phelps, Hope Reformed Church was not even part of Classis Holland, as were the other churches of the area, but of Classis Michigan, since the latter classis consisted of English-speaking churches. Third Reformed, too, switched to the Anglophone Michigan Classis in 1921 because its new minister, James M. Martin, could speak no Dutch. After Dutch disappeared from the pulpit in West Michigan, Holland Classis was reorganized to include Hope and Third churches; see Bruins, *The Americanization of a Congregation,* 58, 202n.

Protestant model of education and a more evangelical Protestant one.

"Local Morality" and Churchly Vigilance

This may suggest that the development of Hope's Middle Way was the result of a careful, or at least calculated, balancing of interests. That is only partly the case. The Middle Way was also the result of serendipity, achieved through a conflicting set of forces that counteracted each other, or held each other in check, over time. It is important to understand these forces that acted upon the college and what kind of effects they had on the college's history. Chief among these factors was the influence of a very conservatively minded subculture that resisted change and assimilation, and which continues, though to a lesser extent, to exert its influence over the college today.

In 1930, president-elect Wichers received a piece of unsolicited advice from Hessel Yntema of the Johns Hopkins University. Hope College, said Hope alumnus Yntema, drew its strength from its affiliation with the RCA and "from its being an intimate part of the Dutch settlement in western Michigan." But if this was a strength, Yntema also thought it a danger, and thought Wichers as president "should guard against too narrow a control over its policies either by the ecclesiastical point of view or by the local community of Holland." Hope, he said, must not only be a training school for clergy, but a "liberal college" — including the social sciences, which he thought had been neglected at Hope.[36] Yntema's observations highlight the significance, whether for good or for ill, of the church and "the local community of Holland" in shaping Hope College.

Religion was more than just one part of life for the Dutch Calvinists who settled West Michigan.[37] Religion was the central ordering principle of life for these settlers, in public and in private. Bible read-

36. Hessel E. Yntema, letter to Wynand Wichers, 31 October 1930, in "Wichers, Wynand: Correspondence — Election of President of Hope College, 1930-1931," JAH.

37. See for this view, among others, Albert Hyma, *Albertus C. Van Raalte and His Dutch Settlements in the United States* (Grand Rapids: Eerdmans, 1947), 256.

ing and prayer after every meal was the norm. Perhaps even more important was church attendance (two or even three times a Sunday) and avoiding all work on the Christian Sabbath — essential hallmarks of Dutch Calvinism in both the Old and New Worlds. Furthermore, all members of the church were expected to carry themselves with Christian decorum — under penalty of falling under the ecclesiastical discipline of the elders. Instruction in the Heidelberg Catechism — the most widely used of the Reformed confessions of faith — and the Bible were considered an essential part of any child's instruction. All these were common features in all of the Reformed churches in Western Michigan till at least the mid–twentieth century.

It can hardly come as a surprise, then, that Hope College made correspondingly stringent demands on the spiritual and moral lives of its students. Particularly in the first half century of the college's existence, there was a decided emphasis on facilitating the spiritual transformation and maturation of Hope students. Influenced by a conflation of American evangelicalism and Dutch Calvinism, Hope presidents like Gerrit Kollen placed great importance on Hope students committing themselves to actively follow Christ. Until the First World War, the college routinely and publicly reported the number of professed Christians, tracking the rising percentages of confessing believers from the first year at the preparatory school to the senior year of college. In 1902, for instance, President Kollen reported at the start of the Day of Prayer that of the seventy college students at Hope, sixty-three were professing church members, and that three of the remaining seven were "professing Christians."[38] (Praying for the conversion of the others, whether in the college or the preparatory school, was in fact one of the reasons for the Day of Prayer.) Thirty years later, Christian Broek of the Board of Trustees could inform the RCA's General Synod that 80 percent of Hope's students were church members, and that some 83 percent attended Sunday School.[39] Until well after the Second World War, Hope College continued to draw students who were mostly Reformed, mostly religiously observant, and mostly conservative in their political and social views.

38. "Day of Prayer," *The Anchor,* February 1902.
39. Minutes of the General Synod of the Reformed Church in America, June 1932, 65.

As the *1928 Milestone* observed, there were "three roots" to the Christian life at Hope College. The first was daily worship in the chapel.[40] From the first days of the school, students were expected to attend chapel daily at 8 a.m. — a tradition that would end only with the ending of required chapel in 1970. It is interesting to note that for decades there was no mechanism in place to enforce attendance, except for the pre-college-age students at the Hope Preparatory School. There was, of course, a great deal of social pressure on college students to attend. But even in those days when Hope was full of aspiring would-be missionaries and ministers, attending chapel did not always command unflagging religious enthusiasm, as a couple of *Anchor* editorials observed in the 1910s. One urged,

> A great many of us come in five or ten minutes late. . . . After we are seated, many of us take up our text-books and look over or even prepare the assignments of the day, or, if by any good fortune, we have all our lessons prepared beyond a doubt, we take this opportunity for a social chat with our neighbor. . . . A regular attendance at chapel worship, provided we do it in the right spirit, is the only way to start the day right. Let's DO IT FOR HOPE.[41]

It was only when the growing enrollments following World War I weakened social control that the Board of Trustees considered introducing a chapel attendance system in 1922, a proposal immediately rejected as impracticable owing to the fact that Winants Chapel already had one hundred seats less than could accommodate all the students.[42] Even after the dedication of the capacious Memorial Chapel in 1929 (renamed after President Emeritus Dimnent two years later), the college administration refrained from enforcing attendance, insisting that chapel was "required" but not "compulsory."[43] An effective system of monitoring student chapel attendance was finally introduced under

---

40. First in a simple wooden structure, then in what is now Winants Auditorium (1894), and then in the current chapel completed in 1929.

41. Jay M. Dosker, "Aftermath," *The Anchor*, 29 November 1916; see also "That Chapel Question," *The Anchor*, 20 October 1915.

42. "Report of Religious Activities Committee of Hope College . . . March 29th, [19]22," in Hope College Board of Trustees, File Minutes, 1922; JAH.

43. *Hope College Bulletin*, 1930-1931, 77.

President Wichers in 1936 — only a few decades before its abolition at the end of the 1960s.[44]

As a corollary to the duty of weekday worship, the college also assumed students would attend church on Sunday, and until the First World War the college catalog insisted that permission *not* to attend church could only be granted by the president. After 1918, Hope College presidents no longer made any claim to enforcing church attendance, but the stated expectation in the college catalog that students attend church remained until the end of the Second World War. This expectation reveals that even if Hope insisted that there were "no religious tests" for attendance, there was a common assumption that students would attend church. But what kind of church? The catalog said nothing about this question until the Dimnent presidency (1918-1931), when it offered students the full range of churches in Holland — eight Reformed, six Christian Reformed, two Baptist, and one each of the following: Episcopal, Methodist, Wesleyan, Seventh Day Adventist, Roman Catholic, and Independent Mission.[45] This presumably non-directive description of students' religious options may have been found too nondirective in a school whose student body remained almost wholly Protestant; in the 1930s the catalog noted only that in addition to the eight Reformed churches, there were also "many other evangelical churches" (i.e., Protestant churches) in town.[46] In any event, most Hope students would have participated in a nearly daily ritual of worship services while attending the college.

The second "root" was the central importance of the YMCA (founded at Hope in 1879) and the YWCA (1901). Until the early years of the twentieth century, they were the only student organizations on campus, and they remained the most important for the first half of the century. They were responsible for Bible studies and prayer meetings on campus, where they promoted missions and actively supported missionaries. They also promoted Christian character (including "true womanhood" in the YWCA). Both organizations expanded their activities to social activities, such as beach parties, by the late 1920s. In the

44. *Hope College Bulletin, 1936-1937, 14.*
45. *Hope College Bulletin, May 1926, 46.*
46. *Hope College Bulletin, 1931-1932, 16.*

end, though, their importance would be eclipsed by the rise of other student organizations with more specific niche appeals.[47]

Finally, the third root was the faculty — "the friends and advisors," as the 1928 yearbook put it, adding, "To them we can look as examples of the best, and to them we can go for a religion that is correct."[48] The college expected its faculty to serve as laudable Christian examples both in terms of faith professed and — perhaps more important — the kind of life they led.

In addition, the college enacted numerous restrictions aimed at preventing activities that might retard the development of Christian character. As a Hope College document to the U.S. Department of Labor in 1925 quaintly put it, students could be expelled for "improper conduct based on local morality."[49] In the early years of the college, as church historian W. H. S. Demarest summarized about student life during the 1870s, the rules were particularly strict:

> [S]tudents must be in their rooms by ten p.m.; they must not smoke on the college premises except in their rooms; they must not attend dancing parties; there must be no singing or practicing music except in regular course of instruction; they must make no unnecessary noise; no sawing or splitting of wood; no throwing of snow balls or other missiles within two-hundred feet of a building; ball, quoits, leap-frog, [and] other games must be only at the southeast part of the campus; there must be no gun-powder or deadly weapons on the premises; there must be no disorder in any building at any time; no disturbing of classes or decorum, [and] no defacing of property.[50]

Some of the college restrictions remained on the books for a long time. Card-playing, for example, was condemned by the college until 1930, when it disappeared from the list of unacceptable vices in the *Hope College Bulletin*. Smoking — except in the privacy of one's own room — remained prohibited throughout the period. It was not until the 1930s

47. Drawn from *The Anchor* (1887-1945) and *Milestone* (1916-1945).

48. "Religion," *1928 Milestone*, 81.

49. "Petition for Approval of School for Immigrant Students, U.S. Department of Labor," 2 April 1925, in Dimnent Presidential Papers.

50. Demarest, "The Men Who Built Hope," 14.

that women students were expressly forbidden (in the catalog, at least) from smoking at all, and not until 1944 that the "fine womanly qualities" of Hope's co-eds were officially cited as the virtue that justified the tobacco prohibition.[51] Presumably, the mores of the Roaring Twenties, and later, the newly-gained social independence of women during the Second World War, had made it thinkable for women students to smoke.

It was not until the late 1880s that, as a result of the rising popularity of the temperance movement in Protestant America, the consumption of alcoholic beverages was forbidden, as was the frequenting of saloons.[52] This was a reflection of the fact that the Reformed Church had become as enthusiastic a champion of temperance, and later prohibition, as any of the Protestant denominations that came to support these causes. A 1918 advertisement for the college noted that the town of Holland — in addition to offering a "healthful climate" and "superior church privileges" — also had the positive distinction of having "no saloons."[53] After Prohibition ended in 1933, the college catalog was explicit that the use of both "drugs" (subsequently replaced by the word "narcotics") and "liquor" was prohibited on campus. It was a principled stance against alcohol that would endure until the 1960s and that, in an understated way, continues to this day.[54]

It is difficult to know to what extent students complied with these prohibitions, or even to what extent the college systematically enforced them. President Vennema (1911-1918) reportedly disciplined three students (all sons of ministers) after catching them at card-playing on a Sunday afternoon.[55] It seems probable that college restrictions were more frequently flouted in the 1920s and 1930s as American society — and American churches — developed more permissive attitudes toward these pastimes. These changes are no more starkly evident than in a letter Vennema wrote to Dimnent in 1919, a year after re-

51. *Hope College Bulletin,* 1936-1937, 14; *Bulletin,* 1944-1945, 17.

52. Demarest, "The Men Who Built Hope," 14.

53. *1918 Milestone,* 158.

54. Unlike other mainline schools, Hope policy forbids the use of alcoholic beverages in campus building and at official functions, and Hope's Haworth Center, though often serving a clientele with no relation to the college, does not serve alcohol.

55. Dimnent, letter to Muilenburg, 12 February 1924, in "Correspondence — Teunis Muilenburg, 1924, 1934," Dimnent Presidential Papers, JAH.

signing the presidency of Hope and having taken up a pastorate in New Jersey, where dancing was already more accepted than in the Midwestern RCA. In a passage with an offensive racial slur that was all too common in those days, he fairly burbled with excitement:

> For the first time in my life, as chairman of a Com[mittee] of Arrangements, I arranged for a dance in connection with the Welcome Home Reception of the 66 boys from our Township, and, take it from me, *it was some dance.* . . . The music was imported from New York. It costs us $75.00 besides transportation and keep, but the money did not come out of our missionary society's exchequer but from the pockets of men who have not much heart for other things and so I shed no tears. Those coons from the big town were some musicians and clowns. Glad to say, nothing coarse or objectionable, but jazz — the real thing — jazz.[56]

One case from the 1920s — again involving dancing — illustrates both the college's approach to upholding its own standards and the difficulties in doing so. In a 1924 letter President Dimnent felt obliged to write to the Rev. Teunis Muilenburg about his son:

> I learned this afternoon that Cornelius took one of the college girls to a dance in the city last Friday night . . . and that the girl was guilty of evasion of the Hall rules and of falsehood in the matter. . . . The girl has been put under discipline in keeping with the practice at Voorhees [Hall]. What your son shall be asked to do will depend on the outcome of our conversation tomorrow. I consider him more at fault tha[n] I do the girl as the invitation would have come from him. . . . I shall not minimize this part of the incident with your boy. I should like to know whether you are in accord with his attendance at public dances and shall appreciate a reply to this inquiry at once.[57]

The Rev. Muilenburg was "deeply grieved" to hear the charge, and "disgraced by the act of Cornelius," but seemed to regret most that

---

56. Papers of Ame Vennema, "Correspondence to Edward Dimnent," 14 July 1919, JAH.

57. Letter, Edward Dimnent to Teunis Muilenburg, 9 February 1924, in Edward D. Dimnent Papers, "Correspondence — Muilenburg, Teunis W., 1924, 1934," JAH.

Dimnent — whom he had long known — would suggest that the elder Muilenburg approved of social dancing. Dimnent replied that the attitude of the home was essential in determining how the student would be judged by the college, since he held church and home most responsible for the excesses of the "modern" generation, including the local "dancing club":

> They belong to the "modern" group who laugh at oldfogyism [sic] and are ready for any fling. They are not bad — just young and without moral responsibility. They are the product of their own homes, of the prevalent attitude toward liberal habits, of the church and its compromise with customs of the present-day magazine and book fiction. The girls are half-dressed or less, the boys are cigaretteists [sic] more or less advanced and they are just "crazy to dance." Of course there is without doubt amongst them one or more of each sex physically tainted — every such crowd has its taint. . . .
>
> Some of our Reformed Churches have adopted the dance in their young people's gatherings; these churches must not expect a lone college administrator to insist that the dance is taboo. The remedy? The teaching of moral responsibility to the youth in home and church — with an insistence that will not be silenced.[58]

If dancing remained a "taboo" subject at Hope until the early 1960s, other restrictions stood the test of time less well. First to fall was the college's principled Christian objection to intercollegiate athletics as a frivolous waste of time. By the 1890s the *Hope College Bulletin* felt obliged to warn against this increasingly popular activity even as it offered physical education:

> Classes in dumb-bells, Indian clubs, chest-weights, etc., are held daily at such hours as best accommodate the student. . . . By a proper use of the advantages offered in this direction, they acquire the physical strength needed to endure the mental strain incident to student life.

58. Letter, T. W. Muilenburg to Edward Dimnent, 11 February 1924; letter, Dimnent to Muilenburg, 12 February 1924; Dimnent Papers, "Correspondence — Muilenburg, Teunis W., 1924, 1934," JAH.

> While physical culture is valued highly, it is not encouraged at the expense of education and morality. Believing that intercollegiate activities have a strong tendency to interfere with the regular college work, and that they are generally not helpful to the development of moral Christian character, it is held that a denominational college like ours cannot afford to support them.[59]

That playing at least some sports carried with it a moral stigma is evident in a 1904 *Anchor* article, in which editor-in-chief Abraham Muste noted something of a divide in the student body. On one side were the aloof and "pious" Christians, and on the other, those who "put a liberal interpretation on their duty, are irregular at chapel and prayer-meeting, say cuss-words when they don't feel well, and play foot ball and basket ball. . . ."[60]

But by 1904 the college's official objection to intercollegiate athletics was already under pressure. The *Hope College Bulletin* of that year omitted its statement on intercollegiate athletics, noting instead that a new gymnasium — made possible by a $20,000 gift from Andrew Carnegie — would soon be built, chiefly for basketball.[61] The age of spectator sports had come to Hope College — not least with the arrival of "the Pull" (an annual tug-of-war between a team of male freshmen and a team of male sophomores across a river near campus) in 1898. And in 1904, too, Hope's baseball team broke through "the crusted shell of conservatism" (as Muste's friend and later prominent clergyman Benjamin Bush wrote) by playing a successful season against other schools.[62]

Yet Hope trustees, overwhelmingly consisting of clergy, remained resistant to participation in the Michigan Intercollegiate Athletics Association, and Hope teams were forbidden from playing out of town. In 1913, the men's basketball team ignored this rule and was suspended, prompting a student demonstration in support of the team at Holland City Hall. Various petitions to allow intercollegiate athletics were opposed by president and trustees and it was not until America had entered the First World War that the trustees, initially by the

59. *Hope College Bulletin*, 1897-1898, 51-52.
60. "Week of Prayer," *The Anchor*, December 1904. The editor went on to say that both groups could learn a bit from each other.
61. *Hope College Bulletin*, 1904-1905, 58.
62. *Hope College Annual*, 1905, 88-89.

narrowest of margins, lifted the ban on intercollegiate athletics.[63] And it was only in 1920 that Hope and Calvin College faced off in the first game of their intense basketball rivalry. If hostility to intercollegiate athletics was the mark of a Christian college, it was a touchstone that the most stalwart of subsequent defenders of Christian education at Hope apparently forgot after the First World War. To the contrary, under such devout coaches as Jack Schouten and Russ DeVette, it has often seemed that the intercollegiate athletics at Hope College have been among the most overtly Christian of the school's programs. Other forms of competition, such as rhetorical and theatrical performances started in 1936 between freshman and sophomore women at the inspiration of music professor John B. Nykerk, also apparently raised few concerns.

But theatre in general, associated for centuries with deceit and licentiousness, did not so easily escape the watchful eye of Holland's traditional-minded religious community. After months of entreaties, students in 1905 were finally permitted to perform the Greek tragedy *Antigone*. Women students in the play, however, were not permitted to perform in public out of concern whether "a Dutch audience [could] endure the decollete dress" of the ancient Greeks.[64] In the long run, plays — and actresses — were to become an established feature of Hope College life. Several pageants (the most traditional and moralistic of all plays)[65] and the Senior Play, an annual affair in the 1920s and 1930s, bear witness to this. Moreover, by the early 1920s Hope students were attending movie theatres in droves. One *Anchor* editorialist complained about the practice of "rushing" movie houses — a practice he condemned as insensitive to community standards, which remained reserved toward the cinema.[66] The creation of a theatre department would have to wait until after the Second World War, and even then suspicion of it had hardly disappeared. Art too was sometimes suspect.

Finally, there is one unique aspect of Hope College life that was shaped by its "local morality": the burgeoning of fraternities and sororities, which were initially founded as "literary societies" prohibited

---

63. Wichers, *A Century of Hope*, 148-50.
64. *Hope College Annual*, 1905, 153.
65. For a more extensive discussion of Hope's pageants, see pp. 88-93.
66. "Rushing Movies," *The Anchor*, 12 December 1923.

by the college from having any national affiliations. Literary societies were common in nineteenth-century American colleges, and Hope was no exception; Philip Phelps founded the Fraternal Society at Hope in 1863 in emulation of its namesake at Union College, Phelps's alma mater. By the 1890s, the "Fraters" were joined by other literary societies (the Meliphon and the Cosmopolitan being the first to follow), the number of which continued to grow until the Second World War.

What distinguished Hope from many other Protestant colleges was not the existence of literary societies, but a continued objection on the part of the college to national fraternities, which in other schools often supplanted the older literary societies in the two decades before the First World War. For years the *Hope College Bulletin* explained its opposition to the national organizations in this way:

> We have no Greek letter fraternities, which are very often expensive to the students and are apt to divide them into discordant classes. As the student life is largely the formation period of the professional man's character, and as a man's influence and usefulness depend much upon his sympathy with men, irrespective of classes, it is therefore desirable that a democratic spirit should characterize the Christian college. Moreover, plain, economical living is encouraged, in order that the young, not favored with an abundance of this world's goods, may be able to acquire a liberal education.[67]

For the administration of Hope College, at least, opposition to Greek letter societies lay not in their quasi-Masonic qualities (which one might have expected), but in the expense and social inequality they engendered — sins in a subculture that still valued thrift and was characterized internally by a relatively narrow range between rich and poor. In any event, opposition to national fraternities was sustained by consciously Christian considerations, even if these considerations might strike one as more social or political in nature than strictly religious. One might say that Hope chose a middle course: fraternities and sororities with secret rites of initiation were permitted, in contradistinction to many Catholic and conservative Protestant schools, but national organizations were kept at bay.

67. *Hope College Bulletin,* 1913-1914, 81.

In summary, Hope College remained strongly rooted until after the Second World War in the "local morality" of the Western Michigan Dutch, with its exacting behavioral prescriptions and a religious outlook that was both staunchly orthodox and pietist. The conservative nature of the subculture and the institution was furthered sustained by ethnicity and language, which kept the Dutch American settlers more isolated from cultural and religious trends in the wider society. These Reformed believers were different from the theologically similar Presbyterians around them because they were Dutch immigrants, or the children of immigrants, imbued with language and traditions that separated them from American WASPs. It seems plausible to suggest that Hope remained more conservative for a longer period of time than most Midwestern Presbyterian schools because of its "Dutchness."

Yet both the college and the wider Dutch Reformed subculture loosened their moral restrictions and widened their theological vision over time. "Evangelical" religion at the college prior to the First World War had been decidedly revivalist; by the 1920s, as we shall see, it was still imbued by an enthusiastic spirit; by the 1930s, the tone was still "evangelistic," but without the "so-called high pressure evangelism," as board members assured the General Synod of Hope's annual Week of Prayer in 1932.[68] The old hostilities toward some ostensibly sinful pastimes had also weakened over time, both at the school and in the church. To the extent that Hope "liberalized" over time, it did so in tandem with the wider religious culture around it.

Still, the conservative moral and theological sensibilities of the students, faculty, alumni, and board members from the Midwestern RCA served to inhibit or retard whatever "liberalizing" tendencies members of the college community might have entertained. This is most evident in the period after 1925, when laity and clergy alike in the Midwestern RCA were alerted to the dangers of "modernism," whether evidenced in the emblematic Scopes "Monkey Trial" or in the appointment of liberal Protestant professors to New Brunswick Seminary. The understandable perception, too, that morals had slipped in recent years may also have prompted the church to take a harder look at its schools. All these suspicions may have served as the basis for a

---

68. Minutes of the General Synod of the Reformed Church in America, 1932, 65. The shifts noted here will receive more detailed attention in Chapter Four.

letter sent to Classis Holland reporting on the "rumors" that were then circulating about Hope College in Muskegon:

1. There seems to be carelessness in the appointment of instructors. No guarantee that they are in full accord with the standards of the R.C.A. Instructors (some) do not seem to set a worthy example in loyalty to our R.C.A. as to church attendance on Sunday and even in their Christian conduct.
2. The teaching of anti-biblical doctrine or rather philosophy, such as evolution and biological interpretations of these without sufficient antidote.
3. The atmosphere of the College not adding up morally to our standards of Christian ethics. Card playing, dancing and theatre going do not seem to be discouraged but tolerated without much comment and even encouraged (particularly the movie) by the example of some of the professors. In other words, Christian discipline seems to be lax and the sacred traditions of our best Christian homes do not seem to receive a great deal of consideration.
4. The emphasis in the teaching and in the whole system of education, including character building and even exhortation to follow Christ seems to be frequently quite contrary to our accepted principles and methods.
5. The various clubs, college societies, fraternities and sororities have been criticized both as to their character and curious way of doing things.[69]

The second concern in particular prompted a special committee of Classis Holland in 1930 to urge the Hope Board of Trustees to investigate whether there were "members of the teaching staff at Hope College who believe in doctrines and are teaching doctrines which are decidedly modern in character and contrary to our Reformed faith." Trustees were to dismiss such teachers if the rumors were true, and to "brand and suppress" such rumors if false.

The board accordingly called before them two of the five faculty members named: the Rev. Paul Hinkamp and the Rev. E. Paul McLean

---

69. Letter of John Bovenkerk as transcribed by Classis Holland, Minutes of 16 May 1930, 744ff.; Western Seminary Collection, JAH.

— both members of classis, and responsible for the Bible instruction at the college. The other three (not named in any of the minutes) were not interrogated because, as the board minutes explained, they could not be found.[70] The specific concerns regarding either of the men remain obscure, though Hinkamp's recent pamphlet "The Claims of Christ" (1929) may have drawn fire for indirectly questioning the authorship of 2 Peter in an otherwise stout defense of the New Testament's reliability.[71] Hinkamp's theological studies in Chicago and McLean's past pastorates in New York City may also have contributed to the reasons for the hearing. In any event, the board quickly exonerated them and expressed "its utmost confidence in the administration of the college and the integrity and orthodoxy of Profs. McLean and Hinkamp." They assured that "careful inquiry" was always made after the "religious views" of all teachers and that, at any rate, the one-year contracts issued to all faculty was surety enough to ensure that heterodox instructors would be dismissed should they ever appear. Classis Holland protested against the board's facile willingness to clear the charges (we might add that McLean's father, Charles, was on the Board of Trustees), but the matter was apparently dropped, with Hinkamp and McLean serving the college for many more years.[72]

There are many things that we could say about the 1930 effort to rid Hope College of "modernism." That these charges could be made against Hope — and that the board apparently refused to act upon them — may be interpreted as signs that even in the 1930s the college was already on the way to becoming the broadly latitudinarian school that it would become in the 1960s and 1970s. At the same time, through the 1940s at least, the college was subject to denominational oversight that made the outright expression of deviant religious thought and personal conduct too out of line with "local morality" unlikely. Trustees, for example, apparently continued to ask students about the religious

70. Minutes, Hope College Board of Trustees, April 1930, 109, 112, 116.

71. Paul Hinkamp, "The Claims of Christ," self-published pamphlet, 1929, in "Biographical File: Paul Hinkamp," JAH.

72. Minutes, Hope College Board of Trustees, April 1930, 116-17. After the April meeting, Classis Holland urged the Board of Trustees to take its concerns more seriously and open an investigation. The Board of Trustee minutes for the spring of 1931 are missing, so it is not possible to know what they decided to do. We do know that the two named professors remained at the college, however.

orthodoxy of instructors into at least the early 1950s. And more generally, suspicion of innovation and new ideas helped ensure that Hope stayed on a tried and true course in respect to its religious culture. It was to this conservative dominance that Hessel Yntema objected, and he was not alone. Gerrit J. Diekema, state Republican luminary, longtime secretary of the board, and U.S. Ambassador to the Netherlands, complained to the senior McLean from The Hague in July of 1930 of the "destructive criticism" aimed at the faculty and administration and argued that the "worship of the past" at the college "is little less than heathenish."[73] Whether we regard it as "heathenish" or as faithfully Christian, the conservative Dutch Reformed subculture continued to set the moral and theological parameters of the college until well after the Second World War, and arguably to the present day.

Dutch Pilgrims and American Citizens

Taken by itself, however, the deep-seated conservatism of Hope's regional constituency is a one-sided account of the college's history. It is important to realize that not only the Eastern RCA, but the Western church *itself* possessed elements of "the forward and upward look" that Gerrit Diekema — himself a prominent local figure in the history of the college — thought essential to the future of Hope.[74] However traditional-minded the Midwestern RCA may have been in its social, religious, and moral outlook, it also included important elements that limited, even undermined, this conservatism.

The Reformed Church in America was not the only representative of Dutch Calvinists in the Midwest. Of increasing importance and demographic weight was the secessionist Christian Reformed Church, which broke away from the RCA in 1857, a scant decade after the founding of Holland. The central issue surrounding the split was whether the Reformed Church was doctrinally pure enough to be regarded as a "true"

73. Gerrit John Diekema, letter to Charles M. McLean, in the Wynand Wichers Papers, "Correspondence — Election as President of Hope College, 1930-1931," JAH.
74. Ibid.

church, an important issue to many new immigrants. Some of them, like Van Raalte, had suffered persecution in the Netherlands for breaking away from the state-sponsored church; others had, at the very least, a dim view of the Christian vitality of establishment churches. For example, to many immigrants the singing of hymns rather than psalms in the Reformed Church suggested that the denomination was willing to depart from the unmediated words of Scripture. Of decisive importance was the issue of Freemasonry. In the Netherlands, the Masonic lodges had been strongly associated with "free thought" and irreligion, and Dutch Calvinist immigrants (including Van Raalte) considered lodge membership patently incompatible with membership in a Christian church. In the United States, however, Freemasonry had made strong inroads after 1850 in the memberships of established churches — including the Eastern wing of the Reformed Church in America. The RCA General Synod (dominated by the numerically much superior Eastern churches) refused to condemn Masonry in general, though it permitted individual congregations to bar Masons from membership. For the newer Dutch immigrants of the Midwest, the question was whether such a Solomonic decision was sufficient. Many families and churches left the RCA in the 1880s in protest of the denomination's unwillingness to stand firmly against Freemasonry.

The effects were dramatic. Most of the immigrants from the Netherlands, disproportionately consisting of conservative Calvinists, joined the Christian Reformed Church and not the RCA — and this precisely in a period of the heaviest wave of immigration from the Netherlands.[75] In this way, the RCA's hopes to be *the* church of Dutch immigrants to "the West" were effectively dashed.

That the Christian Reformed Church succeeded in drawing thousands of recent Dutch immigrants to itself affected the size of the Midwestern RCA, but also, and perhaps more significantly, its spiritual ethos. Conservative as it may have been morally and theologically, the Midwestern Reformed Church did not contain the most rock-ribbed of the Dutch Calvinist population. Relatively speaking, Reformed Church members were the theological moderates — and in some cases the con-

75. Elton J. Bruins and Robert P. Swierenga, *Family Quarrels in the Dutch Reformed Churches of the Nineteenth Century* (Grand Rapids: Eerdmans/RCA Historical Series, 1999), 104-7, 130-35.

scious "progressives" — of the Dutch settlements in the Midwest. In relative terms, they tended to be irenic pietists, more interested in cultivating a personal relationship with Christ than in doctrinal purity, an emphasis that characterized the CRC. The Michigan Reformed (even those who knew no Dutch) derisively referred to the Christian Reformed as the *Afgescheidenen,* or Seceders — a biting reference to the sectarian spirit for which they berated the Christian Reformed.

This intermediate, moderate position of the Midwestern RCA exhibited itself theologically in at least three different ways. In the first place, the RCA Midwestern leadership frequently developed a strong dislike for "sectarianism," a spirit that they blamed for the exodus out of the Reformed Church. John M. Vander Meulen, an 1891 Hope graduate and later president of the Presbyterians' Louisville Seminary, described in 1926 the origins of the Christian Reformed Church in these terms:

> A wave of narrow and bigoted separatism swept over the Dutch Reformed Church in the west. . . . In vain did the loyal leaders try to stem the fanatical tide. [But] the split came. And though of course the larger and more intelligent element stayed with the Reformed Church, in one community and church after another the agitators succeeded in carrying a portion of the flock with them to join the so-called Christian Reformed Church in America. It is the darkest page in the religious history of the Hollanders in America.[76]

Evert J. Blekkink (Class of 1883), long-time professor at Western Seminary, harbored similar sentiments, as evidenced in his own account of the "pioneer" mentality written at the end of his long life in 1947:

> There were, also, the supralapsarians of a quarreling type, who overemphasize and overwork the teaching of Paul in Corinthians: "Come ye out from among them" (a passage that has often been seized upon as a ground for numerous unbrotherly divisions among Christian people).
>
> From these few the pioneers suffered . . . from their faultfinding

76. John M. Vander Meulen, "The Antecedents and Early Career of Dr. Dosker," in "Memorials, Rev. Henry E. Dosker, D.D., LL.D., L.H.D., 1855-1926," 1926 pamphlet, 40-41; in Collection, "Vander Meulen, John Marinus"; JAH.

and separative spirit which defaced to some extent the remarkable history of communities of harmony and good-will, and which later led to secession after secession.[77]

In part because of their antagonism toward the Christian Reformed Church, in part because of their own sincere and simple piety, many leaders of the Midwestern RCA made it a studied practice to avoid looking or acting in "sectarian" ways. Within the Midwestern RCA as a whole, laymen and clergy had less of an appetite for monitoring denominational schools to ensure that they maintained doctrinal purity than those within the CRC displayed toward its denominational school, Calvin College. Although, as we have seen, the church did occasionally intervene directly in the life of Hope College, these incursions were less frequent than CRC interventions at Calvin.[78]

The positive expression of the RCA's anti-sectarian orientation was its ecumenical Protestant outlook. From its very beginning, Hope College — in emulation of most other American Protestant colleges — advertised itself as a nonsectarian institution. The *Hope College Bulletin* of 1871 pointed out that the school, though controlled by the Synod, was Protestant but not "sectarian":

> . . . not even in the theological department shall any sectarian test exist [for students]. Any member of any evangelical [i.e., Protestant] church may avail himself of all its advantages, without changing his church relations. . . . Hence the Institution is not sectarian. And since the Reformed Church in America is established on the original basis of the Reformation as it existed before the division into sects — which its very name indicates — the School may be called denominational only in the Protestant sense.[79]

---

77. Evert J. Blekkink, "Theological Convictions of the Pioneers," in *Flowering Wilderness: Containing Twenty Articles by Various Authors in Commemoration of the Centennial Celebration of the Reformed Churches in the West* (Reformed Church in America, 1947), 15. This edition was published by the Reformed Church to mark the centenary of RCA churches in the West. By "supralapsarians" Blekkink is indicating those who take a particular position on disputed fine points of doctrine regarding the fall of humanity from original innocence.

78. Harry Boonstra, *Our School: Calvin College and the Christian Reformed Church* (Grand Rapids: Eerdmans/RCA Historical Series, 2001).

79. *Hope College Bulletin*, 1871-1872, 4.

The open character of Hope was a feature that the college administration stressed frequently in its literature. For many decades, the *Bulletin* contained the following description:

> Although Hope College is denominational, and is under the patronage and support of the Reformed Church in America, yet, by the law of its incorporation, it can have no "religious test." The doors are open, and welcome is given to all who submit to its scholastic regulations. As a Christian school, however, it inculcates gospel truths, and demands a consistent moral character and deportment.[80]

The 1905 yearbook also expressed the wish that the "college spirit" would, "in its relation to the Reformed Church," show "devotion without bigotry," that is, without a sectarian spirit.[81] And in a 1916 advertisement the college billed itself as "an institution of the Reformed Church in America" and also as "Christian but not sectarian."[82]

It is telling that the college frequently coupled its denominational affiliation with its nonsectarian character. Clearly, the official ties with the RCA were essential to the college, not only for reasons of financial support, but because it catered very largely to members of the Reformed Church. At the same time, Hope College was emphatic in wanting to transcend the parochial and become, in effect, a school that was eager to reach out to a much wider range of Protestant Christians.

Rejection of "sectarianism" in the Midwestern RCA also meant a quicker and easier abandonment of the Dutch language than was the case among the Christian Reformed — a choice made easier by the fact that most Dutch newcomers were joining the CRC. Thus, the two Reformed bodies also differed over to what extent "Americanization" was to be embraced, or held at arm's length. In fact, the language issue — and the concomitant issue of Americanization — was perhaps the most fundamental dividing line among Dutch colonists through the first decades of the twentieth century.[83] Though this line cut across denomina-

80. *Hope College Bulletin,* 1897-1898, 43.
81. *Hope College Annual,* 1905, 21.
82. *The Anchor,* 22 November 1916.
83. "There were two divergent views," wrote A. Pieters almost a century ago, "as to the purpose of the Hollanders in coming to this country. One was that the settlers should come to America, but not be of it." The other, she noted, was the pro-Americanization party, consisting of settlers willing, even anxious, to conform to Ameri-

tions, generally the Reformed felt more at home in the United States than did the Christian Reformed. And from the very beginning, Hope College was clearly envisaged by founders like Van Raalte and Phelps as an agent of Americanization.

Several factors drove the institution to become an engine of Americanization. Hope's early and strong identification with American culture stemmed from the fact that the Midwestern Reformed operated within a denominational body that, until the 1960s, consisted of a majority of almost wholly assimilated, English-speaking Easterners. And, as we have seen, the vital role of important Easterners served to Americanize the ethos of the college from its earliest years. But it was not only Easterners who were responsible for this Americanization. The Midwestern RCA leaders themselves were often passionate advocates of a full-fledged participation in American life, beginning with Van Raalte himself, who clearly saw the fledgling college in the light of a broader American vision. For the college's founders, the task ahead lay in the winning of the American "West" and the world for Christ, not in the defense of classic Dutch Calvinist theology. And in concrete terms, the choice from the beginning to use English as the language of instruction — and to follow an American college curriculum — set the stage for Hope students and alumni to imbibe freely from the wells of both American Protestantism and civic patriotism. The author Arnold Mulder, a 1907 Hope graduate, explained it this way in 1947:

> The college was an American institution of higher learning established by Hollanders and descendants of Hollanders. And it is such today. Its students learn far more about the Puritans of New England than about the Walloons of New Netherland; they become much more intimately acquainted with the writings of Milton and Shakespeare than with those of Vondel and Bilderdyke. Quite properly so; they are Americans, not Hollanders . . . and the men who established such institutions as Hope College intended from the beginning that they should be wholly American in character.[84]

---

can habits and to learn the English language. For this citation and other background information, see Siebe C. Nettinga, "The Church in Michigan," in *Tercentenary Studies, 1928: A Record of Beginnings* (Reformed Church in America, 1928), 441-59.

84. Arnold Mulder, *Americans from Holland* (Philadelphia and New York: Lippincott, 1947), 208-9.

There was no doubt, then, about Hope's solid identification with *American* life. The polite distance with which the Council of Hope College (later known as the Board of Trustees) regarded the Netherlands is evident in their official thanks to Queen Wilhelmina for having knighted President Kollen in 1907:

> . . . we gratefully recognize the interest of her Majesty in her *former* subjects and their descendants and we assure her Majesty that, *though citizens of another country*, we still *remember with affection* the Fatherland over which her Majesty rules and will ever pray for its prosperity [emphasis added].[85]

The First World War and the intense unleashing of American patriotic fervor further solidified Hope's self-identity as an *American* institution. Patriotism as an essential virtue seems to have had its heyday in the Hope of the 1920s. Building "a strong loyal Americanism" became one of the chief educational aims of the college in the mid-1920s, and Flag Day became an important college ritual.[86] Around the same time, too, the college catalog included a Pledge of Allegiance, which, in addition to a promise to defend the Constitution and uphold the U.S. in "all righteous causes," also contained as credos such statements as "I believe in America" and "I believe that in the providence of God America was founded to promote righteousness toward God and justice amongst men of all races, creeds and color."[87] Hope's traditional antipathy toward "religious tests" and "sectarianism" did not apparently preclude open institutional support for the civil religion of "Americanism." On the contrary, Hope's less doctrinaire culture encouraged "Americanism," since American patriotism was seen as a natural expression of the broader outlook that a positive, nonsectarian Christianity evinced. Hope presidents from Dimnent to Lubbers (if not later) came to see Hope College as a pillar supporting American civil and political traditions such as democracy.[88]

85. Council of Hope College, Minutes, April 1907.
86. "Hope College Alumni Newsletter," 1923, 7; for photographs of the flag ceremonies, see, *Anniversary Bulletin of Hope College*, 1926, 100-101.
87. *Anniversary Bulletin of Hope College*, 1926, 103.
88. For a striking but by no means unique expression of this sentiment, see *The Intelligencer-Leader*, 20 June 1941, which marked the 75th anniversary of Hope College.

On one level, the thoroughgoing impulse of Americanization did not eliminate Dutch ethnicity from academic and cultural life at Hope. The college continued to proudly exhibit its Dutch heritage in a number of ways. From the 1880s until the mid-1930s, the college's Ulfilas Club promoted Dutch language and culture, putting on yearly programs at commencement in the Dutch tongue. The club primarily consisted of pre-seminary students with ambitions to serve in one of the RCA's Dutch-language churches — one of the reasons why the college continued to offer an extensive Dutch program into the 1940s.[89] In a similar vein, the college put out a Dutch-language religious weekly, *De Hope*, which it published from 1865 until a lack of Dutch-language readers forced its termination in 1933. Moreover, the college consciously sought to confer its honorific degrees on either Americans of Dutch origin or famous Netherlanders. In 1901, Hope College gave an honorary degree to Vice President (and RCA member) Theodore Roosevelt, who telegraphed the college to say that he felt privileged to be bestowed such glory by his "own creed and race stock." Seven years later the school awarded an honorary doctorate to the Dutch Calvinist statesman Abraham Kuyper.[90] And the House of Orange maintained cordial ties with Hope College, knighting two of its presidents.[91] Two long-serving secretaries of the Board of Trustees played important official roles in Dutch-American relations: in 1929 Herbert Hoover appointed Gerrit Diekema Minister to the Netherlands, and in the 1940s

89. The Ulfilas Club was named after the Arian missionary who translated the Bible into Gothic in the fourth century. Whether the fact that Ulfilas's theology was reputedly non-Trinitarian was a matter of indifference or simply unknown is not clear.

90. Letter, Theodore Roosevelt to Gerrit J. Diekema, in "Correspondence — Gerrit Kollen, 1885-1910," Kollen Papers; Council of Hope College Minutes, April 1908, JAH. The minutes record that the degree was to go to "Abram Kuiper"; it would be interesting to know if the spelling was corrected on the official degree. Kollen had met Kuyper in the United States and introduced him by letter to Vice President Garret Hobart in the late 1890s, the vice president being a Rutgers graduate and Reformed Church member. Kollen visited Kuyper in the Netherlands in 1906 (a year after Kuyper resigned as prime minister), and it is possible that Kuyper played a role in Kollen receiving a knighthood in 1907 — which may in turn explain why Kuyper was honored by Hope College in 1908. See Kollen's travel diaries for the summer of 1906 in the Kollen Papers, JAH.

91. Not only Kollen but Wichers was knighted into the Order of Orange-Nassau by Queen Wilhelmina, and her daughter Juliana received an honorary degree from Hope in 1941.

Willard Wichers, a nephew of a Hope president, became Consul for the Netherlands in Holland, Michigan. In many ways — from playing as "the Dutchmen" on the athletic fields to the self-deprecating humor about the Dutch and their foibles — Hope College seemed only to play up its Dutch ethnicity and its ties to the "Fatherland."

But looks can be deceiving. Dutch ethnic identity at Hope College was constructed in a way that tended to support a strong identification with *American* life, rather than offering an alternate source of allegiance. The most striking example of this is the frequency with which — from about the 1880s to the 1940s — Holland, Michigan, was compared with Plymouth Rock, and the date of the town's founding (1847) with the first Puritan settlements in Massachusetts.[92] For Hope College there was no closer parallel to be found than in the respective founding of the Massachusetts and Michigan settlements. Already in 1886, the people of the Michigan migration were "de pelgrim-vaders van het Westen" ("The Pilgrim Fathers of the West") to cite D. Versteeg's book, which also made an explicit comparison to the Mayflower landing.[93] In 1941, President Wichers asserted that "the impression made on [American] life and history by Bradford and Brewster and Standish was made again in latter days by Van Raalte and Vandermeulen and Scholte."[94]

Indeed, the fact that Van Raalte and his hardy band were hailed as *Western* settlers further seemed to underscore the epic *American* story of westward expansion. The migration was nothing less than the "westward march of a virile and energetic people," as Wichers put it, and in reading the migration this way he intended to place 1847 at the center of American history.[95] Moreover, the Dutch who came to Michigan were almost never defined in the official stories as "immigrants" — a term often reserved for the "less American" arrivals from Eastern and

92. D. Versteeg made a connection between 1847 and 1620; Dosker, in his brief history of the college, with 1630; Versteeg, *Pelgrim-vaders van het Westen* (Grand Rapids: C. M. Loomis, 1886), 68; Dosker, *Hope College Annual*, 1905, 104.

93. Versteeg, *Pelgrim-vaders*, 68.

94. The comparison is between the leading "Pilgrims" of 1620 and the Dutch leaders of the immigration in 1846-1847; copy of Wichers's speech given upon the conferral of an honorary degree upon Princess Juliana of the Netherlands, 11 June 1941, in "Visit of Princess Juliana to Hope College" in Royal Family of the Netherlands Collection, JAH.

95. Ibid.

Southern Europe. In 1866, an Eastern RCA minister who had helped Van Raalte's group in 1846 could speak of the blessings rendered by "the God of the poor immigrant."[96] However, less than a generation later, such an appellation was declassé: the Dutch-Americans were "pioneers," "settlers," and "colonists" — heroic terms that made the Michigan Dutch central players in the unfolding national greatness of the United States. The *1930 Milestone,* which compiled a directory of all alumni, featured illustrations replete with noble American Indians, seventeenth-century Pilgrims, log cabins, and a prophetic-looking Albertus Van Raalte.[97] Hope College saw itself not as serving a backwater ethnic enclave, but as the visionary achievement of a people who, in bravely settling the Western frontier, had become, like the Pilgrims before them, legendary participants in the great American pageant. Preston Stegenga's *Anchor of Hope* (1954) tried to underscore precisely this, billing his work as "the history of an American denominational institution."[98]

Because this vision of Hope's history was essentially civic and political, the story Hope presidents and alumni[99] told about the college's history was strikingly vague about religion and theology. The self-comparison with the Calvinistic Puritans of New England might be regarded as implicitly religious, but if so, it was implicit only, and never made explicit. More concretely, the theological reasons behind Van Raalte and his associates' departure from the established church in the Netherlands — including that church's tolerance of unorthodox teaching — were scarcely mentioned, nor were the specific theological tenets of the settlers to West Michigan. Instead, Van Raalte and his band were portrayed as a freedom-loving people, escaping persecution of the "state" church — a storyline that very much resonated with the vision of America as a haven for the persecuted yearning for liberty.[100] In a

96. Rev. Isaac N. Wyckoff, "Inaugural Charge," *Hope College Rememberancer,* 1866, 11. JAH.

97. *1930 Milestone.*

98. Preston J. Stegenga, *Anchor of Hope: The History of an American Denominational Institution* (Grand Rapids: Eerdmans, 1954).

99. Including Stegenga's and Wichers's histories of Hope.

100. Though not as such a "state" church (no one automatically belonged to it), the Dutch Reformed Church *(Nederlandse Hervormde Kerk)* did enjoy close ties to the Dutch state in the early nineteenth century, and the government did not make registration of

similar fashion, the Netherlands was seldom cast as the bulwark of the Calvinist Reformation, but rather as a country defending its political liberties against Spanish tyranny.[101] It is telling that Edward Dimnent's pageant "The Pilgrim" (performed at Hope College's seventy-fifth anniversary celebration in 1941) selected as representatives of the Dutch Reformation Erasmus, Grotius, and William the Silent — of whom only the last (and only problematically) could be classified as a Calvinist.[102] Clearly, Dimnent was more interested in selecting the heroes of Dutch "liberty" than he was in portraying the Netherlands as the wellspring of true religion, as the Christian Reformed tended to do.[103]

Indeed, Dutch ethnicity as celebrated at Hope College had little direct connection with covenantal theology or international Calvinism. The Ulfilas Club (which was, after all, largely supported by future ministers) waxed eloquent in 1905 about "brave little Holland" and "the glorious history and excellent language" of the Dutch, but nothing about its theology.[104] In fact, there was arguably an *inverse* relationship between the celebration of Dutch culture and history and the embrace of Dutch Calvinist theology — an inverse relationship between the celebration of Holland, Michigan's annual Tulip Time festival and the belief in TULIP (the acronym for the chief tenets of high Calvinist

---

new religious groups easy, and did for some years actively harass seceders like Van Raalte who did not conform to government policy. In this respect, the standard narrative about persecution was less wrong than one-sided in focus — it left the specific theological motivations of the seceders — from their insistence on singing only psalms to their desire to return to the theology and church order of the Synod of Dordt — out of consideration.

101. See John Lothrop Motley's widely read *Rise of the Dutch Republic: A History* (New York: Harper & Brothers, 1856).

102. Edward Dimnent, "The Pilgrim: The Story of Christian Education," program and script of June 1941 performances of the pageant; "Dimnent, Edward D. — 'The Pilgrim,'" in Dimnent Presidential Papers. Erasmus (1469-1536) remained a Catholic; Grotius (1583-1645), though initially a member of the Reformed Church, was a Remonstrant forced to leave the church following the Synod of Dordt, and moved toward Roman Catholicism in later years; and William the Silent (1533-1584) became a moderate Calvinist when political circumstances suggested it prudent to do so, though most historians consider him to have been more religiously latitudinarian.

103. That being said, Dimnent clearly grasped the distinction between spreading the gospel and exporting the American way of life. See Dimnent, President's message in "Alumni News Letter," 1922; in "Dimnent, Edward D. — Annual Reports," 5; JAH.

104. *The Hope College Annual*, 1905, 54-55. Ecclesiastically, the RCA did maintain ties with churches in the Netherlands.

theology).[105] Indeed, the founders of Holland's Tulip Time were not Dutch. Likewise, it was Hope Church — the church where most of the college's presidents and faculty attended — that was the *only* one of Holland's Reformed congregations to construct a sanctuary in Dutch style (1903), while it was at the same time the only early RCA (or CRC) congregation never to use Dutch in worship.[106] Arguably, the presence of Dutch architecture on Hope's campus (as seen in Voorhees or Lubbers Halls) stemmed as much from the "Holland mania" that swept throughout the United States in the late nineteenth and early twentieth centuries as it did from local ties to the Old Country itself.[107]

In summary, the construction of Dutch ethnicity at Hope in the first eighty years of Hope College's existence tended to consolidate, rather than check, its self-identification as an *American* institution. And the intense desire for Hope to become an *American* institution has had a profound effect on the religious life of the college. It has meant an openness to wider currents of American Protestantism (and later more openness to the varieties of American religion) and to the patterns present in American higher education — including the "secularizing" patterns discussed in Chapter One that, as we will see in coming chapters, occurred through the professionalization of faculty and the specialization of knowledge. Through its consciously American identity, Hope escaped at least some of the narrow sectarianism that afflicted the more solidly ethnic and more theologically militant Christian Reformed Church. At the same time, its desire to partake fully in American life gave the Hope community precious little vantage point from which to critique the shadow sides of American society.

Hope was a college in the middle. On the one hand, its originating vision as a "school of the prophets" coupled with its conservative

---

105. As formulated by the 1619 Synod of Dordt: Total depravity, Unconditional election, Limited atonement, Irresistible grace, and Perseverance of the saints.

106. Actually, Hope Church was architecturally patterned after the West End Collegiate Church in New York City, which its RCA congregation completed in 1892; see Annette Stott, *Holland Mania: The Unknown Dutch Period in American Art and Culture* (Woodstock: Overlook Press, 1998), 155-58. In effect, Hope College and Church were imitating both American *and* Dutch architectural styles at the same time.

107. Stott, *Holland Mania.*

"local morality" retarded wholesale cultural assimilation; on the other, its desire to display "the forward look," to participate fully in American life, and to avoid sectarianism kept it from developing a fortress mentality. Indeed, Hope's environment habituated, as we will see even more vividly in Chapter Three, a "Middle Way" — not just culturally but as part of its academic vision.

In the long run, however, Hope's leaders would have to make hard choices about whether to stand in the mainstream of American society and academic life, or privilege its Christian commitments in ways that might, at the very least, stand in tension with this goal. And here James Burtchaell's warnings discussed in Chapter One about the less-than-salutary effects of pietism are disquieting. Given the pietistic strain in Hope's religious pedigree, would it be able to call on the intellectual and theological resources to remain something other than passive or random at crucial decision points? Could the Middle Way survive without an articulate rationale? And if Hope needed to become articulate in order to have a distinctive, enduring vision, from where within its complex nature would this capacity arise? In the long run, that would depend on what educational aims the college forged in the light of its religious and cultural contours.

3 The Goal of the Middle Way: Elevating Humanity through Educating Christians, 1866-1945

- "A Staunch and Certain Christianity"
- Public Schools and Christian Colleges
- Early Curriculum and Faculty
- "Our Bible and Science Departments Do Not Quarrel"
- Manly Men and Women of Granite
- "Messengers of Hope" and the "Elevation of Humanity"
- A Tradition of Self-Sacrifice and Service

As we have seen, a balanced set of tensions, external and internal, led Hope College to develop its cultural and religious Middle Way. There are a variety of dangers inherent in a *via media:* a habit of facile compromise, a loss of any vivid sense of distinctiveness, smug self-congratulation that one has avoided the dangers of the various extremes over against which one defines oneself. During the first seventy years of its history, what protected Hope's Middle Way from being unduly damaged by these dangers was a compelling *telos* or goal for its educational program — that goal was to shape young men and women into activist Christians who would transform the world through church ministry, missionary endeavors, and service in the public sphere. At stake was not some local good of an enclave community but, with all due seriousness, the hope of the world. Aiming at "elevation of humanity" allowed Hope's Calvinism, its evangelical impulse, and its progressive instincts to all pull in the same direction. Character formation at Hope aimed at producing people who would reliably *do* the things that would elevate humanity. The means to the goal was also clear in this period: Christian faculty with proper piety and character must be hired and in turn form the character of their students. Christian faculty could cooperate in this enterprise without all espousing a uniform overarching or unified Christian philosophical theology. Moreover, given that one important aim of the college was to produce future public school teachers, inculcating a Christian approach to subjects that would *contrast* with rather than be *compatible* with public school curriculum would be counterproductive.

The result was a coherent enterprise that allowed a high degree of specialization and academic freedom — Christian faculty, once hired, could teach the truth as they saw it. Outside the Department of Biblical Literature (later called the Department of Bible and Religion), and perhaps especially in the sciences, in many cases Hope faculty saw truth within their disciplines in ways indiscernible from their non-Christian colleagues at secular universities. Prior to the Second World War (and most especially prior to 1925), Hope's Middle Way resulted in Christians teaching Christians from Christian motives and with the goal of transforming the world for Christ's sake, but outside the religion department that was not thought to necessitate a distinctive Christian pedagogy or subject matter. For good or ill, that made Hope College a natural environment for practicing a "two realms" view of knowledge, and it left as an open question whether, when the winds of change began to blow with increasing force in the mid-twentieth century, the Middle Way would endure.

"A Staunch and Certain Christianity"

Did the Reformed Church in general and Hope College in particular ever have a coherent vision for Christian education, and if so, what was it? In 1903, the Christian Reformed B. K. Kuiper opined — in an apologia for a Calvinist college in Grand Rapids — that Hope College had been weighed and found wanting in this respect:

> [W]e cannot be satisfied with anything less than a Calvinistic college. And Hope is not Calvinistic. In Hope too the doctrine of *election* is ignored, by some openly sneered at; and the evolutionary dogma of *selection* receives homage, at least in the natural sciences. Hyper-Calvinism is rebuked, but genuine Calvinism is not openly and fearlessly proclaimed. If any student leaves Hope with an enthusiasm for Calvinism, it is not in his Alma Mater that he received his inspiration. Calvinism is not held to the students as the one system which will prove able to stand firm as a rock in the midst of the

current sway from God and his word. Surely, Hope is perva[d]ed by Christian influences, but it is precisely this vague type of Christianity which we called more dangerous than open hostility.[1]

Kuiper's comments can be sharply contrasted with those of John E. Kuizenga, a staunchly conservative Reformed theologian who ended his career at Princeton Seminary. Writing of his time at Hope in the 1890s, Kuizenga remembered there was only one redeeming feature of his education:

> Our equipment was shamefully inadequate, our laboratories, for physics, chemistry, biology, did not exist, and our faculty, with one or two exceptions, incompetent. The whole situation was a parody of a college, crying to heaven, save for one thing. That little college represented the determination of the fathers that, while their children should get as much learning as possible, there was one thing that they should not fail to get, and that was the conviction of God. Some of us have suffered all our days for these inadequacies, but we forgive it all in the profoundest gratitude for what they did give us, a living faith, the heart of the great Reformed theology.[2]

President Edward Dimnent was even more unequivocal about Hope's no-nonsense Christian educational vision in a newsletter to alumni in 1921:

> In the midst of all the vaporings which America is befogged with and by today, HOPE COLLEGE must inculcate a staunch and certain Christianity which will palter no "ifs" and "ands" but will prove all doctrines whether they be of God or man, and then, without debate or animadversions, will abide by the truth as it is in Christ Jesus.[3]

---

1. B. Kuiper, *The Proposed Calvinistic College at Grand Rapids* (Grand Rapids: B. Sevensma, 1903), 55.

2. John E. Kuizenga, "God on the Campus," *The Intelligencer-Leader*, 20 June 1941, 33. Kuizenga serves as an appropriate contrast to Kuiper because Kuizenga himself had an educational vision that was shaped by Abraham Kuyper, the neo-Calvinist whose influence would make such a mark on Calvin College.

3. "Hope College Alumni Newsletter," 1921, 9.

So how did the Christian faith more generally, and the Reformed tradition more specifically, intersect with the curriculum of the college? Was Christianity so deep a driving force in what was at least initially a mediocre academic program that it would have an enduring seminal role? Or was it, particularly as Hope's academic luster increased, an expendable item, banished to the margins of academic work and college life?

Public Schools and Christian Colleges

Before we can answer this question, it is important to address what might seem to some Calvinists a paradox: why did the Reformed Church in America develop an abiding commitment to Christian *higher* education while remaining loyal to public education at the primary and secondary school level? An answer to this question yields important insights into what Christian education at Hope College meant — and did not mean — both in the pre-World War I period and to the present day.

Van Raalte himself was a vigorous supporter of Christian primary and secondary education, because he thought systematic Christian instruction was necessary for all members of the Holland "colonie." But already in the 1850s, much to his disgust, Van Raalte encountered resistance among his fellow colonists in creating, and then sustaining, a parochial primary school.[4] This school quickly passed from the scene for failure to secure the financial support of the settlers, who saw no need to fund an additional school when public primary instruction was available.[5] Van Raalte was more successful in his drive to create a secondary institution, which as the Holland Academy, the Hope Preparatory School, or later, Hope High School, persisted until 1938. In addition to their provision of post-secondary instruction, Hope College faculty frequently taught courses at the preparatory school, which until the early twentieth century was numerically larger than the college. By

4. Albert Hyma, *Albertus C. Van Raalte and His Dutch Settlements in the United States* (Grand Rapids: Eerdmans, 1947), 259-60.

5. See Henry E. Dosker, *Levensschets van Rev. A. C. van Raalte, D.D.* (Nijkerk: Callenbach, 1893), 188-200.

the 1920s, however, the days of the preparatory school were clearly numbered; in 1926, only four freshmen entered the school.[6] The rise of good public high schools, the development of an alternative network of schools dominated by the Christian Reformed Church, and indifference among the Reformed for Christian education at the secondary level all conspired to kill Hope High School during the economically difficult Depression years.[7] In this respect, developments in Holland, Michigan, were not much different than elsewhere in the RCA; a network of church-run primary schools in the East folded in the course of the nineteenth century, and the RCA secondary schools in Iowa closed their doors in the years after the Second World War. By the mid–twentieth century, the RCA's institutional ties to educational bodies were largely restricted to three liberal arts colleges and two seminaries.

In fact, many members of the RCA and its denominational leadership were deeply committed to American *public* education on the primary and secondary level. In the 1860s and 1870s, the RCA took a strong stand in favor of the public school (as long as the Bible was taught there) because it regarded it as an essential unifying force in American society.[8] In their enthusiastic support for the public school, the RCA leadership and laity differed little from their counterparts in other mainline Protestant churches. Their commitment to public schools stemmed from a vision — one that at least seemed plausible before the Supreme Court decision of 1962 prohibiting public prayers in public schools — that saw public schools as "nonsectarian," virtually Protestant institutions. And particularly in towns with large numbers of Protestant Christians, there was usually confidence that community morals and locally-bred teachers would ensure that in the *local* public school, at least, prayers were said, that the Bible was read, and

6. *1930 Milestone,* 106; for a pessimistic prognosis of the prep school's future, see Dimnent, "Annual Report to the Board of Trustees," April 28, 1928, Hope College Board of Trustees, File Minutes, April 1928–April 1929.

7. The decline of the Reformed preparatory school also probably stemmed from the vast increase in college students. Christian secondary educational institutions, because so many were going on to college, were no longer an important source for Christian leadership in church and society. From the 1920s on, it was the college, as well as the seminary, that became the focal training ground for these leaders.

8. Ryskamp, "The Dutch in Western Michigan" (Ph.D. dissertation, University of Michigan, 1930), 67.

that a wholesome Christian atmosphere was maintained. (In communities with schools with high numbers of non-Protestants, private schools might well be necessary, the argument often went.) This attitude was buttressed by the widely shared assumption that American democratic ideals and cultural values as propagated in the public schools were largely, if not wholly, commensurate with the Christian faith. Christians, therefore, would be able to exercise a constructive role in America's public schools. More than that, as Christians they *should* exercise their influence in public schools, rather than fleeing the world to cloistered, "sectarian" schools.

Of course, the most striking illustration of this confidence that Christianity and the church on the one hand, and the state and public schools on the other, were working in the same direction came not on the secondary level, but on the collegiate level. Since the 1860s, Rutgers College (dominated by a majority of trustees from the RCA) and the state of New Jersey had closely cooperated in the creation of a larger university. At first, the church maintained strong formal control; until the early twentieth century, bylaws required that the majority of trustees be full members of the Reformed Church (though after 1863 it was no longer under direct church control), and that the president be a clergyman from that body. But because Rutgers also functioned as the state's land grant university, and because the size and scope of this university came to overshadow the classical liberal arts institution once established by the church, it became increasingly difficult practically to maintain, or to philosophically justify, "sectarian" control over the school. That some within the church lamented the formal loss of Rutgers in 1917 cannot be doubted, but the close cooperation between the RCA and the state of New Jersey, lasting half a century, also says a good deal about a Reformed willingness to make common cause with the state in the field of education. Even in the field of *higher* education, then, the Reformed Church's confidence in the beneficial effects of public education, and its deep affinities with American life and political ideals, did not invariably encourage the Reformed to create a network of church-related institutions.[9]

Given all of this, why did Hope College (or any RCA college)

9. See Richard P. McCormick, *Rutgers: A Bicentennial History* (New Brunswick: Rutgers University Press, 1966).

continue to enjoy the strong support of the church? Why not throw their wholehearted support to the emerging state universities? One factor explaining why Hope maintained its ties to the RCA — and Rutgers did not — is that the Midwestern Dutch Reformed, as recent immigrants, were more tied to their immigrant institutions, and were able to sustain these institutions through more stable constituencies of support.

However, other reasons for this continued support were not dissimilar to the reasons Methodists and Presbyterians maintained their own colleges. In the first place, there was the important consideration of *in loco parentis*.[10] Until they went off to college, students could always be kept on the straight and narrow by the proximity of family, church, and yes, Christian-friendly public schools. The big state universities, however, did not always provide a wholesome Christian environment for impressionable young adults. The consideration was largely pragmatic: state schools under (Protestant) Christian influence were benevolent; state schools where this was not the case might justifiably be avoided by God-fearing Protestants, who would then have reason to establish their own schools.[11] Christian colleges were important because young Christian adults would spiritually benefit by attending them in the absence of Christian family and home church. A corollary to this attitude was the argument that it was only in adulthood that Christians were faced with *intellectual* questions to their faith. Through secondary education, students of all creeds needed to be taught the same basic subjects, and only in college did the seriously interpretative spiritual work begin.[12]

Perhaps the paramount reason for continued RCA commitment

---

10. Latin for "in place of the parent."

11. Dosker, *Levensschets van A. C. Van Raalte, D.D.*, 189.

12. For these and other arguments for the public school, see Board of Education, Reformed Church in America, "The Relationship of Public and Parochial School Education" (New York: Reformed Church of America, 1957). This report — which included President Emeritus Wynand Wichers as one of its authors — is perhaps the strongest statement of RCA support for the public school written in a decade (the 1950s) when mainline Protestant support of the public schools was at high tide. In this sense, then, its views should not be seen as identical to views held earlier in the twentieth century, but in general tone and argument parallels the major arguments made by earlier Reformed defenders of the public school.

to post-secondary Christian education was that Christian colleges were seen as training schools for Christian leadership of church and society. The very fact that the church needed ministers and missionaries was often justification enough to support Reformed church colleges, since state universities were unlikely to provide either the education or the spiritual conditions such men and women required. But as these colleges grew in size and the numbers of ministers and missionaries proportionately sank, the vision became more explicitly broad: a Christian college was needed to create Christian leaders in *all* areas of life. President Ame Vennema, for example, believed that Christian colleges undergirded Christian support for *public* schools:

> The objection sometimes urged against the public school system, that it is unchristian, largely falls away when we can have teachers who will carry into the school-room the grace and force of christian personality. We aim to send out for the training of our children and youth such as bear the image of Christ as well as the stamp of the college.[13]

The traditional RCA support for *public* education provides an important context for understanding how *Christian* education was understood in the RCA, and constructed at Hope College. Religious instruction and religious life would be important elements at the college in order to sustain Christians away from home and to prepare them for service in public life. Other subjects would be taught much the same as they had been at the public schools, though always under the tutelage of a convinced Christian — again, in order to prepare Hope's graduates for public life. There would be no systematic efforts, such as those attempted by the Christian Reformed or Catholics to create an overarching view of human knowledge that contrasted with that of the surrounding culture, for the RCA's philosophy of education — however inchoate — possessed no impetus for such an attempt. Rather, the basic knowledge that was taught at other colleges and universities would be augmented by additional religious courses and by the Christian sensibilities of a Christian faculty.

---

13. Ame Vennema, "The Educational Position and Policy of Hope College."

Early Curriculum and Faculty

In this light, it can hardly be a surprise that Hope presidents often proclaimed that education without religion was not complete. This included religious instruction in the classroom, and at Hope such courses took a prominent place. Religious instruction was required all four years, of all students, until well after the Second World War. The first three years consisted of what the *Bulletin* of 1897 called "Bible Study" — a systematic exploration of the New Testament.[14] In later years, the Old Testament was included in the curriculum.[15] In all cases the purpose of Hope's religion courses was clearly not only to impart information, but to encourage personal piety. A description of "the Department of Biblical Literature" made clear in the 1920 *Bulletin* that a literary appreciation of the Bible was the least of its aims:

> In all courses given in this department, the genuinely historical character and divine origin and authority of the Bible are unquestioned. The literary value of the Biblical documents is incidentally pointed out. The object in view is to lead the student to a better understanding and appreciation of the Scriptures as the divine revelation of the righteous and loving will of God for men and the only true way of salvation. The providence of God as evidenced in history is emphasized. The cultivation of devotional habits is enjoined.[16]

In their senior year, Hope students were required to take one or more capstone courses intended to show how Christian theology and morality underwrote the whole collegiate endeavor. Prior to the First World War, this included an ethics course that for a long time used *Elements of Moral Science, Theoretical and Practical*, authored by the former president of Yale University, Noah Porter. Of longer tenure was the

---

14. *Hope College Bulletin*, 1897-1898, 14-16.

15. The initial emphasis on the New Testament in the collegiate curriculum stemmed from the fact that the Old Testament was taught to the younger students in the Hope Preparatory School. The many students who enrolled at Hope on both levels would therefore receive four years of Old Testament, and three of the New. The increase in student enrollment of those who had not attended the Preparatory School probably accounts for the shift.

16. *Hope College Bulletin*, 1920-1921, 19.

"Evidences of Christianity" course, sometimes taught in the Philosophy Department. Hope professor and Rutgers graduate J. Tallmadge Bergen considered the purpose of his course not only to offer "a scientific knowledge of Scripture and Christianity, but also effort is made to lay them upon the heart and make them the rule of life."[17] In the first decades of the twentieth century, the course seems to have aimed at providing a Christian view of the world and, with even more emphasis, defending the "Reasonableness of Supernaturalism" and the trustworthiness of Scripture — including detailed refutations of the "naturalistic explanations of the Resurrection of Christ."[18]

What is striking about Hope's religious curriculum is *not* its originality — it bears much resemblance to course offerings at most American Protestant colleges in the late nineteenth century. Much more striking is how *long* it persisted. Well into the twentieth century, "Bible" remained a standard course in each year of college work. And it was only in 1939 that the "Evidences of Christianity" course — with its very title anchored in a nineteenth-century epistemology now widely regarded as antiquated — was replaced by a new capstone course, "The Philosophy of the Christian Religion." Hope College remained, throughout this period, firmly committed in its religion courses to imbuing students with the truths of orthodox Protestantism. To be sure, there were telltale signs of change in the college catalogs of the 1930s — the Department of Bible and Religion (as it was then known) no longer claimed to read Providence in history, or stress, at least in print, the "cultivation of devotional habits." And in the new senior capstone course, students were now encouraged to "bring their personal religious problems for free discussion" — a hint that religious instruction included more dialogue than had previously been the case.[19] But in form and in content, classroom religious instruction at Hope remained strongly traditional — and outspokenly Christian.

The evident presence of orthodox religion in the departments of "Biblical Literature" or of "Bible and Religion" is not, perhaps, very surprising at a college of the sort Hope was earlier in the twentieth century. But what of the other departments on campus? Did their cur-

---

17. *Hope College Bulletin,* 1899-1900, 37.
18. *Hope College Bulletin,* 1934-1935, 33.
19. *Hope College Bulletin,* 1939-1940, 35.

ricula bear the stamp of Christian belief? Ame Vennema in his inaugural address of 1913 argued that here too Christianity made a difference:

> . . . whether history is taught as the record of a series of disconnected happenings, or the evolving of the plan and purpose of an over-ruling Providence, [and] whether biology is taught upon the theory of spontaneous generation, or whether every form of life, from the jelly-fish to the arch-angel, is held to proceed from the one great Fountain of Life. . . .[20]

How a Christian vision of education worked itself out in practice, however, varied enormously. Still, patterns emerge that suggest how Vennema's theistic vision of education was — or was not — carried out at the school.

Perhaps because of an aversion to "sectarian indoctrination," the Hope curriculum tended — at least outside of the Religion Department — to be less systematic in the way it worked out Christian principles. Hope's curriculum "from the beginning was not basically different from the curricula of other liberal arts colleges in America."[21] Henry Ryskamp's distinction between Calvin and Hope, made in 1930, still serves as a useful guide in this respect:

> Hope has always been a Christian College but has not been characterized by such a careful attempt to indoctrinate its products [as has Calvin]. It has aimed at a practical Christian life, its attempts to-day being not so much the development of a theoretical well-sustained Calvinistic point of view as the giving to its students of real "religious experience" as one student put it. It makes much more of inspiring talks and conferences that awaken the youth to a desire to go out and "do" things. Calvin stimulates a desire to sit down and "think it out." It has, therefore, introduced such subjects as Philosophy, Sociology, and organic science . . . because it is desirous that in these branches the student be trained in accordance with Reformed principles. Hope has turned more strongly to the more cultural branches in order to give its youth a foundation for

20. Vennema, "The Educational Position."

21. Arnold Mulder, *Americans from Holland* (Philadelphia and New York: Lippincott, 1947), 208.

the well-rounded life of a Christian man or woman. In the last few years it has become known also for its teaching of the natural sciences with a view to preparation for teaching and medicine.[22]

Outside of the Religion Department Hope's practically minded, rather anti-theoretical Christian vision put its emphasis on Christian *faculty,* not on Christian *curriculum.* From the start, Hope required its faculty to be members in good standing of a Protestant church. Many faculty members were Dutch and Reformed by birth and creed — judging by the admittedly imperfect measure of Dutch surnames, they constituted the overwhelming majority of faculty throughout the nineteenth century. Between the First and Second World Wars, they roughly numbered anywhere from half to almost two-thirds of the professoriate. Outsiders who taught at the college also often joined the Reformed Church when they arrived in Holland — frequently Hope Church, the least Dutch and most broadly evangelical of the RCA churches in town. History teacher Metta Ross, a newcomer to Holland who received her bachelor's degree from Hope at the age of thirty-six and soon joined the faculty and became a member of Hope Church, recalled rather matter-of-factly that to teach at Hope meant going to a Reformed church.[23]

That did not mean finding suitable piously Protestant — let alone Reformed — faculty was always an easy task. President Dimnent, in his own inimitable way, explained in 1918 the difficulties of hiring to an Iowa RCA pastor angered at the fact that Dimnent had just hired a Christian Reformed pastor to teach religion at Hope:

> Let me know of a man trained to physics and I'll hand him the job at once — but he must not be a mason, he must be a church member, he must be willing to work on a maximum of fifteen hundred a year, he must not dance, play cards, frequent the theater, he must know how to use a knife and a fork and when not to use either, he must be clean in body and mind, he must be enthusiastic for schol-

22. Ryskamp, "The Dutch in Western Michigan," 70.

23. Transcript of Interview with Metta Ross, Oral History Project, 1977, JAH. More research would need to be conducted in order to determine exactly how many faculty chose to attend other Protestant churches in the city, but the number was probably quite low, since RCA churches were able to cater to a wide range of Protestant sensibilities.

arship, for religion, for missions. . . . Big bill, eh? But do you know that we looked for several years for a modern language man who could fill those conditions and we did not get him. We made an especial effort to get a man from our church for the Physics chair and catered to him while he was here only to have him find a job with three hundred more a year in it. . . . Do you appreciate the situation?[24]

Poor salaries — biology professor Frank Patterson was forced to take an additional job as night watchman in the 1920s in order to maintain his family[25] — as well as the constraints of "local morality" did not make Hope an invariably attractive place to teach. These factors only made it harder for the college to find the sufficient "evangelical" (i.e., Protestant) faculty it continued to insist must be hired. And in all likelihood the college did hire faculty who would not have met Dimnent's standard of "enthusiasm for religion" (let alone, it might be added, "enthusiasm for scholarship"). Old wags like telling stories about the godlessness of a long-serving professor famed for telling dirty jokes, or of those who were seen none too frequently in church. Samuel O. Mast, the biology professor (1899-1908) who raised Hope's science program out of its moribund state, was apparently no avid pewwarmer. Raised a Lutheran, Mast told his colleagues at Johns Hopkins — where he took his employ after leaving Hope — that his boyhood days were filled with so much church that he no longer needed to attend.[26] Despite these examples, however, there is little reason to doubt that most Hope faculty were not only observant but sincere Christians who tried their best to set a moral, spiritual, and intellectual example to their students.

To these faculty was entrusted the power, as Vennema put it in his 1913 address, to either replenish "the ranks of the materialist, the agnostic or the infidel . . . or to swell the company of devout believ-

24. Edward Dimnent, letter to Harry Hoffs, 20 November 1918, in "Correspondence from Dimnent, 1918-1919," in Dimnent Presidential Papers, JAH.

25. Patterson's health declined during his seventeen-year service at the college (1909-1926), perhaps through the extra exertions he was obliged to take upon himself. He died of tuberculosis in Arizona in 1931. Biographical file, "Frank N. Patterson," JAH.

26. John B. Buck, letter to Donald Cronkite, 23 April 1981, in biographical file "Samuel O. Mast," JAH.

ers."[27] But in pursuing this aim, it mattered less *what* was taught than *who* taught it. A striking example of this is how the role of one contentious issue — evolution — played itself out at Hope during this period.

"Our Bible and Science Departments Do Not Quarrel"

"'Now class, now class . . . Darwin is all wrong,'" Henry Vander Ploeg recalled hearing while at Hope during the early 1890s, "and then for a lovely hour of haranguing on evolution instead of a math. recitation with Prof. Kleinheksel."[28] Within the larger Reformed community of West Michigan, evolution remained throughout this period closely associated with unbelief, and at least some Hope faculty and presidents felt obliged to take a stand against it. A. J. Muste recalls that as a student at Hope Preparatory School there were books he was not allowed to read, including those on Darwin's theory of evolution — books to be read only by the upperclassmen in the college.[29] Throughout Dimnent's presidency (1918-1931), the "Evidences of Christianity" course sought to consider "the Christian View of the World and its superiority to pantheism, materialism, agnosticism and evolution."[30] At the same time, evolution had its supporters at the college. As early as 1892, student D. J. Werkman defended the study of evolution in *The Anchor*, arguing that "there is nothing in the essential principles of evolution that contradicts the essential principles of Christianity."[31] Although the offering in biology never specifically mentioned evolution, it seems clear that Mast and his successors in that department used evolution as a scientific explanation for the workings of nature. From the first years of the twentieth century, then, the theory of evolution was likely used in the increasingly prominent curriculum of the natural sciences.

Was there a contradiction here? Some alumni thought so in the wake of the Scopes "Monkey Trial" in 1925. Late that year, Hope alum-

27. Vennema, "The Educational Position."

28. *1930 Milestone*, 299.

29. Jo Ann Ooiman Robinson, *Abraham Went Out: A Biography of A. J. Muste* (Philadelphia: Temple University Press, 1981), 9.

30. *Hope College Bulletin*, 1920-1921, 47.

31. D. J. Werkman, "Evolution and Christianity," *The Anchor*, June 1892, 135.

nus and RCA pastor George Heneveld attended a meeting featuring fundamentalist preacher John Roach Stratton in a blistering attack on evolutionism entitled "Monkey Men and Monkey Morals." Stung by Stratton's attacks, Heneveld spoke out at the gathering, saying that he was a Christian evolutionist. As he recounted in a letter to Dimnent in December of 1925,

> I told them something like this. "I am a minister of the RCA, graduate of her college and Sem. in the west. Our Dept. of Bible and Science do not quarrel, they agree, always have. . . ." Told them evolution was kept in the background, not stressed but it was there. . . . Told them our students did not have their faith wrecked as so many nowadays do. . . .

But now, Heneveld noted with consternation, he had learned that President Dimnent, key faculty members, and the Council of Hope College had recently and publicly weighed in *against* evolution — presumably because community sentiment had prompted them to do so. Had he been wrong in his understanding of the college's position?[32]

Heneveld was not the only one to be disconcerted. One of his ministerial colleagues, the staunchly anti-evolutionist A. W. De Jonge, was surprised to learn from Heneveld at the Stratton talk that certain faculty at Hope College, like biologist Frank Patterson and religion professor Albertus Pieters, were "evolutionists." De Jonge and another colleague both promptly wrote to Hope College Council President Gerhard De Jonge, who in turn wrote to Pieters, asking for a "statement in regard to your own position on this question, and also in regard to the position of Dr. Patterson."[33]

Pieters's response was telling. Hope alumnus, longtime missionary to Japan, deeply pious and staunchly orthodox, Pieters enjoyed a spiritual stature like few others at Hope. His nuanced explanation deserves to be quoted at length:

---

32. Letter of George Heneveld to E. D. Dimnent, 10 December 1925, in "Correspondence to Dimnent, 1924-1929," Dimnent Presidential Papers, JAH. Heneveld asked Dimnent for a candid response, but any reply Dimnent may have sent is not extant in his papers.

33. Letter of Heneveld to Dimnent; letter of Gerhard De Jonge to Albertus Pieters, 10 November 1925, in biographical file "Albertus Pieters," JAH.

I am not an evolutionist. Brother Heneveld is mistaken about that. An evolutionist is a man who is convinced that the doctrine of evolution is true [and] who forms his world-view, or philosophy of life, upon that basis. . . . I am not convinced that evolution is true . . . although I can see there is much to be said in favor of it. . . . My opinion is well expressed in the following words of Ludwig Heck: "[Human descent from apes] is a plausible hypothesis, although it has not been irrefutably demonstrated. . . ."

As to Dr. Patterson . . . I am sure that he does not teach the evolution of man from the lower animals as a proven fact. . . . He is too much of a scientist for that.

[But] Dr. Patterson certainly teaches the theory of evolution. He must do that, of course. Young people do not come to Hope College to remain ignorant, but to be instructed in what is being said and discussed in the world to-day.

However, of this I can assure you with confidence, that Dr. Patterson neither believes nor teaches any view of evolution that rules God out. Whatever he accepts and teaches he holds together with the earnest conviction that God is the creator and ruler of all things, and that whatever natural process there was, most certainly took place under the divine guidance and control, working towards a purpose in God's mind.[34]

What mattered to Pieters was not what Patterson taught about evolution — whatever counted for a good education would determine that — but that Patterson be able to square what he taught with his own Christian convictions. Since neither Pieters nor Patterson (who himself attended the venerable Gerrit Diekema's Men's Bible Class at Hope Church)[35] could be reproached for a lack of piety, their position on evolution itself was tolerated, even respected within the college community — if discreetly downplayed for the wider Dutch Reformed constituency. In the end, it was the strength of the professors' personal

34. Letter of Albertus Pieters to Gerhard De Jonge, 10 November 1925, in biographical file "Albertus Pieters," JAH.

35. Letter of Frank Patterson to G. J. Diekema, 18 April 1928, in biographical file "Frank N. Patterson," JAH. Patterson was forced to leave the college in 1926, not for reasons of any controversy, but for his failing health. Pieters also left in 1926, to teach at Western Seminary.

example and their Christian faith and character that gave students a Christian education at Hope College.

In the end, evolution never became a contentious issue at the college — though in 1925 it briefly appeared as if it might — nor did any other intellectual issue outside of the Religion Department, with the exception, as we shall see again, of theatre when it was introduced after 1945. There were, of course, occasional flare-ups, as in 1930, when several faculty were briefly investigated for their views (see Chapter Two). And texts with bad language, or impious attitudes, might generate some anger or hostility on the part of students or parents. But for the most part it seems that Hope faculty were permitted — as long as they could demonstrate that they were moral and pious Christians — to teach what they wished in their classrooms. The strength of this approach was that it encouraged a fair measure of academic freedom by allowing for a variety of insights and perspectives from a (limited) range of seasoned and informed Christians. The weakness — at least in the long run — was that it raised the question of whether it mattered that they were Christians, if Christian faculty actually did not teach their subjects in a different way than their non-Christian counterparts. Would the fact that Hope's Bible and science departments did not quarrel eventuate in the Bible and science departments ceasing to talk at all to one another? Many Hope science faculty, at least in the earlier part of the twentieth century, may have avoided enacting the "two-realms" view of knowledge characterized by Sloan and discussed in Chapter One by articulating for their students how they reconciled their theology with their science. Yet it is far from clear that all did. If they did not, of what import was it for the fulfilling of their duties as Hope professors that they were Christians? And if it were of no import, why insist that they be Christian at all?

Manly Men and Women of Granite

But at Hope College the chief aim of education was not to make consistent Calvinist intellectuals but to instill Christian *character* in its students. Here, too, Hope College hardly deviated from the emphasis on character so stressed in American colleges through the early decades of the twentieth century. Nor was the emphasis on character foreign to the wider RCA. In his inaugural 1906 address as president of Rutgers, the last clergyman-president of that college, William H. S. Demarest, espoused that Christian education meant

> that men who teach shall be not only of fine scholarship but of fine character and reverent life, whose fellowship shall be a force of noble education. It [means] the clear uplifting of spiritual values of manhood for coveting and attainment by student life, the standard of supreme allegiance to God and saving trust in Jesus Christ whom He has sent.[36]

As part of its "do" culture, Hope subscribed to a broader American Protestant emphasis on producing people of strength and character who put principles into action. In fact, the college advertised itself as promoting "scholarship and development of Christian character."[37] As one *Anchor* article from 1893 put it, doctrine was only the foundation for Christian manhood — character must follow. Or as another *Anchor* article opined several years later, religion provided the basis for a "seriousness and earnestness" that would enable Christians to execute faithfully their tasks in the world. A 1916 student editorial argued that Hope needed to create "a perfect manhood" acquainted with "the science of right living."[38] By the 1920s, Dimnent had transformed character into "personality" — Christians who in their own persons touch the world and thus reveal to it "the Personality of the Eternal Ages."[39]

Because Hope College's vision of education focused heavily on the character and personality of each individual, the tasks of each individual were often prescribed along gendered lines. In 1913, Vennema exhorted,

> What the world needs always, but especially now, is men, manly men; and women, womanly women; men and women who are truth-fed and conscience-led, to whom right is supreme and duty

36. William H. S. Demarest, "Inaugural Address by the President," in *The Inauguration of William H. S. Demarest as President of Rutgers College* (New Brunswick: Rutgers College, 1906), 36.

37. See the advertisement in the *1916 Milestone*, 147.

38. [Prof.] John Tallmadge Bergen, "The Student and the Bible," *The Anchor*, November 1893, 17; [Prof.] J. B. Kleinheksel, "The College as Safeguard," *The Anchor*, June 1896, 142; "Hope's Greatest Need," *The Anchor*, 22 November 1916.

39. "Thy Pound Hath Gained" (fundraising brochure, Hope College, 1922).

paramount, who will not sell their birth-right of honor for the pottage of material gain or worldly glory. What society needs is men and women, educated and christian, who will lead the forces of good and of God in the great battle against selfishness and greed, against oppression and injustice, against political chicanery and wickedness in high places.[40]

In the *1927 Milestone* the Alethian Society (a sorority) wrote of "the struggle for well-balanced, winsome womanhood" and their male counterparts in the Emersonian Society stated the aspiration to become "a Christian and a gentleman."[41] Samuel M. Zwemer, a Hope alumnus and the RCA's greatest missionary leader, was more explicit than most in what "character" for each sex meant, in his 1921 address at the college:

> Blessed is the college woman whose strength and stability of character remind you of granite; on whom you can press the burden of a whole social fabric without crushing or disintegrating her character, the woman of grit and grace and graciousness — of power and purity and polish — of character and culture and kindness, whose life and influence in the home and community outlast the ages and stand out in the horizon of history like the Pentelic marble of the Parthenon.

For Hope men, Zwemer only needed to make a slight alteration to Psalm 1:

> Blessed is the college man who walketh not in the council of the ungodly nor standeth in the way of sinners not sitteth in the seat of the scornful — but his delight is in the law of the Lord and in his law doth he meditate day and night . . . and whatsoever he doeth, it shall prosper.[42]

However this gendering of character may strike us from our own cultural vantage point, Christian character formation remained one of the abiding educational aims of the college. As the prominent clergyman

---

40. Vennema, "The Educational Position."
41. "Emersonian Society," *1927 Milestone*, 122.
42. Samuel M. Zwemer, "A Stone and a Tree," *Hope College Bulletin*, 1921, 13-14.

Henry Dosker expressed in 1905, "the greatest honor" of Hope College consisted in the fact *that it is a moulder of character.*"[43]

Character building and the cultivation of "personality" at Hope clearly entailed more than a curriculum. What seemed to impress visitors and alumni about Hope College in the early part of the twentieth century was its "Christian atmosphere," as Dutch noblewoman P. van Haersma de With expressed it in 1935.[44] Charles Brown of the Yale Divinity School spoke of "the wonderful spirit of the people" at Hope College. Hope students themselves spoke of "the Spirit of Hope," an embodiment of the school's ideals, which the 1923 yearbook defined as "knowledge, love, service."[45]

Atmospherics are intangible considerations, and any historian attempting to describe such ungraspable essences as "school spirit" risks saying more about the author than about the school, especially when every American college claimed to have its own unique school spirit. What can be said, though, is that Hope's aims of fostering Christian character through Christian example and Christian community created a campus culture in the early decades of the twentieth century that embodied what some have called a "positive Christianity": nondoctrinaire in theology (within the confines of Protestant orthodoxy), practically-minded, cheerful in spirit, and attentive to the personal welfare and growth of its members. Stated in these general terms, the atmospherics at Hope of a century ago do not seem to be so very different from the way those now at Hope College often like to cast their own vision of the community.[46] If much has changed, perhaps much has stayed the same as well.

But did this "Spirit of Hope" translate into a compelling educational or social vision? What larger ends did the emphases on a "positive Christianity" and on character formation serve? In this respect, Hope before the Second World War was directed by a powerful set of spiritual impulses that not only shaped its campus culture but arguably distinguished Hope College from many other American Protestant colleges.

43. *The Hope College Manual*, 1905, 107.

44. P. van Haersma de With, letter to Wynand Wichers, 4 June 1935, in "Wichers, Wynand — Correspondence Presidential Years, 1931-1945," Wichers Presidential Papers, JAH.

45. 1923 yearbook on knowledge, love, service.

46. See Chapter One, pp. 19-26.

"Messengers of Hope" and the "Elevation of Humanity"

For the Hope student Albertus Pieters, there could only be one purpose of Christian higher education. It was nothing less than "the elevation of humanity" — an elevation that could be accomplished only through spreading Christianity. Two years before traveling to Japan as a missionary in 1891, he wrote in *The Anchor:*

> We rejoice in our strong vigorous life, in our superior education and in our Gospel privileges. But all these things lay us under supreme obligations to our benighted brethren. All these things testify against us if we fail to use them for the benefit of mankind. The sunshine that fills our life pleads with us eloquently in behalf of those who sit in darkness. We who enjoy these gifts of God are in a measure responsible for the gloom which covers the nations. It is our duty, who have received light, to become again the dispensers of light.[47]

It is this task — "the elevation of humanity" — that served as the conscious, driving force for Hope College in its first six or seven decades as a liberal arts institution. And for most Hope students and alumni of this period, the duty to elevate others could not be separated from the essential task of evangelism and missions.

In the early twenty-first century, it may seem strange, perhaps offensive, to see Christian evangelism linked to the impulse to educate, elevate, or "civilize" the rest of the world, or to link various forms of secular progress with spiritual improvement. The vision articulated at Hope College from its very inception in 1866 to around 1930 was that all these elements belonged together. Perhaps this can be most easily understood by looking at how Hope's identity as a *Western* college informed its wider mission to the world. "West" initially meant the American West, and as we have seen for clergymen like Van Raalte, it meant that "Western" institutions like Hope must produce ministers and missionaries who would win the American West and the world for Christ. While one natural outgrowth of this vision was that the RCA undertook strenuous efforts to establish missions among the Western American Indians in the late nineteenth century, it just as nat-

---

47. Albertus Pieters, "Our Responsibility," *The Anchor,* April 1889, 100-101.

urally undergirded the creation of institutions, both public and private, that would promote Christian society and all its benefits.

A Hope alumnus, the Rev. Albert Pfanstiehl, wrote back to his alma mater in 1887 about the important insights raised by Josiah Strong's enormously influential book, *Our Country*, written a couple of years before:

> If it is true that the character of the United States is to determine the character of the world; and the West is to determine the character of the United States, it follows with momentous significance to the young people of the West living now, that they are very likely to determine the moral and religious destiny of the world!! . . . [O]ur colleges and schools have a responsibility in this matter . . . for they have much, if not all, to do with determining the characters of our young people, at least the class of young people — the educated — from which largely will be chosen those who will fill places of trust and responsibility.[48]

Through the 1920s, Hope College students and alumni drew evangelistic zeal from the fact that their school was a Western one, placed by Providence in a pivotal role to affect the tide not only of American history, but the world itself. Dimnent, himself bred on the Strongian current influential at Hope while he was a student in the 1890s, chose to underscore the importance of Hope College's "purposeful Christian education" in the 1920s by stating:

> Western Civilization is Destined to Rule the World
> Western Colleges and Universities Produce Western Civilization
> The Great Men of the Future will be the Product of Western Schools . . .[49]

Clearly, Dimnent employed two different definitions of "Western." But the blurring of the two definitions is in fact a good illustration of Dimnent's belief that Christian schools in the Western United States held the keys not only to the future of the Christian church, but to the Western civilization that rested on Christian principles. Dimnent in

---

48. A. A. Pfanstiehl, "From our Alumni," *The Anchor*, December 1887, 3.
49. Advertisement, *1922 Milestone*, 191.

fact saw the world locked in conflict between the Christian West (though he harbored doubts on how Christian it was) and the polytheistic East. But Christian influences were badly needed in both hemispheres, and Hope's mission remained "the civilization and redemption of this world," as Dimnent put it in 1922.[50] "The world has need of you," as student Anne Whelan exhorted Hope in 1920.[51]

Yet, of course, Christian work would differ in different parts of the globe, as the 1916 Pageant made clear. In it, the Spirit of the Orient, followed by representatives of Eastern countries, beseeches the Spirit of Hope:

Spirit of Hope,
Have mercy on our need.
O send to us thy help!
Thy kindly culture send us, to refine our ways,
Thy wisdom to illume our ignorance
But most of all, O gracious Spirit,
Send us thy loving gospel, send thy Christ!

Then the Spirit of the Occident arrives, "followed by the people of the West":

We, too, have need of thee
Wisdom and culture, these we have, but Oh!
Give us ministers to tell of God,
And teachers, merchants, lawyers, serving Him,
Physicians like the One in Galilee
O Spirit, give us these.

The Spirit of Hope accordingly sends "Messengers, Envoys of Hope," to the Orient, and provides the Occident "Christians to work in your midst."[52]

It is not difficult to find fault in the vision or verse of Dimnent's

50. Dimnent, "The President's Report," in *The Fifty-fifth Annual Report of the Council of Hope College,* in "Dimnent, Edward D. — Annual Reports," in Dimnent Presidential Papers, JAH; letter to Rev. James de Pree, January 4, 1922, in "Correspondence from Dimnent, 1922," in Dimnent Presidential Papers, JAH.

51. Anne Whelan, "The Heritage of Hope," *1920 Milestone,* 122.

52. *1916 Milestone,* 128.

pageant. There is, of course, the rather facile cultural superiority of "the West" and the implicit support of various forms of Western imperialism in various "Oriental" countries that made Christian evangelization easier, even possible. And it is probable too that racist assumptions of the day shaped the contours of Hope's great vision, despite Hope's student missionary group's assertion in 1917 that it "never thinks in terms of race, color, or national boundary, but strives only for the evangelization of the whole world."[53] And, of course, there is the problem of conflating so many ideals — as if Christianity and America and Western Civilization and liberal arts education and material progress were unproblematically co-extensions of one another.

But it is precisely this conflation of ideals that made the vision to elevate humanity — spiritually, culturally, and materially — so powerful and compelling. Margaret Sangster's processional hymn (sung for four decades at Hope commencements until 1946) captures the apparent seamlessness of Hope College's broader vision.

Her children bear her lessons forth
To many lands and far
And East and West and South and North
Her pride those children are. . . .

For God and native land and man
In every clime and zone
We pledge our strength for what we can
Before Jehovah's throne.[54]

This vision unified the aims of Christian piety with a liberal arts education, and provided a deeper and wider purpose for every field of

53. *1917 Milestone*, 73. The need to overcome racial and ethnic prejudices was at least occasionally recognized as an imperative, as illustrated when the Student Volunteer Band presented the missionary play "The Color Line" to local churches in the course of the 1933-1934 school year; "Student Volunteer Band," *1934 Milestone*.

54. Margaret E. Sangster, "Hope," *Hope College Annual*, 1905, 130. Sangster was not a Hope College graduate, but was a writer from New York who wrote frequently in RCA magazines. Wynand Wichers reports that the song originates from a 1907 visit Sangster made to Hope, but a copy of her text "Hope" can be found in the 1905 annual; Wichers, *A Century of Hope* (Grand Rapids: Eerdmans, 1968), 177-78.

study. It was, in fact, a vision of Christian education that could meet with the wholehearted support of the rural churches and more sophisticated urban congregations of the RCA. It also unified traditional Christianity with a progressive vision of a new and better world that less conservative Protestants desired. Hope alumnus James Muilenburg, who would become a noted Protestant biblical scholar, wrote in 1925 while pursuing a doctorate at Yale:

> While her halls are filled, for the most part, with a special group of students of a particular faith and a particular national heritage, Hope College has been able to ward off the stigma of provincialism because of her broad charity and splendidly heroic missionary attitude. While the dangers of intolerance are ever near, she has liberally kept herself informed of activities of men and nations outside.[55]

Hope's educational vision also unified the aims of evangelical religion — concerned primarily with the salvation of the soul — with a civic Calvinism that demanded the reformation of society in accordance with divine norms. For Hope's vision, whatever Calvin College supporters like Kuiper might say, *was* Calvinistic insofar as it believed that the calling of the Christian was to transform culture.[56] "Elevation" and "uplift" — recurring themes in Hope's self-described mission — did not apply only to the soul, but to the improvement of society as well. Hope, then, might not have been Calvinistic in having a parochial academic program but might be said to be Calvinistic in its broad vision for a world made better by the gospel, and by the charge to its students to "reform, elevate, revolutionize" the globe.[57] Or, as Siebe Nettinga described the mentality of the Western RCA more generally in 1928, "world-conquest" — not "world-flight" — was the aim.[58] At

55. *1925 Milestone*, 141.

56. H. Richard Niebuhr gives a classic analysis of how different Christian traditions view the Church's relationship to its surrounding culture in *Christ and Culture* (New York: Harper, 1951). Among his five categories "Christ transforming culture" is the one that characterizes Reformed Christianity (in contrast to, for example, "Christ against culture," a characteristic Anabaptist stance).

57. "Editorial," *The Anchor*, June 1914, 28.

58. Siebe Nettinga, "The Church in Michigan," in *Tercentenary Studies, 1928: A Record of Beginnings* (Reformed Church in America, 1928), 452.

Hope College, revivalist religion went hand in hand with Calvinistic elevation.

There is no better articulation of Hope's world-historical mission than Dimnent's pageant play "The Pilgrim" of 1941. Dimnent necessarily figures prominently in this story, not only because of his presence on the campus for more than a half century, or because he was fonder of sharing written insights with others than other Hope presidents, but also because he was considered at the college to be a genius (he made money in the stock market during the Depression) and a visionary. And visionary in scope "The Pilgrim" was. Its protagonist was none other than Humanity, whose quest for "a perfect welfare" begins in darkness and then proceeds to the Ur of Abram, Egypt, Old Testament Israel, Calvary, the European monasteries, "the Reformation and the Liberation of Men" in the early modern Netherlands, and then to the settlements of the New World, ending, of course, in Holland, Michigan, and Hope College. There "the eternal quest of the Pilgrim is realized in so far as earth and this life permits," with Christian faith, freedom, and education finally united together as Providence intended. The great climax of the pageant follows as "children representing all the domestic and foreign mission fields" of the RCA, from Brewton, Alabama, to the Amoy Mission in China, enter the stage. Each group of children is in turn led by a "Leader," and together they "symbolize the ideal of service which is the aim of Hope College." The pageant then ends with the singing of Handel's "Hallelujah Chorus."[59]

Dimnent's pageant — the last to be performed at Hope College — was the most grandiloquent of Hope's pageants, all of them performed by students for the wider community. But it did not diverge substantially in theme from the pageants of 1916, 1926, and 1936, which all stressed the God-appointed task, to put it in the words of the 1926 production, to "send heralds forth to summon all the peoples of the world."[60] The "uplift of mankind" remained the central purpose of Hope College.

59. Edward Dimnent, unpublished summary of "The Pilgrim"; "The Pilgrim: A Pageant in Eight Episodes: In Commemoration of the Seventy-Fifth Anniversary of the Charter Grant, May 14, 1866"; "The Pilgrim: The Story of Christian Education," Dimnent Presidential Papers, JAH.

60. *1926 Milestone*, 177.

A Tradition of Self-Sacrifice and Service

But was Hope College really exceptional in both vision and practice in respect to this ideal? "Other colleges and universities," Zwemer said in his 1921 address, "have traditions and ideals of sport, of social privilege, of special lines of scholarship, of orthodoxy, or ecclesiastical loyalty." But Hope, he continued, was different:

> [O]ur Alma Mater has one great tradition and ideal. It is that of self-sacrifice and service. Van Vleck and Voorhees Hall are the little Westminster Abbeys of the men and women who made good. We love those walls and their old traditions, a record of heroism.[61]

Zwemer's claim of Hope's distinctiveness is, of course, exaggerated. But there can be little doubt that when it came to Christian missions, Hope alumni were far above average: they heeded the call to "heroism, adventure, sacrifice and death," the elements of which, according to future missionary Nettie De Jong, were the reasons youth was drawn to missions.[62] For about four decades in particular (from about 1885 to 1925) Hope College sent out an impressive number of missionaries to either foreign or domestic destinations — including a large number of women. By 1889, 11 out of Hope's 134 graduates to date had given themselves to missionary work; that percentage (just over 8 percent) remained constant until around 1920.[63] John R. Mott, the leader (along with Samuel Zwemer) of the Student Volunteer Movement, claimed in 1910 that no college had sent more missionaries to proclaim the gospel than had Hope. In the early 1920s, at the peak of missionary zeal at Hope, the college was sending over forty students a year into missions, roughly a quarter of the graduating

---

61. Zwemer, "A Stone and a Tree," 12. Van Vleck was at the time a men's dormitory, Voorhees a women's.

62. Nettie R. De Jong, "Young People and Foreign Missions," *The Anchor*, December 1905, 4.

63. Albertus Pieters, "Our Duty," *The Anchor*, April 1889, 101; "Member and Vocations of Hope's Alumni Retabulated by Secretary," *The Anchor*, 12 January 1921. Professor Paul Hinkamp spent a summer compiling these results — results that themselves were probably lost in the Van Raalte hall fire of 1980. The Student Volunteer Band in 1921 tallied the percentage of former and present missionaries at 15 percent, but this is probably too high; *1920 Milestone*, 61.

class.[64] The work of the "Messengers of Hope" in places such as the Basra(h) Boys' School in present-day Iraq or the impoverished American South occasionally resulted in their students choosing to study at Hope. As early as the 1870s, four Japanese students studied at the college; in 1932, James Carter Dooley of Brewton, Alabama, was the first (and only pre-Second World War era) African American to graduate from Hope College.[65] English professor Clarence De Graaf stressed this accomplishment in 1943:

> We at Hope can . . . point with pride to a number of orientals, Indians, Negroes and representatives of other minority groups who have come to us for some years on our campus. [And] the college has reached out to other races through the large numbers of missionaries, teachers and doctors who have graduated from our school.[66]

With the presence of these still small numbers of students of different cultures and different ethnicities, it is possible to contend that Hope College made strides — however modest — against the cultural superiority and racial stereotypes that afflicted not only the Dutch of West Michigan but much of American society.

The number of missionaries produced by Hope declined sharply, however, in the course of the 1920s. Just as the Student Volunteer Movement itself shrank nationwide as missionary zeal declined along with idealistic patriotism in the Twenties, the "Student Volunteer Band" (SVB) found it impossible to sustain its numbers in that decade. From a high of forty-three members in 1921, the SVB was down to twelve in 1928 — a number it would struggle to maintain until its dissolution in 1934, when it was replaced by the "Christian Workers' League," an organization that no longer catered only to aspiring missionaries.[67] Hope continued to send out a significant number of mis-

64. "Never before in the history of Hope College has God called so large a number of men and women to labor in his vineyards the world over," the Student Volunteer Band claimed in the *1920 Milestone*, 61; see also the *1921 Milestone*, 61.

65. Christian Shuck, "Minority and International Student Report," document prepared for the Joint Archives of Holland, 2003. For all the available material on James Carter Dooley, see the *1932 Milestone*.

66. Editorial, *The Anchor*, 27 October 1943.

67. See the *Milestones* of 1935 and after.

sionaries for the RCA and other denominations after the 1920s, but no longer in either the relative or absolute numbers of earlier years.

But missionaries, of course, were not the only bearers of the Christian message. The high numbers of Hope alumni who entered the ministry have already been discussed; in 1929 — when the number of missionary and ministerial alumni was already in decline — roughly 500 of the college's 1350 graduates were pastors, pastors' wives, or missionaries.[68] And in 1932, Hinkamp estimated that perhaps a quarter of the students were interested in some kind of "religious work," down from previous decades, but enough to indicate "that the Christian influence was still active on the campus."[69] And this did not include those who were preparing to become teachers in public schools — a vocation, as we have seen, itself considered an important area for Christian witness in society. Nor does it include the variety of Hope graduates who, whatever their major field of study and their eventual career, learned from their alma mater the essential task of uplifting humanity through the force of their Christian character and convictions.

The question hanging over Hope College at this point was whether a Middle Way aimed at character formation for Christian service, but also linked with an American ideal of progress and individualism, was a durable vision. In 1921, when Hope's halls were called "the little Westminster Abbeys of the men and women who made good," it seemed clear that the good that people aimed at was the good of *others,* and that that good was sought for Christ's sake. As Hope's religious ethos shifted after the world wars, coming more and more to identify making good with personal accomplishment and advancing national (rather than identifiably Christian) agendas, would Hope's collective memory retain any clear notion of *why* it pursued a Middle Way, and how a Hope education was to differ from that available at any respectable liberal arts college?

68. See Chapter Two; "Hope Memorirl [sic] Chapel Dedicated in Fine Style Last Friday Night," *The Anchor,* 12 June 1929.

69. "Y.M.C.A," *The Anchor,* 7 December 1932. Only 12 percent of freshmen who matriculated in 1935 expressed the intention of entering religious work — half of what it had been the year before. This number seems to have been abnormally low for the 1930s, but more research is needed to make definitive claims; "Statistics of Frosh Given," *The Anchor,* 30 January 1935.

4 Continuity and Change within Hope's Middle Way, 1925-1963

- "Evangelistic" to "Evangelical," 1925-1945
- Controversy and Control, 1945-1953
- Sacrificing the Spirit to Survival? 1953-1963
- The Babe and the Bathwater

"Hope College is proud to be a member of that large body of Liberal Arts Colleges that are called Christian," the college *Bulletin* proclaimed in 1945. Moreover, the *Bulletin* continued, Hope "is not colorless so far as Christianity is concerned. It is definitely Christian in character and does not shrink from the duty and obligation to help the Church redeem the world to Christ. . . . A spacious and beautiful chapel assists the Christian Faculty in making possible a religious atmosphere that parents will appreciate when they are thinking of sending their sons and daughters to College."[1]

This picture of a safely ensconced and undisputed Christian identity, to the extent it is true at all, is a more accurate description of the last half of the 1950s than the years immediately following the Second World War. Indeed, the *Hope College Bulletin* of 1945 (as most college catalogs) did not, of course, note serious concerns voiced by some about Hope's spiritual condition and direction. There were many RCA parents in the late 1940s who suspected that Hope's religious atmosphere was hardly Christian enough for their sons or daughters. All this would prompt the college leadership, spurred by an active Board

---

1. *Hope College Bulletin,* 1945-1946, 5. This passage was probably written by Wynand Wichers, the president of Hope College from 1931 to 1945. These words first appear in the 1931-1932 "Year Book," i.e., the college catalog.

of Trustees, to strengthen its ties to the RCA in the years after 1945. Perhaps more significant, the Board of Trustees would take the initiative in ensuring that Reformed-centered Protestantism would be made manifestly predominant at the college.

"Evangelistic" to "Evangelical," 1925-1945

The concerns harbored by some about the religious identity of Hope at mid-century can only be understood against the background of subtle changes that were occurring in the period between the world wars. It should not be assumed on the basis of our discussion thus far that between Hope College's founding as a liberal arts college in 1866 and the end of the Second World War little changed. Indeed, the controversies to which we have already alluded illustrate that shifts in the religious ethos of the college were already recognizable enough to be of concern to some in the 1930s.[2] To anyone like Dimnent, who came to the college in the early 1890s and who retired from teaching in the early 1940s, asserting that we can speak of one unchanging religious mentality and spiritual vision throughout this period would have seemed a palpable absurdity. He could have pointed to any number of changes, obvious and subtle, that had transformed the school in the course of their lifetimes.

However, from a vantage point of the early twenty-first century, it is obvious that the most dramatic shifts in religious life at Hope College took place in the explosive growth and social changes that rocked not only the college but all of American higher education in the wake of the Second World War. Compared to what came after, Hope College was a placid pond of tranquility from its inception as a college until ex-G.I.'s took advantage of government largesse to enroll. Hope remained overwhelmingly Dutch in ethnicity and Reformed in religion, with a large number of its graduates called to serve the college and denomination in a variety of ways. Restrictions on dancing and abhorrence of alcohol, if weakened, remained in place, and "local morality" continued to determine in unspoken ways the mores of the college. Though the science departments had become known for innovation, many of

2. See Chapter Two.

the other departments — certainly not least religion — remained traditionalist in orientation. And a collective memory of Van Raalte and his pilgrims — however ornamented with mythical elements in college pageants and panegyrics — kept the school tied to its original founder and mission. If some critics lamented in 1945 that Hope College had not yet fully entered the twentieth century, there were many enthusiastic alumni who celebrated the constancy of its vision and the persistence of its Christian ethos.

But all these important lines of continuity must not obscure the fact that Hope College changed in these years, particularly after the First World War. In the first place, the school was simply growing larger, especially in respect to its student body. Until 1890, graduating classes of well under ten were the norm, and twenty-five years later thirty students constituted a good year. By the end of the 1920s, graduating classes were nearing one hundred, though further growth slowed during the Depression. Economic and social demand for a widely expanding professional class meant that Hope College was not — could not be — a school chiefly for ministers and missionaries. Though most students in the 1920s and 1930s were sincere Christians, growing enrollment and differing vocational goals, combined with a more secular ethos in American society after World War I, made the Christian climate at the college more diffuse than it had been in the revivalistic days of President Kollen. Critics complained that students knew their Bible less than ever before; moreover, cars made the allurements and temptations of Chicago easier to reach, and radios and movies exposed students to ideas and lifestyles that would not have been countenanced before the war.[3] One does not have to hold to the simplistic view that Hope students of 1905 were pious saints and those of 1925 were profligate sinners to see that the Christian atmosphere at Hope faced a new series of challenges after World War I than it had had to face before. As future president Irwin Lubbers noted in 1930, "the breakdown of tradition during the war and immediately after" and "the endangering of spiritual development of

3. "Our young RCA people do not know what their heritage is either in traditions or in doctrine handed down to them or in the accomplishments of the promoters of the Church in America," President Dimnent wrote the Rev. Peter Moerdyke (Class of 1866); Dimnent, letter to Moerdyke, 12 March 1923, in "Correspondence from Dimnent, Dec. 1922–Oct. 1923," Dimnent Presidential Papers, JAH.

youth in a period of religious uncertainty" had made the 1920s a diffi-cult decade for Hope College.[4]

Accompanying this trend was a subtle change, as we have seen, from what might be called "evangelistic" religion to "evangelical" re-ligion in the late 1920s and early 1930s. Reporting "decisions for Christ" and the "conversion" of students as a way of demonstrating to the church the high spiritual tone of the college fell into disuse after the First World War. Broad if imperfect indicators of students' inter-ests — the college newspaper and yearbook — also focused much less on the religious mission of the college after the mid-1920s. The YWCA and YMCA played a declining, though still important, role in campus life, as many of the activities that it had organized for the whole stu-dent body were now taken over by more task-specific student groups. A student intent on entering the ministry reported in 1939 that he had "often" heard students speaking of "the general failure of religious life on the campus," and he wondered if the introduction of a short prayer "in all our classes" might not raise the spiritual tone.[5] It is not that the theological content of students' faith had changed very much — the YWCA and YMCA continued to exhibit the same evangelical piety and purposes (often in contradistinction with college chapters elsewhere). But it does seem that religious fervor abated, as a more moderate and sedate "evangelical" (understood then as synonymous with Protestant) faith increasingly set the tone at the college. Chapel talks came to have a broader focus than to encourage student piety; for example, Dutch Consul General Henry van Coenen Torchiana in 1932 addressed chapel on "Good Citizenship in International Rela-tions on the Pacific."[6] More important, the general *tone* of religious ex-pression was more subdued and less zealous after 1925 or 1930 than it had been before. The period at Hope before 1930 was essentially re-vivalist and missionary in thrust. The period from roughly 1930 to 1960 (the Wichers and Lubbers presidencies), when the college pri-marily considered itself a Protestant community, was situated firmly in an orthodox but centrist spirit and orientation in contrast to Funda-

4. Irwin J. Lubbers, "President Dimnent — An Appreciation," *Christian Intelligen-cer,* 16 July 1930, 466-67, in "Dimnent, Edward D. — Tributes," in Dimnent Presidential Papers, JAH.

5. Harold Mackey, "Let the Sparks Fly," *The Anchor,* 2 February 1939.

6. "Subject of Talk is Good Citizenship on Pacific," *The Anchor,* 13 April 1932.

mentalism.[7] Hope English professor Lubbers — probably saying more about himself than his superior whom he was praising — characterized this Middle Way as follows in 1930:

> In a period when men were losing their grip on religion by deserting their creeds, and others were losing theirs by defending their creeds, President Dimnent guided the destinies of Hope College so that young people in their formative years might develop their personal faith and character through genuine religious experience.[8]

Creedalism had never been an emphasis at Hope, and in this respect Lubbers's emphasis on "religious experience" could be traced to Van Raalte himself. But by 1930 this distinction was used to define Hope not only over and against the confessionally minded Christian Reformed, but also over and against literalists and fanatics now associated with Fundamentalism. The Hope College of today — neither closely fitting a conservative "evangelical" nor a "mainline" model — clearly found its origins in this emerging attitude.

As Hope College grew larger, its academic program also grew in size and quality. In the nineteenth century, not a single Hope faculty member possessed an earned Ph.D.; by the time of the First World War, several did. By 1930, four of roughly thirty faculty possessed a Ph.D. (two of them, Gerrit Van Zyl and J. Harvey Kleinheksel, were foundational figures in the natural sciences); a decade later, this had climbed to seven in a slightly larger faculty. Many more now had Master's degrees, or had spent at least some time (a summer or a semester) in graduate school. Perhaps more importantly, professional standards became factors to which all faculty paid more attention, as made necessary, for example, through the rise of accreditation agencies. In Wichers (1931-1945) the college had a president who, though having no doctorate of his own, paid more attention to developments in the

---

7. After the Scopes Trial, and the rise of the Fundamentalist-Modernist controversy, there was an effort by leaders in the RCA — including Classis Holland — to refrain from joining either camp, and maintain a moderate high ground that preserved them from apostasy on the one hand and marginalization and obscurantism on the other.

8. Lubbers, "President Dimnent," 467.

academic world, in part because of his own graduate education at what is now Western Michigan University.

Just how the gradual process of professionalization had an impact on the religious orientation of the college is a complex issue, of course. Certainly it was not true of Hope faculty to say that the higher the degree, the greater the measure of religious doubt. But it seems likely that more faculty came to see their mission as one of tension between — as Wichers himself felt — affirming and defending Christianity on the one hand and maintaining academic standards on the other.[9] This perceived dualism between academics and faith, already present in the way many Hope faculty thought of the academic enterprise, widened as academic expertise and religious faith came increasingly to seem at best unrelated and complementary spheres of life.

Finally, there were changes in how those at Hope College understood their essential mission, "the elevation of humanity." Through the 1920s, national and religious aims, American and Christian ideals, had barely been distinguished; to serve one was to serve the other, since the advancement of "Christian civilization" was the goal. By the 1930s, and especially in the 1940s, as America mobilized to fight the Nazis and the Japanese, this changed. References to a Christian society, persistent through the 1920s, were replaced in World War II by a renewed commitment to democracy, whether at home or abroad. It was support for a democratic America — and a democratic world — that now became the most pressing mission. Christian conscience and Christian institutions now came to be seen as bulwarks of democracy — religion in the service of a laudable secular ideal which itself needed religion in order to thrive. "Hope thou in God — This is the need of Democratic Education," John Dykstra, President of the Board of Trustees, intoned in 1941.[10] The language of citizenship, as evidenced in the initial "Aims of Hope College," became a new way for Hope faculty and students to express Christian responsibility. And one graduating senior in 1945 wrote about the tasks that lay ahead in the postwar world:

9. Wynand Wichers, "Inaugural Address," 12 October 1931. Personal Archives of Elton Bruins.

10. John A. Dykstra, "Hope Thou in God," *The Intelligencer-Leader*, 20 June 1941, 34.

Again, we look to the Directions for Living and here learn it is our duty as individuals to live sinlessly before God and *for* our fellow man; it will be our duty as Christian citizens to live not selfishly unto our own nation, but unto the whole world.[11]

There were students who did not think that Hope College was doing enough in the fight for democracy, not least in terms of racial prejudice. As *Anchor* editor Connie Crawford put it in 1943:

It is just about time we loyal Dutchmen took a look at the scoreboard. We might be surprised to find it filled with a host of [u]ncompleted passes and fumbles concerning racial-relations right here on campus and in our little college town. Why, we don't have any racial problems here at Hope. We have no other race here but the good Caucasian stock! . . . What makes the Christian college of ours so exclusive? — So exclusive that other races or religions are afraid to enroll in our course of study? America, the melting-pot of nations — Holland, Michigan, the melting-pot of Dutchmen.[12]

Increasingly, the mission of the college — and not least its religious mission — would be understood in terms of its contributions to democratic society at home and abroad. This was itself another Christian vision of "elevating humanity." But what ties if any did this new participation and involvement in democratic life share with an older Christian vision, still strongly represented at the college, which emphasized personal conversion and faith in Christ as the heart of true transformation? The Second World War was only the starting point of the debate surrounding this question.

Some readers may regard the changes at Hope College after the First World War as a story of spiritual decline, when the college lost its spiritual fervor. Some may regard it as a story of progress, in which the college slowly moved out of the confines of which Yntema had complained in 1930.[13] The point here, however, is to underscore that already in the period between the two world wars the Middle Way had

11. "Hope College Looks Forward to a Bright Future," *1945 Milestone,* 95.
12. "Human Football Is Still a National Sport," *The Anchor,* 13 October 1943.
13. See p. 40.

become more and more diffuse. This was due to the college's gradually expanding size, its increasing academic ambitions, and perhaps especially its tendency to conflate its Christian mission to elevate humanity with the national goal of making the world safe for democracy.

Hope College in 1945 could have gone in several different directions. It was characterized by a number of elements among which there was rising tension: the proximity of a conservative religious constituency, a convinced if non-doctrinaire Christian ethos, a rising academic reputation and increasingly professionalized faculty, and a deep commitment to participate fully in American life. Before 1945, many at the college could believe — or hope — that these various elements traveled in the same direction. In the years after the Second World War, many at Hope found it increasingly difficult to articulate a common vision of how academic life and Christian faith related to each other.

Controversy and Control, 1945-1953

In the first postwar years, most Protestant colleges in the United States sought to fortify their religious mission in the light of new challenges and responsibilities. For many presidents of these colleges, the past crises of depression and war taught that democracy required morally and spiritually discerning citizens, and the future, with an American nuclear superpower facing a formidable communist adversary, demanded no less. Only the timeless virtues of the West's spiritual heritage, they believed, could effectively arm America against the perils of the future. Hope alumnus Irwin Lubbers, who became president of Hope in the summer of 1945, regarded the church-related college, with its theistic and moral education, as a vital asset of American democracy.[14] On this score, at Hope as well as elsewhere, religious moderates like Lubbers could make common cause with more conservative churchmen about the necessity of rethinking the connection between liberal arts education and Christian faith.[15] The challenge was to do

14. See, for instance, Irwin Lubbers, "My Hope for Christian Education is the Reformed Church," in Irwin Lubbers, Office of the President, "Board of Education — RCA," JAH.

15. A call for such reflection came, interestingly, in the student newspaper; see the editorial "Hope Needs Re-valuation," *The Anchor*, 25 April 1946.

this in a period of rapid growth, when the number of students and faculty — many of them without much connection to the founding faith of the various colleges — was changing the face of American higher education.

Despite this widespread and renewed commitment to church-related higher education, there were those among Hope's constituency who questioned how well the college was executing its Christian mission. After the war, RCA conservatives, whether in the pew or the pulpit, became alarmed at both the moral decline of postwar America and purported moral and religious laxity at Hope College, which itself was undergoing a boom in enrollment and faculty hires. An overture to the Hope Board of Trustees by the Classis of Chicago in 1946 noted that "there is a growing suspicion that our College is not as positively Christian as the church to which she belongs wants her to be." At the top of these concerns was the Hope College faculty. Among examples of worrisome conduct at Hope the overture named were the "Professor who works on his boat in his yard on Sunday afternoon, disturbing the peace and rest of the Lord's Day until neighbors complain," and a play that contained profanity, a bar room scene, and "which ridicules our belief in eternal life."[16] Nor was the Classis of Chicago the only body to voice these worries. In a 1947 brochure directed at the Midwestern Synods of the RCA, the Dutch-born minister Henry Bast asserted in effect that Hope had employed many liberal, even nominal, Protestants:

> Hope College hires professors for its faculty without regard for Christian conviction, except that they be Protestant. I spent five years on the faculty of that institution and know what is going on; and if anybody wants to check this, let him look at the religious background of the present faculty at Hope College. It ought to be enough to shock the most indifferent.[17]

Intensifying the worries of conservatives like Bast about the Hope College faculty was the fear that the Eastern wing of the Re-

16. Classis of Chicago to Board of Trustees, 6 June 1946, in Minutes, Hope College Board of Trustees, 18-19 June, JAH.

17. Henry Bast, "An Appeal to the Ministers and Laymen of the Chicago and Iowa Synods" (N.p., 1947), 6.

formed Church, which supported RCA membership in the Federal Council of Churches and its post-1950 successor, the National Council of Churches, held altogether too much power in denominational institutions.[18] The college itself stood on the fault line of increasing friction between the more moderately conservative Protestantism of the Midwestern RCA and the moderately progressive Protestantism of the Reformed churches on the Eastern Seaboard. Situated as it was in Western Michigan, Hope catered mostly to the conservative Reformed constituencies of the Midwest, from which a not insignificant number of its faculty was drawn. But it also, as we have seen in Chapter Two, had strong historic and financial ties to the more theologically liberal Reformed churches of New York and New Jersey, who also supplied the college in the late 1940s with up to a fifth of its students.[19] Many of Hope's faculty, whether of Dutch Reformed origins or "imported" from outside the tradition, felt more at home with a less conservative form of Protestantism, less precise in its theological convictions and more reticent in its religious verbiage. Regardless of their precise theological views, many faculty members resented these new intrusions by conservatives within the RCA into college life. In 1947, a number of them signed a resolution to the Board of Trustees, proclaiming "that the members of our body are loyal, efficient, and devoted to the cause of Christian education and the best interests of the Reformed Church in America." They supported Lubbers as president against external encroachments on his prerogatives.[20]

One short-lived expression of a less conservative vision of the college was the faculty-written and presidentially sanctioned "Aims of Hope College," published in the Hope College *Anchor* in May of 1946 and intended as a preface to the curricular changes being advanced by

18. Bast, "An Appeal," 7-11.

19. One imperfect measure of this is the number of students attending Hope in the fall of 1949 from New York and New Jersey: 244 out of a total of 1124 enrolled (21.7 percent). Obviously, not all of them would have been members of the RCA, but the great bulk of them certainly were. "Annual Report of the Registrar, 1949-1950," found in Irwin Lubbers, Office of the President, "Board Meeting, Fall 1950," JAH.

20. The resolution was signed by such longstanding luminaries as the chemist Harvey Kleinheksel, Dean of Men Milton Hinga, the maestro R. W. Cavanaugh, historian Metta Ross, and Dean of Women Elizabeth Lichty; Irwin Lubbers Personal Papers, "1945 — Transition Year — Central to Hope," JAH.

the Lubbers administration. The result of drafts written by various faculty members in the spring of 1946, its final version was penned to a large extent by John Hollenbach, a young professor of English who was already on a trajectory that would propel him into prominence at the college for the better part of four decades.[21] The document spoke of advancing "Christian leadership in church and society." To do so, it pledged, along with more secular goals, to inculcate in the Hope student "an understanding of his relationship toward God," enabling him to fulfill "his responsibilities toward God and his fellowmen" and to give him "religious and moral principles that really act as the touchstones for all his actions."[22] Hollenbach apparently resisted efforts by more conservative faculty to present a more explicitly Christian "Aims of Hope College" to the Board of Trustees,[23] but despite this conflict neither he nor Lubbers seemed to have been prepared for the storm of criticism that the document aroused within the Reformed Church.

The 1946 attempt by the faculty to define the aims of the college, in fact, was *the* catalyst for the attacks on the college by both the Classis of Chicago and Bast, because it had opted for a few theistic utterances instead of a more Christocentric or biblically-inspired philosophy of education. Prominent board member (and future director of church relations at the college) Rev. Dr. Jacob Prins wrote a stiff note to Lubbers in June of 1946, panning the proposal as "a serious blunder." Moreover, he warned that the "matter becomes the more serious because the sharp differences of opinion within the faculty have become known in the church [as] both sides of the so-called factions have spoken outside." It was essential, Prins thought, to end suspicions within the RCA as to whether Hope College was a Christian college, worthy of denominational support.[24]

At that time (and until 1968) Hope College's Board of Trustees still consisted — with only three exceptions on a board of forty-two

21. Hope College Faculty Minutes, 3 December 1945–6 May 1946, JAH. Hollenbach later became Dean of the faculty.

22. "Hollenbach Compiles Statement of Aims For Hope College From Work of Faculty," *The Anchor,* 29 May 1946.

23. Prins to Lubbers, in Irwin Lubbers Papers, "Board Meeting, June 1946." This assertion seems indirectly sustained by looking at the various contributions made by faculty members on the Aims in the Faculty Minutes of 1946.

24. Ibid.

members — of representatives from either the General Synod, regional synods, or from various local classes of the RCA.[25] The vast majority of trustees, therefore, were either RCA clergy or elders, making Hope College, at least in governing structure, a denominational school *par excellence*. Mainly though not exclusively representing conservative constituents in the Midwest, these trustees were not only able but willing to exercise what they saw as their responsibility, in a time of spiritual peril, to keep Hope College close to the churches they represented.

Accordingly, a committee within the Board of Trustees, led by Prins, set about to draft a more specifically Christian "Aims of Hope College," which was published in 1947. Although Hollenbach was able to persuade the board to make the "Aims" more concise,[26] it was nonetheless a *tour de force* of pious Christian purpose, containing a long "Standard of Faith" built around the Apostles' Creed. It also made explicit, as the earlier catalog and statement had not, the college's ties with the RCA and, moreover, faith in Christ as a qualification for appointment at the college. It sought to offer a liberal arts program on "a distinctively evangelical, Christian basis, through a Faculty whose faith is in Jesus Christ and whose practices harmonize with His teachings." Aiming at cultivating Christian leadership, it also saw it as the college's responsibility to cultivate Christian character and faith. Finally, as a community, Hope College was to "interpret all of life on the basis of revealed truth presented in the infallible Word of God," and "to arouse a keen awareness of the power of unseen spiritual forces in the world and their importance in the total pattern of living."[27]

Furthermore, the Board of Trustees endeavored to screen more rigorously the faith commitments of faculty. To be sure, Lubbers had from the beginning made an effort to introduce his all-Protestant faculty to church-related issues at faculty meetings, and in 1949 he stated

---

25. Even the three non-ecclesiastical members were expected to be members of the Reformed Church. Later, in the 1950s, the board composition was widened slightly, made larger, and included six non-ecclesiastical representatives from the alumni association.

26. Irwin Lubbers, Office of the President, "Prins Correspondence with John W. Hollenbach — Re 'Aims,'" JAH.

27. "The Aims of Hope College," *Church Herald,* 20 June 1947. The word "evangelical" meant orthodox Protestant; in 1947 it carried with it a somewhat different connotation than it does today.

at the annual faculty retreat "that the Christian college is the kind of vitalizing force in American education which is being more and more consciously sought after."[28] It was not as if Lubbers and his administration paid no attention to the church background of prospective faculty. Lubbers needed no prompting to play the churchman, rebuking one (ultimately successful) candidate in 1945 for having scorned his RCA roots and attending fundamentalist Wheaton College instead, and warning him that he would have to explain his choice during the interview.[29] In the late 1940s, too, Hollenbach (as Acting Dean) sent out letters to pastors of candidates asking whether each candidate would "fit into [the] type of college" that was affiliated with the RCA. But for some board members, this was not enough, especially since at least some letters were rather summary and said all too little about a person's faith; all that one (successful) candidate's pastor wrote (in 1947) was that he was "a splendid Christian man, a Protestant."[30] At the prompting of the Particular Synod of Chicago, the board in 1951 put into place a Committee on Instruction, largely consisting of trustees, which would screen incoming faculty. (Students were now also to be screened by the Admissions Committee as to their religious convictions and their support of college aims.) The Committee on Instruction was "to sit down with prospective teachers to acquaint them with our spiritual heritage, aims and requirements so that they may thoroughly understand before they become members of the faculty exactly what is expected of them."[31] Those expectations included being "an active Christian" which demonstrated itself in the "active participation in those activities which promote the Christian program of Hope College."[32]

28. Hope College Faculty Minutes, 15 September 1949.

29. "It would be rather difficult," Lubbers lectured the candidate in a letter, "to explain the conflict that would arise from taking a job at an institution [Hope] which you were not interested in attending [as a student] when there appears every good reason why you should have done so." Biographical file, Faculty Member A, JAH.

30. Biographical file, Faculty Member B, JAH.

31. "Report of the Executive Committee of the Board of Trustees of Hope College to the Particular Synod of Chicago," 2 May 1951, in Board of Trustees, "Secretary's Resource Materials," 14 June 1951, JAH.

32. Board of Trustees memorandum quoted in Preston J. Stegenga, *Anchor of Hope: The History of an American Denominational Institution, Hope College* (Grand Rapids: Eerdmans, 1954), 216-17.

On occasion, the Board of Trustees — or the conservative constituency it represented — could put pressure on Lubbers to rid the college of suspected heterodox elements. As early as 1946, Prins urged Lubbers to "release" four Hope employees on the grounds that they did not "enhance the cause of Christian education in general nor Hope College in particular."[33] Lubbers resisted the pressure to do so, though he did suggest to one of the four — a theatre professor whom Lubbers had just hired to start a dramatics programs — that he show a willingness to edit "a few lines" from plays. In order to assist him, Lubbers also wrote to professors at Chicago Theological Seminary and Bob Jones College (an eclectic combination of schools) to produce a list of "some dramatic productions of real quality which are at the same time distinctly Christian."[34] But Lubbers did on occasion intervene more forcefully. In the spring of 1947, the college, under "denominational pressure," released the part-time instructor in Dutch, who had only been at Hope for a few months, when it became known that she was a Christian Scientist.[35]

In another incident, trustees saw it as their duty to directly investigate a faculty member about whom students sent home disturbing reports — and about whom President Lubbers seemed to do nothing. And in 1953, Classis Zeeland, with the Board of Trustees' approval, appointed a special committee "to investigate the spiritual life" of a professor in the college's English Department. She was widely reputed to

33. Prins, letter to Lubbers, "Board Meeting, June 1946."

34. Biographical file, Faculty Member C, JAH. Writing in 1949, the faculty member wrote to Lubbers and Board of Trustees President John Dykstra, complaining of the incessant objections to his work, including to the most recent college drama, "The Late Christopher Bean," in which characters utter "damn" and "My God." He concluded, "I believe that I have done no play . . . which is not in the best tradition of Christian education." The Theatre Department more than any other would elicit shock from Hope's constituency.

35. Stegenga, *Anchor of Hope*, 223. Stegenga does not mention the affiliation of the dismissed faculty member, but her biographical file notes it. The dismissed faculty member, a Dutch subject, seems not to have changed her view of Hope as the best place she had visited in America, writing Lubbers and the faculty upon her departure, "The extreme cleanliness, which is next to Godliness, of this city guided my visitations and the religious standard of the town and the College opened a new perspective on the U.S. . . . I can therefore gratefully say, Hope College in Holland has made me appreciate the United States." Biographical file, Faculty Member D, JAH.

take walks during Sunday worship services and, worse, to profess opinions in the classroom that contradicted the Christian sensibilities of the students. It probably did not help that she was, as Lubbers put it, "an eccentric person in her dress," "rather aloof in her social life," and "short in patience with students who do not attain the level of excellence she desires."[36] Classis Zeeland "investigated" the professor because they were worried about hiring people who, though perhaps Christian, "will find it hard to blend in with the total Christian atmosphere of the college life." The committee did not meet with the professor herself, but met with Lubbers, Hollenbach, and Dean of Men Milton Hinga, faculty whose professional and theological inclinations made them prepared to defend, if not very stoutly, a teacher they considered highly effective but a political liability. They admitted that she did not have a strong religious background, had not adjusted to Hope as she should, and that if she did not evidence a "change of spirit" that "we shall have to let her go." At the same time, they pointed to her membership at Hope Church, the Reformed congregation that was the haven of progressive Protestants in town (to which all three men and a large percentage of the faculty also belonged), and her new interest in the "great Christian writings of Milton and others." Satisfied with the administration's answers, the committee chose no further action other than to admonish the administration not to hire faculty members on the hope that they would be converted to Christian faith while serving at Hope.[37] The English professor, not wholly happy with Hope's conservatism and perhaps sensing pressure from Lubbers to shape up or ship out, departed the college soon thereafter for another position.[38]

In order to bolster the Christian character of the college, the Board of Trustees also undertook to regulate the most vexing of "social evils" at Hope — dancing. The local morality of the Midwestern RCA, shaped as it was by American evangelicalism, still held considerable sway over Hope's views concerning personal behavior, and the

36. From the vantage point of the twenty-first century, we wonder how much of the "eccentricity" perceived here was a product of sexism.

37. Irwin Lubbers, Office of the President, "Classes and Synods — Report of Agent on Christian Education, Spring 1954, Classis of Zeeland," JAH.

38. The professor continued for some years to have a cordial correspondence with Lubbers, whom she regarded as her advisor and benefactor; Biographical file, Faculty Member E, JAH.

college *Bulletin* of 1947-1948 reminded students that "the college op-pcses drinking, gambling and hazing in all forms." Moreover, be-cause of "its esteem for fine womanly qualities" (a phrase dropped in 1951), Hope also "discouraged" female students from smoking.[39] Dancing was a particularly knotty problem in the 1940s, because it was at once openly practiced without qualm by many students and opposed by others — students, parents, and church folk alike — as a form of licentiousness. In 1948, the board moved to officially ban dancing from campus, and to formally disapprove of student dance hall attendance, but to tolerate faculty-chaperoned dancing at other venues. This compromise looked like something less than the anti-dancing policy many Reformed churchgoers expected from their col-lege. The Classis of Grand Rapids told the board in 1950 that it was "disturbed" that Hope's student council and the college's society par-ties were sponsoring dances, and that the administration might thus be encouraging "the modern dance." This, the classis believed, was one reason why church-college relations were not as strong as they could or should be. The faculty, however, believed that "real progress had been made in solving the baffling problem of dancing." In the end, the board did little more than underscore the policy it had set out in 1948, a policy that would be revoked, in favor of on-campus danc-ing, in the early 1960s.[40]

In summary, the late 1940s and early 1950s witnessed an attempt by the conservative wing of the RCA — usually through the Board of Trustees — to reestablish Hope College as a bastion of Protestant or-thodoxy and impeccable moral conduct. Nowadays, their efforts seem archaic at best, probably to many as authoritarian and, at least in the case of the investigated faculty member, an imitation of the witch-hunts then being conducted by Joseph McCarthy in the U.S. Senate. But leaving aside the content of their proposals, it is worthwhile to point out that various church boards took the relationship between the church and the college it had spawned seriously. They held, as indeed moderates like Lubbers also held, that Hope College was (to use Lub-

39. *Hope College Bulletin*, 1947-1948, 23.
40. Addenda to the Minutes, Hope College Board of Trustees, 14 June 1950, JAH.

bers's words) "of the church, by the church and for the church."[41] They maintained the idea, often since abandoned or attenuated, that church-related colleges are not merely academic institutions, but spiritually rooted in a specific faith tradition — and accountable in their mission to a wider body of believers.

Yet the church's interest in Hope College was neither sophisticated nor sustained. It was not very sophisticated in that it contained plenty of piety and yet, despite a few fine phrases, displayed a far less vivid and refined sense than had been present before the two world wars of how the school's academic mission related to the Christian faith. The Reformed Church's pietism in this period — having either lost track of its quest to "elevate humanity" or having collapsed it into pursuit of the "American way" — did not offer a compelling answer as to why the church connection mattered in the academic pursuits of the college, and this would be one source of the "crisis" of the 1960s. And it was not sustained in that the investigation of the English professor at the end of 1953 signaled the end of the synods' and classes' efforts to supervise directly the spiritual and moral life of the college. Even Classis Zeeland registered some embarrassment for investigating a Hope faculty member (they were not an Inquisition, they wished to assure the college functionaries with whom they met), and the exercise was not repeated.[42] From the mid-1950s on, the Board of Trustees, and the church bodies it represented, would exercise vigilance almost wholly through the Committee on Instruction's guarding the gates of faculty hiring. The board left the rest of governance of the college's religious identity to the administration, exercising a broader, less intrusive oversight, and increasingly turning to securing denominational funding for the college.

Sacrificing the Spirit to Survival? 1953-1963

"We are encumbered," President Lubbers addressed the board in October 1955, "with much business today. The deeper concerns of Hope

41. Lubbers, "President's Report to the Board of Trustees of Hope College," June 1950, in Hope College Board of Trustees, "Secretary's Resource Materials," 15 November 1950, JAH.

42. "Report of Agent on Christian Education, Spring of 1954"; Donald Buteyn, letter to Irwin Lubbers, 16 September 1953; in Lubbers Papers, "Classes and Synods," JAH.

College must perforce be held in abeyance. . . . The spiritual and intellectual concerns which are nearest my heart are constantly stifled by the stark reality of the material struggle for survival of the college."[43] Lubbers made these remarks specifically in order to persuade the board to reorganize the college's corporation in order to make its governance more efficient. But the "abeyance" of deeper spiritual concerns might well be regarded as characteristic of Hope College from the mid-1950s to the mid-1960s. This assertion must be made with care, of course, lest it be thought that the college was void of all spiritual vitality in that era. There were many thoughtful Christian students and faculty on campus, actively practicing their faith inside the classroom and out, and President Lubbers exercised his responsibilities of strengthening spiritual life on campus and sustaining good relations with the churches with diligence. At the same time, the fairly conservative Protestant culture of the college arguably did not reflect very often, or very deeply, on the changes gradually transforming the college. Hope was growing in size and stature, altered by bin-busting numbers of students, the professionalization of its faculty, and its increasing reliance on government and industry — in distinction from the church — for its financial support. But it was only after 1965 that the tension between the college's religious heritage and its academic trajectory became a matter of public debate. For the time being, the relationship between Hope's Protestant identity and its academic mission remained largely unexamined.

If the Board of Trustees was preoccupied with shoring up the spiritual estate of Hope College in the late 1940s, by the mid-1950s a new businesslike approach had set in. Like elsewhere in the West, "the end of ideology" had come to reign at Hope College, as a whole range of technical challenges, from campus logistics to creating new debts and reducing old ones, demanded most of the board's attention. The minutes of the board got longer and longer in the course of the 1950s, but the amount of space devoted to religious matters, relatively and absolutely, fell off sharply — a downward trend, incidentally, that would continue through the Van Wylen presidency. The reorganization of the

43. Minutes, Board of Trustees, 21 October 1955, JAH.

board in the late 1950s, though not yet altering the preponderance of ecclesiastical representation, divided it into various committees, each responsible for its own area of expertise, an arrangement which probably tended to underscore the businesslike tone of the meetings.

Moreover, the RCA's crisis of confidence in Hope College was now largely, if not completely, a thing of the past. The board's high-visibility statements on the Christian identity of the school — and the willingness of board members to defend the school's reputation — helped assuage fears among church folk. The litany of complaints and concerns fell off. For various reasons, RCA congregational and personal giving to the college rose some 300 percent in the first ten years after the war, and would continue to climb in absolute numbers in the years ahead.[44] In the 1950s, the denomination launched fund drives that would give Hope additional monies, though not at the rate promised or expected by the college.[45] RCA giving did not reverse Hope's increasing dependence on other sources of income, but it did generate optimism that the church would remain an important source of financial support.

By this time, too, Lubbers had won the confidence of both the board and the RCA constituencies, not least because of his adroit sensitivity to a variety of religious concerns. A moving chapel speaker and personally pious — some say particularly so after a car accident in which he was badly injured — Lubbers was typically friendly and conciliatory. As with many effective presidents, there was something Sphinx-like about his persona, and Lubbers's official correspondence suggests that there were few letters he received — regardless of their actual content — that were not met with warm affirmation. Born in Wisconsin, a lifelong member of the RCA, and former president of another RCA school, Central College of Iowa, Lubbers could both speak the language of his Midwestern constituency and understand the concerns of his faculty. He was adept at forging a religious discourse and style that knew how to stress piety without ever giving the impression

44. Minutes, Board of Trustees, 12 October 1956, JAH.

45. According to Lynn Japinga, 2 February 2002. Part of Hope's quibble with the RCA allocation system was that the denominational money was divided evenly among its institutions of higher learning (initially including the two seminaries), which had the effect of giving the largest institution — Hope — the smallest amount of money per student.

of overdoing it. Adumbrating an irenic Protestant pietism in the WASP world of the 1950s was easier than it subsequently would become, but Lubbers possessed more than enough diplomatic sense to pull it off.

In articulating these sentiments, Lubbers did not shy away from proclaiming to the board, who doubtless appreciated his sentiments, that his aim was to make Hope College "the BEST CHRISTIAN COL-LEGE in America and the world."[46] What Lubbers meant by "Christian" in those days was, of course, "Protestant," but the term also stood in contrast to merely "Reformed." In a 1956 address (which Lubbers said was the best commencement oration of his presidency), former Hope president Wynand Wichers lauded the college for both being faithful to its "Calvinistic" heritage as well as the RCA, and for having a spirit that "has never been parochial or sectarian but always ecumenical."[47] Hope College during the Lubbers presidency remained unflinchingly Protestant, but the college's historic stress on being "ecumenical" prepared the path for greater religious inclusiveness in the 1960s, when definitions of ecumenicity in American society were substantially widened. Hope College was a "comprehensive Protestant" school that regarded itself as a "comprehensive ecumenical" one.

Lubbers did not neglect to insist on the religious responsibilities of his faculty, who were expected throughout his presidency, as they traditionally had, to attend chapel and lead it. In collaboration with Dean William Vander Lugt, the administration also attempted to instill in faculty what it meant to teach at a Christian college. Vander Lugt, perhaps more than anyone else at the college in this period, showed a perennial interest in the purposes of Christian higher education; it was he more than Lubbers who tried to engage the faculty on this issue. The year 1955-56, Vander Lugt reported to the board, was devoted to emphasizing this theme in particular.[48] But already in 1945, faculty were urged to read and discuss such articles as "Rethinking the Christian College" in *The Christian Century*. In subsequent years — in fact,

46. "President's Report," in Board of Trustees, "Secretary's Resource Materials," 31 May 1957, JAH.

47. Wynand Wichers, "A College of Distinction," in *Hope College Alumni Magazine*, October 1956, 13-14; Irwin Lubbers, letter to Wynand Wichers, 5 June 1956, in Wynand Wichers Papers, "Correspondence — Post-Presidential Years, 1945-1969," JAH.

48. William Vander Lugt, "Dean's Report," in Minutes, Board of Trustees, 1 June 1956, JAH.

until Vander Lugt retired from the college in 1972 — it was the norm for the faculty to hear a lecture or discuss some aspect of Hope being a college of the church at the pre-college conference or faculty retreat. Lecturers included Dr. Theodore Gill answering the question "How Is College Teaching and College Learning Christian?" (1957) or the RCA Board of World Missions' Rev. Edwin Luidens, who spoke on the role of the college in the church's mission (1965).[49]

The faculty was also engaged in rethinking, in the mid-1950s, the curriculum of the college to better "equip" the "liberally educated Christian person . . . to live effectively in the modern world," as Hollenbach put it in 1953.[50] The new curriculum was based on the various aspects of the human condition, from the "biological" to the "psychological."[51] It easily accepted the premise that "man is a religious being," and continued to assign to the Religion and Bible Department the charge of giving Christian instruction to Hope students, albeit with fewer credit hours than before. It was heavily against giving "Man as a moral being" a status in the curriculum, and this component failed to make it into the catalog. An integrative capstone course was proposed, designed for students to develop "a more integrated and more intelligent philosophy of life" and the precursor to the current Senior Seminar program. Opinion was evenly divided between faculty supporters and opponents, presumably because critics questioned whether such a course was really valuable for students who might benefit from more Bible, or more science.[52] This too failed to make it into the program. What is perhaps most striking, however, about the "integrative" component of the curriculum is that the specific justifications for it were wholly atheological. It articulated broad personal and ethical aims for the capstone course, rather than explicitly tying it to the creation of a "vital Christian philosophy" in each student, as the *Hope College Bulletin* continued to claim as the school's purpose into the 1960s.

Into the early 1960s, Hope College was, at least after the worries

49. Hope Faculty Minutes, 6 September 1958 and 22 March 1965, JAH.

50. "Report of the Study Committee to the Faculty," Hope Faculty Minutes, 30 November 1953, JAH.

51. "Curriculum Discussion #2," Hope Faculty Minutes, 16 February 1955, JAH.

52. "Hope College Faculty Balloting on Curriculum Areas Outlined by the Core Curriculum Study Committee, by Area and by 'Straw Vote Question,'" Hope Faculty Minutes, April-May 1955, JAH.

and wrangling of the late 1940s, and much as it had been in the 1920s and 1930s, a school that took its Protestant Christian signature more or less for granted. As a result of the board's hiring policies of 1951, its Committee on Instruction screened candidates and presented all new faculty for approval to the Board of Trustees, noting up through the mid-1960s each new faculty member's denominational affiliation. All were Protestants, many were Reformed, and a sizable percentage were from denominations with close kinship to the RCA: Presbyterians or Christian Reformed. By the early 1960s, non-Reformed Protestants were better represented on the lists.[53] But beyond shutting out non-Protestants, there is little indication that Lubbers or anyone else was as zealous in gatekeeping as Henry Bast, rightly or wrongly, would have wished them to be. It seems likely that alumni and other candidates from the Dutch Reformed "pipeline" were not much vetted at all, since their pedigree was thought guarantee enough that they would "fit in" with the school's religious culture. For "fitting in" was what Lubbers and many others at Hope cared about: they wanted self-selecting faculty who either knew the Protestant college scene or showed promise in adapting to it. That meant being a churchgoer and, at the very least, not being a religious controversialist. It also meant looking and sounding as though one could fit in. Lubbers on one occasion undermined the candidacy of a man seeking employment at another RCA college, writing that, even though he seemed a sincere Christian, he did not look or sound as if he were "the ideal sort of person for a Reformed Church school."[54] It was this kind of not very reflective Protestantism, often more cultural than religious, that would be challenged at Hope in the course of the 1960s.

If the faculty at Hope was uniformly Protestant into the early 1960s, its student body was scarcely less so. Nowadays, perhaps one in

53. Precise numbers are difficult to come by for the period, since either the Committee on Instruction did not present denominational affiliations to the Executive Committee every year, or some of their reports are no longer extant in the Board of Trustees material. In 1960 — to pick one year randomly — Hope hired four members of the RCA, two Presbyterians, two Methodists, and one from each of the following denominations: Baptist, Christian Reformed, Lutheran, and Society of Friends; Joint Meeting of Executive and Building Committees, Board of Trustees, 9 August 1960, JAH.

54. See, for instance, Lubbers, letter to J. L. De Vries, 22 June 1955, in Lubbers, Office of the President, "Northwestern Junior College," JAH.

five students at Hope comes from the RCA; in the 1950s, it was closer to two out of three. In 1954, over 66 percent of Hope's 877 students claimed the RCA as their denomination; the rest were overwhelmingly Protestant, with four Roman Catholics, two Buddhists, and five reporting no religion.[55] This composition changed, but relatively slowly; in the fall of 1963, toward the end of this period, almost 62 percent of Hope's 1,571 students were RCA, with some 15 Roman Catholics, seven without a recorded faith, one Unitarian, and one "Mohammedan." Despite its dramatic increase in size, Hope remained, from the standpoint of its student body, a strongly denominational college.[56] Moreover, a high percentage of Hope's students went off into RCA (or some other Protestant) ministry or missionary work; between 1949 and 1957, one in eight of *all* graduates enrolled in a seminary after leaving Hope.[57] The Centennial Census of 1966, marking Hope's centenary as a college, tallied that one out of eight *men* graduating from Hope between 1953 and 1967 entered a seminary "immediately" following graduation.[58]

Hope's spiritual climate in the 1950s still could be fairly characterized as pietistic. Setting the tone for religious life at Hope was chapel, required of all students, Protestant or not.[59] The college provided all new students with a "Chapel Etiquette," which kindly but firmly reminded them that though "sleep and study are both good . . . chapel is clearly not the time or place for sleep or study!"[60] Eight a.m. services, which students sometimes attended in pajamas, probably made the former particularly tempting. Many students, reflecting back later, remembered thinking chapel attendance a "game," and tried to chisel

---

55. "Registrar's Annual Report," 4 November 1954, Board of Trustees, "Secretary's Resource Materials," 3 June 1955, JAH.

56. Recorder's Report, 1963-1964, *Hope College Bulletin*, 1964, 155.

57. "Hope Graduates Entering Christian Ministry, 1949-1957," Board of Trustees, "Secretary's Resource Materials," 29 May 1958, JAH.

58. Cited in "The State of Religious Heritage at Hope," *Hope College Alumni Magazine*, January 1968, 5.

59. In 1948 the Executive Committee of the Board of Trustees affirmed their policy that all Hope students attend chapel and take Bible courses (including Roman Catholic ones). The Bishop of Grand Rapids had recently barred Catholics from attending such exercises; Minutes of the Executive Committee, Board of Trustees, 30 January 1948, JAH.

60. "Chapel Etiquette," undated document though probably written between 1947 and 1951, Chapel Committee folders, JAH.

away at the number of times they were required to appear. Others are glad they attended chapel, and were made to, agreeing with the administration's assertion that collective worship was an integral part of the Christian community that Hope aspired to be. In any event, the chapel program presented challenges for the administration, not only in trying to make the services as winsome as possible to a captive audience, but in monitoring chapel attendance. From the early 1950s through the mid-1960s, ever more elaborate means were devised, from assigned seating to ticket machines (dubbed "slot machines" because of their levers and the annoying clicking sounds they made), in order to accurately record student attendance so that slackers could be punished, some eventually facing the possibility of suspension from school.[61] Mandatory chapel was further faced with the complication that Dimnent Chapel was no longer large enough to hold all students at once, prompting the college to drop required chapel attendance in the early 1960s from five to two days a week.

The school, moreover, promoted an annual Religious Emphasis Week, another example of Hope's "value-added" approach to religion,[62] usually featuring a well-known clergyman.[63] Student-led spiritual life was spearheaded by the YMCA and YWCA (replete with their own *Anchor* column, "Y's Word") until the two merged into the Student Christian Association during 1959. Bible studies were also common. A review of *Anchor* articles pertaining to religion in the 1950s suggests a student body that was staunchly committed to an orthodox Protestant faith, although it is striking how *little* students wrote about religion — the 1960s showed a far greater interest in the subject. Perhaps it was because they took Protestant piety so much for granted. But Hope did not wholly lack reflection and debate over spiritual matters. *The Anchor* did carry (still rather restrained) critiques of the chapel policy, the unreflective nature of religious life at the college, the arbi-

61. James Michmerhuizen, "Slot Machines Incorporated," *The Anchor*, 9 October 1959.

62. This was also the criticism of *Anchor* editor-in-chief John Fragale in "'A Rose By Any Other Name,'" *The Anchor*, 7 February 1958.

63. Lubbers drew the line occasionally on who could speak on such occasions; for instance, he prevented the invitation of well-known itinerant evangelist Rev. Donald Barnhouse, a Presbyterian, to head up Religious Emphasis Week; Lubbers, letter to Henry Voogd, 18 December 1958, in Lubbers Papers, "Religious Emphasis Week," JAH.

trariness of its rules, and the provincialism of its ethos. And there were occasional challenges by those who did not think Hope was Christian enough; one student in 1958 lamented the talking and laughing during communal mealtime devotions and *The Anchor* placing advertisements for films.[64] But these voices did not significantly challenge the religious tranquility of Hope College until the first half of the 1960s.

The Babe and the Bathwater

A 1960 report suggested that the growing size of Hope College threatened the Christian liberal arts nature of the school, and that it would have to make hard choices about whether to become a small, less liberal-arts oriented university, and whether to raise money to hire more faculty or to cap enrollment.[65] The decision to hire many new teachers brought in a new generation of faculty who, though still wholly Protestant, often had not been formed by church-related colleges or who, at any rate, were most shaped by the sensibilities of the research universities where, in ever increasing numbers, they had been trained. Hope was quickly moving into intensive contacts with the wider academic world. In 1961, it joined the newly-formed Great Lakes College Association.[66] In rising numbers, Hope's professors and students were the recipients of outside grants; the mid-1960s in particular witnessed an impressive number of prestigious scholarships being awarded to the college's top students.[67] Moreover, the college itself received foundation grants and federal and state money. All of these developments in the early 1960s provided new opportunities to substantially boost the academic programs of the college and seek recog-

---

64. Henrietta Ket, "Letter to the Editor," *The Anchor*, 21 November 1958.

65. "Report on the College Program, 1959-1960," Board of Trustees, "Secretary's Resource Materials," 2-3 June 1960, JAH.

66. Presently, the Great Lakes Colleges Association includes Hope, Albion, Antioch, Denison, DePauw, Earlham, Kalamazoo, Kenyon, Oberlin, Ohio Wesleyan, Wabash, and Wooster.

67. Wynand Wichers, *A Century of Hope* (Grand Rapids: Eerdmans, 1968), 259-64. Professor Charles Huttar remembers his first students (he arrived in 1966) as notably among his best — a view shared by others as well about the mid-1960s. Interview with Huttar, Holland, Michigan, 17 January 2002.

nition of its growing quality. By 1958 Lubbers was making inquiries about Hope's chances of being granted a Phi Beta Kappa chapter.[68] From this time onward, hard questions arose. Could Hope College remain a "sectarian" school and still receive desired government grants and loans? (This question was only answered in a qualified affirmative later in the 1960s.) And did its religious affiliation make it less attractive to private philanthropic institutions like the Ford Foundation?[69]

Moreover, the quality of Hope's community was also changing. It was becoming at once less prone to religious expression and reflection in some contexts, and more aware of, and more interested in, the wider world around it. This was evidenced, for example, in the *Hope College Alumni Magazine*'s changing subject matter in the late 1950s and early 1960s, with its shift from religious themes to the international sites where Hope students and faculty had studied.[70] Moreover, relatively few of the faculty hired in the early 1960s, in contrast to the generation before them, saw much virtue in "fitting in." As the new sensibilities of the 1960s spread even into West Michigan, it increasingly became the community's responsibility to tolerate dissenting voices in its midst, rather than the individual's obligation to adapt to the community. Hope students too were becoming more critical of the status quo, whether expressed in James Michmerhuizen's satirical "Notes from the Underground," which began appearing in *The Anchor* in the autumn of 1962, or in an earnest 1964 article by Wes Michaelson, in which the future General Secretary of the RCA urged a deeper and more dynamic Christianity than the rule-bound religion he found dominant at Hope.[71] After 1963 in particular, students increasingly demanded that they be treated as adults and be allowed to live their lives with fewer rules and regulations.

68. Letter, 5 November 1958, from Lubbers to Dr. Laurence M. Gould, President of Carleton College and of the United Chapters of Phi Beta Kappa, Phi Beta Kappa Topical File, JAH.

69. In 1964, the Ford Foundation turned down Hope's application for funding because it thought that the Reformed Church ought (first) to provide the college with more money; Minutes, Executive Committee, Board of Trustees, 28 May 1964, JAH.

70. *Hope College Alumni Magazine*, all issues, 1956-1965.

71. James Michmerhuizen, "Preamble to Year: A Three Ring Circus," *The Anchor*, 14 September 1962; Wes Michaelson, "Christ and Campus: Quo Vadis Hope?," *The Anchor*, 20 November 1964.

None of these changes spelled an obvious and abrupt end to the Protestant college that Hope had been. The "Profile Report" of June 1965, written by a cross-section of Hope's faculty, affirmed the college's definition as a "four-year liberal arts program, largely pre-professional and basically Protestant-Christian value-centered."[72] This phrasing was a paler version of the theological hardiness of earlier statements, but at the same time it did not signal a marked departure from Hope's religious identity. Still, there was a growing uneasiness about what the changes of the past few years were doing to the college in religious terms. An *Anchor* editorial of October 1965 by future seminary president John M. Mulder was not entirely sure that the Christian identity of the school would be sustained in an age of religious skepticism and with the imperative of chasing after big money. Still, he thought,

> There seems to us to be some way of being a fine academic institution without throwing out the babe with the bath water. There also is no reason why Hope College should be a Bible College [that] gives a second-rate education. We insist that there is some validity to the idea of a Christian college, no matter how nebulous that idea may be. We are concerned, however, that the idea is not lost in the activity of the day or the expediency of the moment or in the attractiveness of easy money. It ought to infect the everyday decision[s] of many for it is as real as iron nails and rough hewn crosses.[73]

Mulder's editorial launched a renewed discussion about whether Hope was staying true to the highest ideals of its spiritual legacy, or whether it was indeed "throwing out the babe with the bath water." That debate would be a recurring theme throughout the twentieth century and into the twenty-first.

By the 1950s, the philosophy of Christian education enacted at Hope College had long been essentially a two-realms approach,[74] with two fundamental ways of knowing truth, one scientific or evidentiary,

---

72. Profile Committee, "Directions for Hope College in the Next Decade, 1965-1975," in Board of Trustees, "Secretary's Resource Materials," 1975, JAH.

73. John M. Mulder, "Looking Ahead with Hope," *The Anchor*, 22 October 1965.

74. See Chapter One, pp. 11-12.

the other religious or revelatory. By mid-century this approach had become so ingrained as to be unreflective. Nearly everyone at Hope in the 1950s (and afterwards) thought that the ethics and spiritual wisdom that sprang from religion ought to have some role in properly *applying* human knowledge. But at the same time it was seen by increasing numbers of faculty as having little role in the actual *production* of knowledge. For many faculty, though by no means all, the Christian character of the college was best sustained not in a college-wide curriculum that was at all times explicitly Christian, but by the Bible and Religion Department, the chapel program, the YWCA and YMCA groups on campus, and in relationships between faculty and students. In particular, there was a drive in the late 1950s to improve the quality of the chapel program, because it was assumed that it was in the chapel (and not the classroom) where the spiritual life of the campus lay. This essentially compartmentalized view of religion did not preclude the interaction of Christian conviction with the subject matter of the classroom — which some instructors chose to foster — but neither did it demand it. As we have seen, this two-realms approach was one reason why evolution was taught at Hope during this period, and before, and only occasionally contested.[75] This approach afforded Hope faculty members freedom to take whatever understanding they regarded as most proper between their religious convictions and their academic endeavors. For philosophy professor D. Ivan Dykstra, it was "freedom of the spirit," which cultivated "the active and open mind," that was Protestantism's great educational insight. Religion gave inspiration, not content, to education. As the prominent faculty member explained in "An Introduction to Liberal Education" — required reading at Hope in the 1960s and 1970s — "the only way a chemist or philosopher can do anything that can contribute toward religious belief is to point out the finiteness of all chemistry's and all philosophy's achievements. This [will] not guarantee religious belief, but . . . hold open a relevant place for it."[76]

Dykstra's vision was common in Protestant colleges at mid-century, and it was common at Hope College. But because the college

75. Paul Fried, "Hope's History and History at Hope," *The Anchor*, 28 October 1966.

76. D. Ivan Dykstra, "An Introduction to Liberal Education," 76-78, JAH.

did not require or expect a distinctively Christian perspective in the academic activities of the college, and because the earlier goal of molding Christians to be agents of the "elevation of humanity" became much more diffuse and faded from view, it became hard for some to see the relevance of faculty candidates' faith commitments to their ability to contribute to Hope's mission. This set the stage for a protracted debate between those who thought that adhering to the Christian faith was essential for teaching at Hope College, and those who did not.

5 Crisis for Hope's Middle Way, 1963-1972

- Piety versus Competence
- Search, Confrontation, and Liberating Minds
- Enacting a Socially Relevant Christianity
- A Lengthening Hyphen in "Church-Related"?

As we have seen, Irwin Lubbers sought to move Hope College forward academically while remaining true to Hope's tradition. He appropriated and updated Hope's self-conception as a practitioner of the Middle Way: "[Hope's] course was set at the time of its founding as a middle course. . . . Recognizing that the car which takes the middle of the road runs the greater danger of accident and even catastrophe it seeks to utilize the improved three lane thoroughfare as a means to more rapid progress, pulling out of the middle lane when signs along the way warn of danger ahead."[1] After the Second World War, the Middle Way had now become the passing lane — the path of bold, yet not rash, innovation.[2]

As we have seen, many of the forces that test the endurance of Christian mission at church-related colleges had been evident — though often with subtle effects — in Hope College's history before the 1960s. The college moved from tight control over students' extracurricular activity to an increasing number of concessions allowing for

1. "Hope College as a Factor in the Assimilation of Netherlanders in American Life," n.d., Lubbers, "Addresses, 1953-59," JAH.
2. The middle lane of this period could be used, in level places where visibility was clear, by cars traveling in either direction that wished to pass slower cars ahead of them. Such arrangements increased in rarity, presumably as the fatality rates on such roads escalated.

what would once have been seen as "worldly" behavior. At the same time, it expanded in size and became somewhat less religiously homogeneous. Relatively early in relation to these shifts, Hope's curriculum developed into an embodiment of a two-realms view of knowledge that tended to compartmentalize Christian reflection; many faculty began to take for granted the assumption that they should teach their disciplines in ways indiscernible from that of their colleagues at secular institutions. Despite Lubbers's vision of Hope's occupying the passing lane, most of the changes occurring were gradual — even as the rate of change was accelerating. During the first three quarters of the twentieth century, hindsight would make the past, when compared with the accelerating change of any given present, appear to be a period when Hope's religious identity was relatively stable.

And the prevalence of continuity underlying change was more than illusory — in no small part because Hope possessed many of the features that Robert Benne points to as being preservative of religious identity, including structural links between the college and its founding denomination through the mandated composition of its Board of Trustees and attention to the religious commitments of faculty when hiring. Continuity was also encouraged by Hope's geographic location in the generally conservative Midwest.

Against this picture of relative continuity, the Calvin Vander Werf era (1963-70) stands out in vivid contrast. In no period of the college's history does Hope's trajectory look more like the standard one toward secularization described by James Burtchaell and George Marsden. Changes in hiring patterns at Hope signaled a new openness that seemed, at least to some, to shift swiftly from an ecumenism that included both Protestants and Catholics to a pluralism that found any religious preferences in hiring unimportant. These changes in hiring stemmed from the college's rising academic ambitions, coupled with a desperate shortage of qualified potential instructors. Hope's self-description, insofar as it concerned religious matters, became more vague and broadly humanist. At the same time, rules governing student life became more and more latitudinarian. Would Hope's Middle Way endure in light of these changes, or was Hope on its way to becoming just another formerly church-related college?

Piety versus Competence

Few people in Hope's history have been more controversial than Calvin Vander Werf, Lubbers's successor to the college presidency in 1963. Praised for rescuing Hope from religious obscurantism and condemned for wrecking it on the shoals of secularism, Vander Werf in fact inherited a college already on an impressive academic trajectory and malleable as to how its Christian heritage related to its future. Criticized for an erratic administrative style, Vander Werf, as president during years of social turmoil and severe growing pains that haunted many of America's colleges, faced many problems not of his own making. Moreover, save for not standing in their way, he had little to do with many important changes in the college's religious life, such as the controversial ending of mandatory chapel. Nevertheless, before his abrupt departure from the college in 1970, Vander Werf pursued crucial policies that would substantially alter the religious face of the college.

Vander Werf was, like Lubbers, a Hope alumnus. He had also been away from his alma mater and the RCA for a quarter century before returning to lead the college. He had served for many years at the University of Kansas. In addition to apparently helping to recruit Wilt Chamberlain to the Kansas basketball program, he had made his mark there as the leading light and chair of the Chemistry Department. The son of an RCA minister, Vander Werf had belonged to "a very liberal Congregational church" in Kansas, as William "Wild Bill" Hillegonds, his confidant and the college chaplain, put it.[3] Vander Werf's drive for academic achievement, particularly in the natural sciences and even more particularly in chemistry, his long hiatus from the Reformed Church, and his essentially liberal Christian vision of higher education would help shape the contours of his legacy as president.[4]

There is no better expression of Vander Werf's vision for the college than his inaugural address of 1963. There he raised, as other commentators had, the specter of Protestant colleges "passing into

3. Bill Hillegonds, letter to James Kennedy, 9 August 2001.
4. "Cal . . . was a bit uncomfortable with the RCA" because of being away from it for a long time, Hillegonds opined; Hillegonds, letter to Kennedy.

oblivion, slowly miring in a morass of mediocrity" as rapid social change and accumulation of knowledge swept them aside. Vander Werf declared himself up for the challenge, though he feared "that the hour is already late for us to cast aside self-satisfied smugness." But the necessity of upgrading technology and providing the liberal arts program with a global orientation did not mean a departure from the "eternal verities of the Fatherhood of God and the Brotherhood of man." Quite the contrary:

> We are pioneers in the era of breathless change, when revolutionary upheaval is the order of the day, and we must learn to live in a state of perpetual surprise. But . . . we at Hope College must hold fast to the changeless, the abiding faith of our fathers which is as real and relevant today as ever.[5]

Vander Werf believed, as had Lubbers, that religiously based liberal arts education was a counter to the misuse of the modern world's technological might, and he had no desire to cut Hope loose from the church. But as a New Frontiersman charged with propelling Hope College into the Space Age, Vander Werf placed a premium on high-octane professional performance.[6] If there was a mantra for his presidency, it was that "piety is no substitute for competence" — a message he liked repeating to faculty and board alike. For example, Vander Werf wrote to Chairman of the Board Hugh De Pree in 1968: "We can never at Hope College allow a certain surface piety, formal church connections, or a wide variety of church activities to become a cover-up, by faculty or staff, for non-performance of duty, for incompetence, or for just plain slothfulness."[7] Accordingly, the president set about to raise the standards of excellence at the college. His high demands ex-

5. Calvin Vander Werf, "The Inaugural Address," *Hope College Alumni Magazine,* January 1964, 5-13.

6. "New Frontiersman" is a phrase borrowed from the sociologist B. Weston, who is writing a history of Centre College; Weston presentation, Rhodes Consultation on Higher Education, Memphis, 3 November 2001.

7. Though not as such an argument for disregarding religion as a criterion for hiring, in Vander Werf's mind the high priority given to professional competence came pretty close to being a reason to give religious commitment vanishing small weight; Vander Werf, letter to De Pree, 6 January 1968, in Office of the President, "Correspondence, Hugh De Pree," JAH.

tended to the athletic program and to the support staff he hired. And they certainly applied to his faculty, especially the impressively strong science faculty, whom he regarded as the leaven by which the college's academic loaf was to rise. All this meant finding the highest quality scholars to work at the college, even if this required that Hope look beyond its Protestant base to get them.

Two more or less synchronic developments strengthened the hand of Vander Werf and a sizable number of faculty members who thought that professional competence was the decisive criterion in faculty appointment.[8] The Protestant pool of candidates, at least in some fields, was thought to be too shallow to ensure excellence. Finding "suitable" Protestants had not always been easy — as President Dimnent had discovered in his search for a physicist decades before — but with the number of students dramatically up, and the number of M.A.'s and Ph.D.'s woefully inadequate, it became much harder in the following decade. In 1963 the Church Relations and Religion Committee of the Board of Trustees restated its commitment to hiring "faculty with both a deep Christian commitment and a high level of scholarly competence," but admitted it was hard to find candidates with both assets.[9] Even if Protestants could be found, William Vander Lugt complained two years later, there were all too few candidates who could relate their spirituality to their work.[10] Until the early 1970s, when the number of Ph.D.'s suddenly exceeded positions available, this tension would only grow, and even then not disappear. Perhaps a more conservative Hope president than Vander Werf would also have been tempted to change the "Protestants only" hiring policy that was maintained through the mid-1960s.

Going hand in hand with this development was the growing sense that the Protestant qualification for faculty membership was

8. The one exception was the Bible and Religion department, which Vander Werf, on the basis of preliminary evidence, was willing to stock exclusively with conservative Protestants.

9. Minutes, Hope College Board of Trustees, 30-31 May 1963, JAH. In order to find qualified personnel, the committee recommended that Hope find promising graduate students and pay for their education, and provide grants to faculty members to explore "the relationship between their individual disciplines and the Christian religion."

10. "Report of the Dean of the College," Board of Trustees, "Secretary's Resource Materials," 3-4 June 1965, JAH.

both arbitrary and unhealthy. One faculty member, hired in 1963, remembers answering a query from his prospective chair about his religious affiliation by saying he was Congregationalist and getting the reaction, "Oh, thank goodness you're not Catholic."[11] Such reactions seemed increasingly repugnant. In the first place, fewer Protestants saw the sense in excluding Catholics, as the two branches of Christianity drew nearer to each other after Vatican II. Moreover, there were others who now thought religious affiliation said nothing very important about a person's real spirituality or character, and that it would be legalistic to insist on something like church membership. In any event, maintaining a faculty with a shared religious commitment was less vital for proponents of a new hiring policy than (to use the buzz word of the time) "ventilating" the stuffy Protestant provincialism of the college. In this respect, Hope's emerging hiring policy in the 1960s could be labeled as intentionally pluralist,[12] though, given the mad scramble for qualified faculty in the 1960s, and Vander Werf's academic vision of excellence, it is difficult to discern just how "intentional" it was.

The first person to broach the subject of altering the hiring policy to the Board of Trustees was Dean of the College Vander Lugt, who, after complaining about a dearth of good candidates, asked,

> Why is it that we cannot hire people of Roman Catholic or Greek Orthodox faith? When I think of scholars such as Augustine and Thomas Aquinas. . . . I find it difficult to say to them that they do not qualify for membership on our faculty. Aren't we as one part of the Church of Christ saying to another part of His Church, we do not want to have fellowship with you? Does the outside world understand this policy?[13]

In June 1966 Vander Lugt reported to the Board of Trustees that the first non-Protestants had been hired: a member of the Greek Orthodox Church, and another without religious affiliation. Presumably to re-

---

11. Charles Aschbrenner, letter to James Kennedy and Caroline Simon, 18 February 2002.

12. See Chapter One, pp. 17-18.

13. "Report of the Dean of the College," Board of Trustees, "Secretary's Resource Materials," 3-4 June 1965, JAH.

assure trustees, the dean added of the latter: "He is a 'seeker' and is open to the influence of the Spirit. I predict that, living in our environment, he will come to a decision on this important issue."[14]

After 1966, the board received no further official reports about new faculty, and when the board was reorganized (see below) it no longer reviewed incoming members. Though the trustees did not officially modify the "Protestants only" hiring policy, by 1967 or 1968 the college was hiring Roman Catholics and a range of other non-Protestants as well. A 1965 motion by a trustee to allow non-Protestant Christians onto Hope's faculty was tabled, and the board did not revive the issue of hiring until 1971. Even then, no official action was taken.[15] Possibly the board was too badly divided over if and how to modify the policy — or too busy with other pressing matters, of which there were many in the late 1960s. In any event, the evidence suggests that the Executive Committee of the board let the president, his dean, and the chairs hire at their own discretion after 1966.

If the Board of Trustees was undecided about how to describe the role of religious commitment in faculty hiring, those who wrote the college's application for Phi Beta Kappa had no such hesitations. "New faculty members and staff are selected upon the basis of their interest in liberal education, their interest and ability to work closely with students . . . and upon their competence in their professional discipline," the application stated; "There are no religious, political, or other special conditions required of faculty members."[16] The only vestiges of Hope's Christian identity extant in the application were references to its founders having sought "religious freedom in a new land," along with its desire to help students confront "great philosophical and religious questions of man's being, of his relation to his fellows, to his environment, and to his Creator" and come to terms with their "personal, social and spiritual being."[17] Was Hope stretching the ex-

14. "Report of the Dean of the College, Board of Trustees, "Secretary's Resource Materials," 2-3 June 1966, JAH.

15. Minutes, Board of Trustees, 21-22 October 1965, 6-7 May 1971, and 21-22 October 1971, JAH.

16. General Report presented for consideration by the Committee on Qualifications of the United Chapters of Phi Beta Kappa, 27 September 1968, pp. 83, 84. Phi Beta Kappa Topical File, JAH.

17. General Report presented for consideration by the Committee on Qualifica-

tent of its secularization in order to court Phi Beta Kappa approval, or was the application an accurate description of the hiring policy enacted at Hope — if without the Board of Trustees' explicit blessing, at least with its acquiescence?

Whatever the case, neither Vander Werf nor his dean in the late 1960s, Morrette "Morrey" Rider, had the least desire to discourage good prospective candidates by stressing the college's religious character.[18] Historian Bill Cohen, who describes himself as having a secular Jewish background, recalls that Rider and others placed little emphasis on the religious dimension of the college during the interview that led to his appointment as Hope's first Jewish faculty member in 1971.[19] Vander Werf's apparently active role in dramatically deemphasizing the religious "aims" found in the college catalog until 1964 stemmed from his desire to attract a broader range of faculty. Nor was the 1969 Faculty Handbook particularly specific about religious expectations of faculty, specifying only that all tenure-track faculty at Hope "give evidence of . . . sympathy toward its purpose."[20] Religious faith, now much more diffusely defined, could still strengthen a candidate's application, but this depended on the particular department making the hire.[21] There was probably still scrutiny

---

tions of the United Chapters of Phi Beta Kappa, 27 September 1968, p. 1. Phi Beta Kappa Topical File, JAH.

18. Rider told G. Larry Penrose, successful candidate for a history position in 1970, "not to sweat the religious stuff," or words to that effect. Interview with Penrose, Holland, Michigan, 3 January 2002.

19. Caroline Simon, interview with Bill Cohen, 19 September 2003.

20. Hope College Faculty Handbook, 1969, D1, JAH. Previous faculty handbooks had not as such articulated Protestant church membership for faculty members; the ones between 1959 and 1964 stipulated that faculty members "give evidence of understanding and believing in the aims of Hope College." Since these aims were so manifestly Protestant, it was doubtless assumed that only Protestants could in good conscience abide by them. The rapid "secularization" of the college's "aims" in the catalogs after 1964 made it easier for a broader range of faculty to affirm its "purpose."

21. The English Department, for example, continued to note the religious commitments (or lack thereof) in its leading candidates, as evidenced in a 1972 document on interviewing candidates, though not *ipso facto* ruling any out on these grounds; Charles Huttar to Personnel Committee, "Report on Modern Language Association Interviews with 26 Candidates," 27-30 December 1971, in Vander Werf Papers, "English Department, 1965-1971," JAH. Other departments probably adopted a similar approach, with some more laissez-faire on religion and a few perhaps stricter.

of religious identity of candidates in some cases even during the height of the liberalization of hiring (1966-72); Cohen recalls that his own appointment was delayed, perhaps because History Department chair Paul Fried needed to obtain special permission from board members to hire a Jewish applicant.[22] Yet under Vander Werf's administration after 1966 there was no longer a religious test for hiring on a college-wide basis; when it came to hiring, Vander Werf's commitment to Christianity in higher education was indistinguishable from his commitment to academic excellence.[23] The result was an academically stronger and more religiously diverse faculty — and more division than ever over the purposes and mission of the school, as religious liberals and conservatives found themselves increasingly at odds.[24]

Search, Confrontation, and Liberating Minds

The 1960s witnessed a widespread pattern of colleges and universities breaking or loosening ties with their founding denominations. Direct ecclesiastical control became a thing of the past among most Southern Presbyterian church-related schools, for example, and the RCA faced the question of whether and how to redefine its relationship to its three colleges. Given the Reformed esteem for covenantal language, a "Covenant of Mutual Responsibilities" seemed a natural conceptual umbrella under which to articulate an agreement that would replace

22. Caroline Simon, interview with Bill Cohen, 19 September 2003.

23. Vander Werf's State of the College Report to the board in October 1969 spoke in terms of "teachers and scholars who possess the plus, the extra," and asserted that Dean Rider lead searches for faculty who "through their living, give substance and witness to the goals and concerns of Hope College. Christian care and concern for the individual student, as a whole person, must indeed come to life in our faculty." These statements, though ambiguous, provide a context that may temper this view if they are not explicable à la Burtchaell (see p. 15) as "befogging" rhetoric; Minutes, Board of Trustees, 16-17 October 1969, JAH.

24. It is interesting to note that by 1971, even Rider expressed his "disappointment" to Hillegonds that many faculty were not choosing to affiliate with a local congregation, and wondered if the chaplain could invite such faculty to the Student Church; Morrette Rider, letter to Bill Hillegonds, 2 March 1971, in Vander Werf Papers, "Hope College — Memoranda — Rider, Morette, 1968-1972," JAH.

structures that in the past provided tight governance linkage of national and regional denominational authority with the colleges. Would the "Covenant" be a fine piece of paper making everyone feel comfortable with complete "disestablishment," or would it help to articulate an ongoing — if less formalized — relationship between Hope, Central, and Northwestern and the RCA?

Though Vander Werf had no quarrel with Hope's cultivating congenial relations with the RCA, the very notion that the church had a right to challenge the academic direction of the college (as Vander Lugt suggested it might) was anathema to him. As the "Covenant of Mutual Responsibilities" between the RCA and its colleges was being drawn up in the late 1960s, Vander Werf saw the document primarily as a place where "the real battle for academic freedom and open inquiry must be fought," and instructed Dean William Mathis in 1967 "to put more teeth into the affirmation of open discussion and free inquiry."[25] It is likely that Vander Werf was most concerned with the 1966 General Synod's charge to its Standing Committee on Higher Education, mandating that it draft an agreement that would ensure that "the church not feel pharisaic when it constructively criticizes the policies of the colleges."[26] In Vander Werf's view, church support for the college was welcome, but when it came to academics, the church should defer to the college. Controversies over the initial attempts to draft the covenant resulted in the formation of a special committee that included two prominent Hope College voices: physics professor David Marker and philosophy professor D. Ivan Dykstra.

The resulting Covenant, approved by the Reformed Church in 1969, is steeped in the New Frontierism and revolutionary spirit of its era. Its preamble asserted that the mission of RCA higher education was to "PROVIDE AN EXCELLENT EDUCATION IN A CHRISTIAN CONTEXT WITHIN A REVOLUTIONARY WORLD," and that the mission of the church was to "break the 'sound barrier' between the

25. Vander Lugt, letter to Vander Werf, 18 September 1967; Vander Werf, letter to William Mathis, 3 May 1967; in Office of the President, "RCA Covenant Statement, 1967-1969," JAH. President Van Wylen would later call this Covenant a "really fine and beautiful document." "The Church Scene," *The Church Herald*, 15 May 1987.

26. Report of Special Committee on Reformed Church in America Philosophy of Higher Education. Minutes of the General Synod of the Reformed Church in America, June 1969, 64.

secular and the sacred."[27] Among many responsibilities, the colleges were to "fearlessly examine the words and works of God and man in the spirit of openness and humility," to maintain a "friendly appreciation for the Reformed tradition," and to "provide an atmosphere of search and confrontation that will liberate the minds, enhance the discernment, enlarge the sympathies and encourage the commitments of all students entrusted to them, so that each may achieve the fullest personal development and self-definition." In turn, the RCA pledged to assure the colleges "full freedom to pursue all truth" while encouraging "their responsiveness to the Lordship of Christ in whom the fullest freedom lies." The denomination also promised to send them students and financial support. Vander Werf seems to have gotten what he wanted — the Covenant's declarations of freedom had plenty of teeth and the church's role was one of encouragement and support. The original vision of helping the church feel less pharisaic when it criticized the colleges had gone by the boards.

Though Vander Werf made every effort to keep the RCA from intruding on the business of the college, he at the same time sought to strengthen Hope's religious mission in tangible ways. Contrary to widespread perception, he did cultivate ties with the Reformed Church, and he continued throughout his presidency to think of the college as a denominational school in the service of Reformed Church students.[28] The number of RCA students in absolute numbers remained static through most of Vander Werf's presidency, but as a percentage it shrank from 62 percent in the fall of 1963 to a little more than 40 percent in the fall of 1970.[29] Declining denominational loyalty was one factor behind the trend, and rising tuition costs — particularly necessary in a time when the endowment was marginal — were simply pricing Hope College out of the range of many RCA families of modest means. Until at least 1966, Vander Werf was committed to

27. Ibid., 65. All capitals in original.

28. Vander Werf's first-line strategy for getting additional funding at the beginning of his presidency was to "draw closer to the Reformed Church"; Minutes, Executive Committee, Board of Trustees, 28 May 1964.

29. In the fall of 1969, the percentage still stood at 47 percent. The 1968-69 school year was the last year with an RCA majority, 1037 out of 1980 students claiming affiliation (52 percent). By the fall of 1970, only 830 of Hope's 2,071 students were from the Reformed Church. Registrar's Enrollment Reports, Hope College, Office of the Registrar.

keeping RCA students coming to Hope by maintaining tuition at the same level, a policy at odds with his other ambitious goals.[30] Over time, though, he had become pessimistic about the church's ability to pay for Hope's low tuition, as church giving by 1968 amounted to no more than 5 percent of Hope's income.

To make things worse, receipts from the churches declined in absolute numbers during Vander Werf's last years.[31] And the president's move to drastically reorganize the Board of Trustees and end clerical control of it, completed in 1968, reflected his view that a church that did not come close to financially supporting the college must give way to sponsors from business and industry who could.[32] (Vander Werf also assiduously courted would-be sponsors like Bob Hope, who shared a name with the college. The entertainer never did succumb to the temptation to give money to the proposed Bob Hope Student Center, even after Vander Werf sent him golf balls.)[33] At the same time, the Vander Werf administration held that the RCA was abandoning its colleges more than the other way around. Reformed Church functionaries, faced with declining revenues and a denomination now badly fractured on everything from the war in Vietnam to a proposed church merger, were only too glad to reduce their support to the colleges so that they could meet their financial obligations on programs that seemed to belong more to the church.[34] The crisis of church-related higher education in the 1960s was often caused by a faltering commitment on the part of the churches to their own colleges. In response to this crisis, Vander Werf, through his representative Stu Post, arranged

30. Trustee Fritz V. Lenel complained to Chair of the Board Ekdal Buys in 1966 of Vander Werf's unrealistic determination to keep tuition low and to do this by, among other things, dramatically increasing church giving; Lenel, letter to Buys, 18 April 1966; Board of Trustees, "Secretary's Resource Materials," 2-3 June 1966, JAH.

31. "Hope College Operating Budget, August, 1968," in Minutes, Board of Trustees, 18 October 1968, JAH.

32. Vander Werf, letter to De Pree, 6 January 1968, JAH.

33. Gordon J. Van Wylen, Office of the President, "Hope, Bob (Campus Visit)," 1964-1982," JAH. Though less persistent, and no more successful, President Gordon Van Wylen also tried to get the celebrity to sponsor "Bob Hope Scholars" at the college, in part by trying to enlist Gerald Ford to talk to Mr. Hope, who was his golfing partner.

34. This, at any rate, was the view of Clarence Handlogten, Vander Werf's business office administrator; "Report of Special Meeting, May 6 & 7 1969," Board of Trustees, "Secretary's Resource Materials," 6-7 May 1969, JAH.

an important Church-College conference in early 1970, trying to improve ties between the two.[35] In fact, Hugh De Pree, in summarizing Vander Werf's performance to the board's Executive Committee in early 1970, credited the president with "improved relationship of the College to the Church."[36]

Enacting a Socially Relevant Christianity

More significantly for the religious ethos of Hope College in the 1960s, Vander Werf's Christian faith prompted him to espouse the cause of social justice at the college, even if it raised the ire of conservatives. For example, he was criticized for the college's decision to invite the African-American comedian Dick Gregory to speak on Civil Rights in March 1968, since Gregory used profanity in his addresses, and would thus desecrate his speaking venue, Dimnent Chapel. Assuring one prominent conservative critic afterwards that Gregory had restricted his cursing to "four simple 'damns' and one 'hell,'" Vander Werf pressed his point:

> We, especially in Holland, have over the years shielded ourselves most effectively from listening to those of God's children whose skin happens to be black. But now the students listened to "their neighbor" and heard him, and his cries of pain, anguish and despair strike home. This is unsettling and disturbing — but can a Christian do less?[37]

Vander Werf's own sympathies for social activism coincided with the temper of many students at Hope. Throughout most of the

35. Calvin Vander Werf, Office of the President, "Church-College Conference, March 11-12, 1970," JAH.

36. Hugh De Pree, memo to Executive Committee, 2 February 1970, in Board of Trustees, "Secretary's Resource Materials," 5-6 February 1970, JAH.

37. Vander Werf, letters to Louis Benes, 18 March and 1 April 1968, Vander Werf, Office of the President, "Correspondence — Gregory, Dick, 1968," JAH. Benes had written to Vander Werf warning him that a caustic letter against Gregory would be printed in the denominational *Church Herald*. Vander Werf called upon all the high-powered RCA functionaries he knew (all of them Easterners) to bring pressure upon Benes to change his mind about publishing the letter. It worked.

God-is-Dead Sixties, *The Anchor's* pages reveal a remarkable surge of interest in the Christian faith — particularly in its practical effects. A large number of students remained theologically conservative, but for many the pietism of the 1950s gave way to social concerns, from protesting the Vietnam War by walking in the Tulip Time Parade in May of 1966 — a demonstration that unleashed controversy at the college and in the town — to sending dozens of volunteers to do summer social work in Chicago.[38]

As students argued with ever more insistence that Christian maturity demanded more individual responsibility and fewer regulations, at Hope as elsewhere[39] the administration felt under pressure to relax parietals, rules pertaining only to women students, and compulsory chapel. In the spring of 1968, some ninety-nine students were suspended for failing to attend chapel, creating a huge challenge for the college.[40] In the last half of the 1960s, Hope students (mostly against), faculty (still mostly for), and alumni argued passionately over the merits and demerits of mandatory chapel. No issue provoked more heated debate.[41]

Hope's chaplain in the late 1960s (and most of the 1970s) was Bill Hillegonds, Vander Werf's pastor at Hope Reformed Church, whom he handpicked as Hope's chaplain in 1965. Hope alumnus, emerging critic of compulsory chapel, and proponent of social change, Hillegonds was above all an innovative chaplain, establishing a Student Church in 1966 (complete with its own elders and deacons) and later, the Coffee Grounds, a deliberately non-traditional Sunday worship service. The chapel program also sponsored a Coffee House where believers could meet skeptics in the hope "that healthy encounter can

38. George Arwady, "Students Protest Vietnam War During Parade," *The Anchor,* 20 May 1966; "Church, Senate Project Gets 75 Volunteers," *The Anchor,* 26 April 1968.

39. In discussing changes in attitudes toward rules governing student behavior, David A. Hoekema notes that *in loco parentis* ("in the place of the parent") has been replaced with, in some cases, a permissive stance he dubs *non sum mater tua* ("I'm not your mother") and, in other cases, by replacing requirements with exhortation and education, a stance that he calls *in loco avunculi* ("in the place of the uncle"). See *Campus Rules and Moral Community: In Place of In Loco Parentis* (Lanham, MD: Rowman & Littlefield, 1994), 140.

40. George Arwady, "Hope to Suspend 99 Students," *The Anchor,* 8 March 1968. A compromise formula was found by which most students were reinstated.

41. See files of the "Religious Life Committee/Chapel Committee," JAH.

take place."[42] Hillegonds's program, though not without its critics, was popular with many students, and it helped give the campus religious focus and purpose in a time of flux. As one faculty member was to remember years later, "I was not then, anymore than I am now, a church going or praying person. But I always felt comfortable in Bill Hillegonds' chapel. . . . Bill was absolutely tolerant. He was also utterly frank and straight from the shoulder."[43] In regard to "the spiritual life on the campus" Vander Werf was given good marks by Chairman of the Board De Pree in 1970, a scant four months before the chairman opted to remove him from office.[44]

Much changed on Hope's campus from the mid-1960s to early 1970s.[45] Many of the last vestiges of Hope's imposition of "local morality" upon students faded from the scene at Hope in the last half of the 1960s. Dancing was first permitted on campus in 1963. Hope's traditional moral opposition to alcohol was muted over time; by the mid-1960s the *Bulletin* toned it down to say only that the college had always supported "voluntary abstinence in the use of alcoholic beverages." By 1970, the college's principled stance on alcohol disappeared from the catalog, though the *Anchor* headline of two years later, "Campus considers beer tap in DeWitt Center" seemed overly hopeful.[46] The dress code was weakened and then abolished. In a sharp break with Reformed sabbatarianism, the library opened for Sunday study in 1967. The restrictions on smoking for female students came to an end, and the last of the gender-specific regulations — the "closing hours" for the women's residence halls — were discontinued in

42. Hillegonds sermon, ca. 1969, in Board of Trustees, "Secretary's Resource Materials," 16-17 October 1969, JAH.

43. Minutes of the Faculty Meeting, 25 April 2000, Farewell remarks by retiring faculty member Earl Curry, JAH.

44. De Pree, memo to Executive Committee, 2 February 1970.

45. *Hope College Bulletins*, 1966-1973.

46. Bob Roos, "Campus Considers Beer Tap in DeWitt Center," *The Anchor,* 27 September 1971. Hopes for a drinking age dropped from 21 to 18 were raised with the passing of the 26th Amendment in 1971, which lowered the voting age. In 1976, Dean of Students Michael Gerrie proposed to allow students to drink in their own rooms, a proposal torpedoed by President Gordon Van Wylen; see "Reservations on a Drinking Proposal," in Van Wylen, *Vision for a Christian College,* ed. Harry Boonstra (Grand Rapids: Eerdmans, 1988), 41-46. The State of Michigan, moreover, made the drinking age 21 again in the late 1970s, further dampening plans for such liberalization.

1974.[47] Parietals for both genders were liberalized, though not abandoned. Finally, compulsory chapel was modified in 1968 at the recommendation of a Blue Ribbon Committee in favor of a "2100 Plan" (requiring twice a week attendance for freshmen, once for sophomores and not at all for older students). This was a portent of things to come; in the spring of 1970, after a study and recommendation of the Religious Life Committee and approval of the Board of Trustees, mandatory chapel was abandoned altogether.[48]

In short, the aim of building Christian character through demanding conformity to various forms of "Christian" conduct was abandoned in the course of the 1960s in favor of approaches that reminded students of their own responsibilities. The 1969-1970 catalog was short and sweet in this respect: "Hope Colleges assumes that all students will conduct themselves as responsible persons, guided by the basic principles of the Christian tradition." By 1972, the catalog was even broader in its ethic: "Hope can only be a true community if members understand and genuinely accept the responsibilities of living together in a meaningful framework."[49] But if the Student Handbook was increasingly devoid of moralistic regulations, it contained increasingly explicit and elaborate prohibitions against, among many other things, firearms, damage to property, and disorderly conduct on campus.[50]

A Lengthening Hyphen in "Church-Related"?

Many members of the Hope community found the spiritual changes of the 1960s a story of progress, years when Hope dispensed with petty regulations in favor of a deeper morality and spirituality, when it moved from a monochrome parochialism to a wider perspective on the world. (Still, by 1970, there only were 76 Catholic students, 4 Jewish students, and 33 students of no religious affiliation on campus, out

47. Hope College Student Handbook, 1962-1974.
48. Minutes of the "Blue Ribbon" Special Committee on Religious Life, 16 March 1968; Religious Life Committee, "Rationale," Board of Trustees, "Secretary's Resource Materials," 28-29 May 1970, JAH.
49. *Hope College Bulletins,* 1966-1973.
50. Hope College Student Handbook, 1974-1975.

of a total of 2071.)[51] Critics, however, lamented what they regarded as the abandonment of the Christian faith as *the* bond that held members of the Hope community together. In 1961, "religious organizations" were at the top of the *Bulletin*'s listed "Student Organizations"; by 1963, they were demoted to the bottom of the page, and by 1967, "the religious dimension" of the school received its own separate heading, apart from the other organizations.[52] This tendency to relegate spiritual life to "optional" status — as evidenced in the demise of mandatory chapel, the de-emphasis on hiring committed Christians, and the apparent waning of a shared moral code — generated the impression among some that Hope was in the hands of people who cared all too little for the Christian nature of the school.

These concerns were heard with regularity after 1965. In that year, outgoing chaplain Allen B. Cook warned that the hyphen in the word "church-related" was getting longer and longer at Hope.[53] Dean of Students James Harvey wrote in April 1966 to Chairman of the Board Ekdal Buys that despite the unseemly behavior of the Fraters and the Knickerbockers, he was being pressured by Vander Werf to tell church leaders "that all was well at Hope" — something Harvey refused to do. Moreover, Harvey, soon to resign from Hope, prophesied that the "current policies will lead Hope to academic excellence and spiritual bankruptcy. This will happen slowly, so slowly in fact that few will become seriously aware of the erosion."[54] In 1969 Harvey would repeat this warning about the drift of RCA colleges in the *Church Herald* in an article that caused a stir within church circles.[55] But it was not as if many RCA stalwarts, or many Hope alumni, had a diffi-

51. Registrar's Enrollment Report, First Semester, 1970-1971, Office of the Registrar, Hope College.

52. *Hope College Bulletins,* 1961-1968.

53. "Report of the College Pastor," in Board of Trustees, "Secretary's Resource Materials," 2-3 June 1965, JAH.

54. James Harvey, letter to Ekdal Buys, 5 April 1966, Calvin Vander Werf Papers, "Hope College — Memoranda — Harvey, James, 1964-1966," JAH. In a somewhat later correspondence between the dean and the president, Vander Werf denied that there was any "drift" taking place at Hope College; Vander Werf, letter to Harvey, 16 June 1966.

55. James Harvey, "The Reformed Church and Its Colleges," *Church Herald,* 12 December 1969; for the effects of the Harvey article, see Gordon Van Oostenburg, letter to Louis Benes, 23 January 1970, in Office of the President, "RCA/Church Herald, 1966-1971," JAH.

cult time believing Harvey. As a recruiter between 1965 and 1969, Jim Bekkering heard an "earful" from RCA churches in the Midwest about how Hope was selling off its spiritual birthright.[56] "I believe Hope is losing its 'first love,' its reason for existence," wrote one 1958 alumnus in 1966 about Hope's apparent waning commitment to Christianity.[57] Congregational giving to Hope declined markedly in the late 1960s in part, it seems, because of conservative fears of Hope's poor spiritual condition. By the late 1960s, an important segment of Hope's students, faculty, alumni, and board members was concerned about the college's lack of a clear Christian mission. In 1969, the newly constituted Board of Trustees reaffirmed the (until then little-used) 1965 Profile Report's "purpose" for the college, which said the purpose of Hope's educational program was "toward the development of whole persons as this phrase is given meaning through the Christian faith." This reaffirmation was probably an indication that board members felt that the Christian identity of the school needed to be shored up.[58]

Did these rising concerns contribute to Vander Werf's abrupt resignation in 1970, as has sometimes been suggested? Not directly, in any event. That Vander Werf had antagonized religiously conservative members of the college's constituency is clear enough. But more important was faculty frustration with, among other things, the president's "lack of communication," and in November of 1969 it passed a resolution that was partly intended as a vote of no confidence in the president.[59] This got the board's attention. A program designed in February of 1970 to improve these relations could not be implemented after Vander Werf's health suffered a complete collapse in the spring. Because of this the Executive Committee decided on 28 May 1970 to "release" him as president.[60] Though Vander Werf continued to advise

56. Interview with James Bekkering, 26 December 2001, Holland, Michigan.

57. Cited in "Quotes from the Centennial Census," *Hope College Alumni Magazine,* January 1968, 7.

58. Minutes, Board of Trustees, 6-7 February 1969, JAH. It was this statement of purpose to which faculty members were asked in the Handbook to show "sympathy."

59. Hope College Faculty Minutes, 24 November 1969. The resolution demanded that the board inform the faculty of all their decisions, which implied that the president was not communicating enough with the faculty.

60. "Presentation to the Executive Committee and the Board," and Fritz Lenel, letter to Willard Wichers, 29 December 1969, in Board of Trustees, "Secretary's Resource

the Board of Trustees on the state of the college into August, he formally resigned in July, and soon took a prominent position at the University of Florida. Religious controversy had played no apparent role in these events. But if disagreement over Hope's religious identity did not directly contribute to Vander Werf's "release," his departure did set the stage for a sharpening of the conflict that had been growing since the mid-1960s.

The vacuum created by Vander Werf's departure, and the nearly two years it took for his successor to take office, prompted members of the Hope community to take stock of Vander Werf's legacy, and to consider how either to build upon it or check it. In 1971, the hiring policy suddenly became a central topic at Hope, discussed vigorously among faculty, students, and, as noted above, the Board of Trustees. Conservatives, now convinced that a high number of faculty were not active Christians, increasingly regarded the hiring policy as the most important avenue left to them to save what was left of the Christian nature of the college. Progressives on the other hand were prepared to defend the hiring policy bequeathed to them by Vander Werf as indispensable to Hope's religious diversity — not to mention its intellectual advance (evidenced, for example, by the success of the Phi Beta Kappa application discussed above[61]). The religious direction of the college, and particularly how religion affected hiring, had now become *the* issue — and a highly politicized one. As then physics professor David Marker recalled, "the only thing worse than academic politics is ecclesiastical politics and here you had both united."[62]

Gordon Van Wylen, the eventual successor to Vander Werf, arrived amidst these contentions. Upon invitation, Van Wylen entered the presidential search late, in the summer of 1971, after the search committee, in consultation with the Board of Trustees, had failed to agree upon any acceptable candidates. Dean of the University of Michigan's School of Engineering, Van Wylen was an effective administra-

Materials," 5-6 February 1970; Executive Committee, Board of Trustees, in "Secretary's Resource Materials," 28-29 May 1970, JAH.

61. The Phi Beta Kappa chapter at Hope was officially established in 1971. Hope College News Release, September 23, 1970, in "Honor Societies — Phi Beta Kappa," JAH. This success crowned nearly a half-century of periodic effort by Hope officials to get a Phi Beta Kappa chapter at Hope College.

62. Caroline Simon, interview with David Marker, 25 August 2003.

tor and an assertive personality, and this doubtless contributed to his successful candidacy among trustees still haunted by Vander Werf's shortcomings. He was, as a student, a charter member of the evangelical InterVarsity Christian Fellowship in the United States (and was active as a faculty member in its University of Michigan chapter), as well as a Calvin College alumnus and a member of the Christian Reformed Church, the more rigorously Calvinistic cousin of the RCA.

For some faculty, the engineer was a man of God's own choosing. "He does not compartmentalize his academic pursuits and his Christian thinking and keep them in separate areas as [is] so often seen at Hope and the American religious scene," wrote one member to the search committee after having interviewed him. He regarded Van Wylen's commitment to a *Christian* liberal arts vision as essential to Hope's future. But most faculty who interviewed him in October of 1971 opposed his candidacy[63] — some explicitly objecting to his overt religious stance, which was perceived as hostile to "maintaining excellence in the secular aspects of [Hope's] educational program," and not being sufficiently ecumenical. In fact, he was thought by some to be downright sectarian. Another senior faculty member sounded a concern that would dog Van Wylen throughout his presidency: he might be planning to turn Hope into another Calvin College.

> His is an unmodified Christian Reformed — Calvin College philosophy, which has to be looked at all the more carefully because it is so very appealing to a simplistic mind. . . . [T]he point is that the Reformed Church and Hope College specifically have never, and have never been expected, to function in [this] sectarian spirit.[64]

Coupled with these concerns were fears of a "ruthless" administrative style, a "bloodletting" of faculty, and a restrictive hiring policy should Van Wylen come to power. Acting on these fears, key faculty members worked hard to prevent his appointment.[65]

63. It should be noted that the number of faculty who actually interviewed Van Wylen was quite small.

64. Evaluations, in Gordon J. Van Wylen, Office of the President, "Presidential Search, 1971."

65. It was a faculty member who in his 1971 report on Van Wylen suggested that the faculty were fearful of a "bloodletting," though he did not believe that this would be

But the Board of Trustees liked what they saw in Van Wylen, who by October of 1971 was the only viable candidate left. Taking over from a search committee badly divided on his candidacy, the Executive Board interviewed Van Wylen during a four-hour meeting at Detroit Metro Airport in November, and presented him to the full board in January of 1972, where his appointment was secured by a 20-0 vote. He had been chosen in part because many board members, themselves theologically conservative, thought that Van Wylen would do something to revive Hope's spiritual condition.[66] Yet their decision did not end the tug-of-war over the length of the hyphen in "church-related." It remained an open question whether that tug-of-war would provide needed mid-course corrections to Hope's Middle Way, or tear the college asunder.

---

the case. "Presidential Search, 1971." To offset negative feedback from faculty, Elton Bruins and five other religiously conservative faculty members met with Van Wylen in December of 1971 to persuade him not to be put off by faculty opposition, and to become president of the college.

66. Minutes, Board of Trustees, 21-22 October 1971 and 21-22 January 1972; Gordon Van Wylen, letter to personal friends, 21 November 1971, in Office of the President, "Correspondence — General," JAH.

6 Hope's Neo-Middle Way, 1972-1987

- Excellence in the Context of Faith
- Negotiating the Shape of the Neo-Middle Way
- Education in the Neo-Middle Way
- Religious Freedom — for Whom?
- Hope's Unsettled Religious Settlement

If the Board of Trustees had any particular ideas they wished to see implemented concerning Hope's religious identity, they did not confide them to Gordon Van Wylen when he entered office in July of 1972. It was basically up to Van Wylen himself, as the emeritus president recalled years later, to chart a new course.[1] In hindsight, he saw himself striving to apply an insight that he had gained from Robben Fleming, who was president of the University of Michigan during the student protest days of the late 1960s and early 1970s. One of Fleming's guiding principles was: *don't lose the middle.* Van Wylen learned from Fleming that while there were valuable insights to be gained from listening to those at the extremes of an institution, it is the "solid core in the middle" that can evaluate and incorporate those insights.[2] Thus the *via media* that Van Wylen forged in the course of his presidency was not so much intended as a resurrection of an old Hope ideal, but was a new pragmatic hybrid, tested only through trial and error. And by the end of Van Wylen's presidency his administration had come closer to creating a consensus on Hope's Christian identity than had been present at any time since the early 1960s.

---

1. Interview with Gorden Van Wylen, Holland, Michigan, 18 October 2000.
2. Gordon Van Wylen, letter to James Kennedy and Caroline Simon, 21 February 2002.

Nevertheless, even in 1987 the nature of Hope's "true" spiritual identity remained a point of sharp disagreement. The history of the Van Wylen administration raises questions that go beyond it: How enduring would Van Wylen's "Neo-Middle Way" be? How dependent was its viability on Van Wylen's vigorous presence, or on circumstances? Was the new Middle Way more or less durable than its late-nineteenth-century and early-twentieth-century predecessor?

Excellence in the Context of Faith

Hope College was not an easy place to govern in 1972, not least because of the rift over the role of religion that had become more sharply focused through Van Wylen's candidacy. The divide between those who thought Hope had been freed from "its Christian chrysalis"[3] and those who mourned the fading of its light — from Reformed and "evangelical, to Christian, to religious, to wholesome, to 'the [intangible] goals of the college'"[4] — made the tensions of the late 1940s seem trifling in comparison. From the beginning, it was Van Wylen's intent to steer Hope on a middle course toward becoming something between a comprehensive Reformed college (like Calvin College) and a pluralist one (like most of its companion institutions in the Great Lakes Colleges Association). Early in his presidency, he attempted to articulate this to a New Jersey Reformed clergyman:

> The possibility of developing a liberal arts college which is of true excellence academically and which retains its commitment to the historic Christian faith is a very difficult matter. I certainly want to avoid any narrow religious approach to liberal arts education. At the same time, I want to avoid the path which many liberal arts colleges have followed, namely to reduce the Christian commitment to a vague moral or ethical dimension.[5]

3. Jon H. Roberts and James Turner, *The Sacred and the Secular University* (Princeton, N.J.: Princeton University Press, 2000), 122.

4. James Tunstead Burtchaell, *The Dying of the Light: The Disengagement of Colleges and Universities from Their Christian Churches* (Grand Rapids: Eerdmans, 1998), 829-30.

5. Gordon Van Wylen, letter to the Rev. Albert A. Smith, 8 February 1973, Office of the President, "RCA — Correspondence, 1972-1976," JAH.

As we have seen, the idea of Hope steering some kind of middle course between conservative Protestant and liberally religious colleges was deeply rooted in Hope College's history; Lubbers, echoing Dimnent, had formulated such an idea before and after retiring in 1963,[6] and indeed, their presidencies themselves could be seen as an attempt to work out some middle way. Nor was the *via media* ideal dead when Van Wylen arrived at Hope, though the definition of "middle" was now up for grabs. Moreover, Van Wylen was particularly well suited to rearticulate a middle way. Unlike Vander Werf, Van Wylen's "sectarian" background gave him a sense that the Christian faith must be privileged in the college's institutional policies, even if that went against the grain of prevailing academic sensibilities or of the general culture. Van Wylen's stance in this regard earned him the gratitude of much of the college's constituency, not least in the conservative Midwestern RCA.[7] At the same time, Van Wylen, like Vander Werf, was largely shaped by a long career at a research university, having lived for years in Ann Arbor. In fact, Van Wylen's intellectual vision was shaped less by Calvin College than by InterVarsity, which was less interested in "Christian scholarship" than in Christians who would be respected in a university setting. His preference for "Christian" as a noun and not an adjective stemmed from this experience, and his more flexible expectations for what constituted the content of Christian academic endeavor set his vision apart from more conservative Protestant colleges.[8]

Van Wylen sought to create a consensus of commitment to this Neo-Middle Way in the first months of his presidency. As an engineer, Van Wylen liked mission statements, taking them seriously as articulations of common commitment and purpose. In the summer of 1972, he commissioned his own committee, consisting of a mix of theological

6. "The Church College," in Lubbers, Office of the President, "Address: The Church College," JAH. See also p. 27.

7. Church giving to Hope, congregationally speaking, improved immediately after Van Wylen became president; one member of the board's Church Relations Committee, Elliot Tanis, reported that "many of the more conservative churches are now welcoming the appeal from the College"; Minutes, Board of Trustees, 18-19 January 1973, JAH.

8. Van Wylen, "What We Owe Our Institutional Heirs," in Van Wylen, *Vision for a Christian College* (Grand Rapids: Eerdmans, 1998), 125.

moderates and conservatives: David Marker (his future provost), Lambert Ponstein of the Religion Department, and Arthur Jentz of Philosophy, to write a "Purposes and Goals" statement that would update the barely-used "Profile Report" of 1965.[9]

The debate over the "Statement" in 1972-73 was a repeat of the debate about "Aims" in 1946 — only now faculty members and not trustees were objecting to the draft statement. Their outcry was that it was too theological rather than not theological enough. The philosophical and religious tone of the first draft (including sections about the purpose of humanity and the salvific role of Jesus Christ) of November 1972 were already toned down in the version of January 1973, and the debate continued thereafter.[10] As Van Wylen later remembered, "Soon after I arrived at Hope I realized that it would not be possible to achieve agreement on a basic, comprehensive, theologically rooted vision or mission statement at Hope College."[11] Realizing this, he let the matter drop for five years until challenged by Board member Hugh De Pree to articulate the essence of Hope's mission in a single sentence. Thus it was that in 1977 or 1978 Van Wylen hit upon a mission statement that would find widespread support across the range of the religious spectrum, precisely because the connection between the Christian faith and the academic programs remained a matter of individual interpretation:

> [Hope is] to offer, with recognized excellence, academic programs in the liberal arts, in the setting of an undergraduate, coeducational, residential college and in the context of the Christian faith.[12]

9. Faculty were also asked by the committee to discuss the Profile Report's first chapter, and send remarks to the committee as feedback; "Memo from the President's Committee on Purposes and Goals," 20 September 1972, in Van Wylen, Office of the President, "Memoranda — Faculty & Staff, 1972-1977," JAH. See Chapter Five, p. 144.

10. "The Hope College Statement of Purposes and Goals," 24 November 1972, in Board of Trustees, "Secretary's Resource Materials," 18-19 January 1973; "Hope College Statement of Purposes and Goals," 29 January 1973, in Board of Trustees, "Secretary's Resource Materials," 3-4 May 1973, JAH.

11. Gordon Van Wylen, letter to James Kennedy and Caroline Simon, 21 February 2002.

12. Gordon Van Wylen, Report to the RCA General Synod, 1978, in Van Wylen, Office of the President, "RCA Reports — 1974-1976 [sic]," JAH. See also Gordon Van

The genius of this statement is that it allowed a sense of shared mission across a wide spectrum of faculty. Religious conservatives, moderates, and liberals, as well as those who possessed no religious commitments, could espouse it. Faculty who took a more integrative approach to faith and learning were also full contributors, enhancing both the academic mission and the Christian context. Faculty who did not identify with the Christian faith, as well as Christians with a two-realms approach to their duties as faculty members and those for whom faith was a private matter, could see themselves as full contributors to the mission by being excellent teacher/scholars, while letting others attend to Hope's Christian context. The studied ambiguity of the phrase "in the context of the Christian faith" allowed not just Hope's middle, but its extremes, to find some level of comfort with this description of the college. Yet Van Wylen could still lapse into referring to Hope as a "Christian college," less of a mouthful though a phrase now resisted by those who thought it made Hope sound too conservatively Christian.[13] The precise wording of Hope's mission, and perceived intentions behind the wording, remained a sensitive issue throughout the Van Wylen years.

But if the lack of a robust consensus on mission vexed Van Wylen's early years, it did not prevent him from taking other steps to strengthen his control over the direction of the college. By 1974, an Advisory Committee appointed by Van Wylen (which included education professor James Bultman, who would become Hope's president in 1999) proposed to reorganize the academic administration of the college into its present structure of a provost overseeing several "divisional deans," instead of a single academic dean.[14] There were

---

Wylen, "Mission in Action," in Van Wylen, *Vision for a Christian College,* 57-64. "Historic" as an adjective for "the Christian faith" was added later, though it is interesting to see Van Wylen using it as early as 1973 in his letter above to Rev. Smith.

13. This is the claim of Larry Penrose, and it is borne out in a now-printed speech to the Board of Trustees from 1985; "Hope College and South Africa," in Van Wylen, *Vision for a Christian College,* 110. Calvin Vander Werf referred to Hope as a "Christian college"; this term began to take on its conservative connotations only in the 1970s, as mainline Protestant colleges dropped the phrase.

14. Initially, there were four deans, but by 1978 the arts and humanities shared a single dean, as did the natural and social sciences. In 1982, the natural and social sciences were each allocated a dean.

several advantages to this system that had nothing to do directly with the religious nature of the school, including the fact that deans were now more accessible to faculty and students.[15] But the intensification of traffic between administration and faculty also had the effect of increased administrative oversight over crucial departmental decisions — not least in the hiring of new faculty. And with the departure of Dean Morrey Rider in 1974, stemming from philosophical differences on this score with Van Wylen, the president was free to appoint a provost (the physicist Marker) and deans who shared his vision on this issue.

Negotiating the Shape of the Neo-Middle Way

As had been feared by many faculty who opposed his candidacy, Van Wylen was deeply committed to the hiring of people "with a mature understanding of and commitment to the Christian faith." (Van Wylen's favorite word was "mature.") In a letter from the end of his presidency, Van Wylen underscored that a prospective faculty member's relation to the Christian faith was one of those "issues that really count."[16] For him, a vibrantly Christian institution required committed Christians. Once the new administrative structure was in place in 1975, Van Wylen, his deans and his provosts, Marker and (later) Jacob Nyenhuis, were well positioned to monitor the religious qualifications of faculty candidates and, if necessary, veto their candidacies on these grounds. The administration's insistence on hiring "mature Christians" elicited different responses from the college's departments, from compliance to the "coaching" of candidates to cries of protest. However, many if not most faculty remained opposed to the hiring policy for its "administrative caprice" (the standard "mature Christian" was not clear enough for some) and its potential to disqualify superior candidates and limit the range of religious viewpoints at the

15. See President's Advisory Committee, "Recommendation for the Academic Organization and Administration at Hope College," in Board of Trustees, "Secretary's Resource Materials," 2-3 May 1974, JAH.

16. Gordon Van Wylen, letter to Gordon H. Girod, 15 May 1987, Office of the President, "Correspondence — General, 1987," JAH.

college.[17] As a result, as former Provost Marker remembers, "there was tension on virtually every hire.[18]

Because of the sharp disagreement on this issue, it was only in the early 1980s that the faculty and administration worked out formal hiring procedures to codify existing practice as it had emerged since 1975. The new statement, much more specific than the 1969 wording of the Faculty Handbook, charged the faculty to find candidates committed to "the historic Christian faith." The bulk of the faculty remained opposed to the hiring of Christians only. Perhaps the most spirited and sustained resistance to the policy came from the History Department, where various members issued many letters and memos articulating why it was wrong to restrict hiring to Christians. They argued that the "religious" test led to parochial "exclusion" and declining academic quality. Additionally, they thought it inherently and hopelessly subjective as a measuring instrument for candidates.[19] In the eyes of some members of the department, a school like Hope that benefited from federal funding in various ways ran afoul of constitutional questions in "discriminating" against non-Christians.[20] Although the History Department acquired a reputation as a siege-engine of rebellion against the administration's policy, the sentiments they articulated were widespread within the college's professoriate, though with variations in rationale.[21] Faculty members voted by a margin of 2 to 1 in the fall of 1983 for a faculty committee's resolution that faculty recruitment policy "be so written as to ensure that the practice of religious exclusivity in hiring will not occur."[22] The board and the president did not find the final faculty statement on recruitment to offer sufficient guarantee that Christian faculty

17. The phrase "administrative caprice" is Larry Penrose's; interview, January 3, 2002. Some evidence of the high level of tension between faculty members and the administration is extant in Van Wylen's correspondence with several departments.

18. David Marker, interview with Caroline Simon, 25 August 2003.

19. Correspondence Among Members of the History Department, Provost Nyenhuis, and President Van Wylen, February 1987 and March 1989. Personal Archives of Bill Cohen.

20. History professor Bill Cohen wrote a closely argued position paper to that effect in 1983. Personal Archives of Bill Cohen.

21. Many faculty members agreed with the historians who advocated more open hiring but differed with them in how often exceptions should be made to the policy of seeking Christian candidates.

22. Hope College Faculty Minutes, 27 September and 4 October 1983, JAH.

would indeed be sought.[23] In response, the trustees passed an addendum to the statement in January of 1984, directing all parties to "strive diligently" (a phrase concerning the interpretation of which administrators and faculty would wrangle throughout the 1990s) in hiring for tenure-track positions to recruit persons of both outstanding ability in scholarship and teaching *and* "mature understanding of and commitment to the historic Christian faith."[24] The eventual policy, enshrined in the Faculty Handbook of 1984, did state that the hiring policy "does not mean the faculty should consist only of professing Christians" while insisting at the same time that "the faculty as a whole be predominantly Christian."[25] In fact, whether these phrases allowed for exceptions to seeking a Christian commitment in new hires or simply acknowledged and protected the presence of non-Christians hired before the 1980s continued to be debated in the 1990s. Whatever the case, the administration, as before 1984, retained the right to veto a candidate on the basis of the candidate's insufficient commitment to the Christian faith. In practice the administration almost never saw the need to deviate from the norm of hiring Christians.

One conspicuous exception to the college's practice of hiring only Christians came in 1983 with the appointment of Michael Silver to the Chemistry Department — just prior to renewed debate over the role of religion in hiring. Silver was a religiously interested Jew whose abilities towered over those of his competitors for the position. His academic abilities won him Van Wylen's serious consideration as a candidate. In the job interview, Silver recalls, Van Wylen asked him if he would one day accept Christ. "Probably not next week," Silver remembers responding. He did not take the president's questions badly because they stemmed, as Silver explained, from evident faith. In turn, Van Wylen felt comfortable enough with Silver to

23. The statement was adopted by the Administrative Affairs Board in December 1983 before the Board of Trustees amended it by its addition. The Administrative Affairs Board is one of three policy-making governance boards of the college; as its name implies, it sets college-wide administrative policy. It is comprised of a roughly equal number of faculty and administrators and also has a smaller representation of student members.

24. Minutes, Board of Trustees, 26-27 January 1984; Gordon Van Wylen, "Faculty Recruiting Statement," in Board of Trustees, "Secretary's Resource Materials," 26-27 January 1984; Minutes of the Faculty Meeting, 31 January 1984, JAH.

25. Hope College Faculty Handbook, October 1984, B1-B2.

recommend his appointment to the board and, as Silver heard to his discomfort some years later, to acquire assurances that Silver would never be denied tenure on account of his religious beliefs.[26] The outcome of the Silver–Van Wylen interview was not a common one, however, either before or after the enactment of the restated hiring policy of 1984.

As we will see in the next chapter, the hiring policy remained a bone of contention that extended beyond Van Wylen's presidency. Influential faculty voices insisted that no more than 80 percent of the faculty needed to be Christian in order to maintain a "critical mass" supportive of the school's religious mission. But for the administration and some faculty, this was not enough; a church-related school demanded palpable Christian commitment of (nearly) all its new members. Hope College was an ecumenical critical-mass school in the composition of the faculty because of hires during the Vander Werf era. But after 1984 it was also a college with a pronounced trajectory toward becoming a comprehensive ecumenical institution as a result of the policy enacted by the Van Wylen administration in making faculty appointments.

Van Wylen's sometimes abrasive administrative style did not invariably endear him to the faculty. But his executive acumen, frankness, and willingness to listen and learn did earn him widespread respect across the campus. With his own firm conviction and the backing of a Board of Trustees that endorsed the idea of striving diligently to hire Christians, Van Wylen's administration recalibrated Hope's trajectory away from the pluralist course it had been taking in the Vander Werf era. Though this did not happen without struggle, it is evidence that Van Wylen had succeeded in not "losing the middle"; he had accurately interpreted and skillfully appropriated Hope's broad religious center.

Education in the Neo-Middle Way

If the faculty's religious composition gradually changed from 1972 to 1987, the academic program did not change much. It was under Van

26. Michael Silver, interview with Caroline Simon, 19 August 2003.

Wylen (and administered by psychology professor Lars Granberg) that the Senior Seminar, with its effort to stimulate a coherent philosophy of life among seniors, was finally implemented, replacing a senior-level religion class.[27] Because of its aim of integrating a student's philosophy of life with learning, because of the subject matter chosen by many professors, and because of the Christian faith of many students, the Senior Seminar had, from the beginning, clear Christian overtones. But the program was intentionally conceived as wide enough to encourage ethical and existential explorations by either students or faculty that were not grounded in the Christian faith. Under these conditions, the implementation of the Senior Seminar was not controversial. Yet the Senior Seminar Workshop, a summer seminar designed to help faculty who would teach the course reflect on how Christianity could inform a philosophy of life, became a place where faculty at Hope discussed — and still discuss — the relationship of faith and learning over the years. Those conversations have nurtured not only the discussion of Christianity in Senior Seminars but broader applications of faith to teaching and scholarship. Because of the range of theological views held by those who teach Senior Seminars, the Workshop has been a place where the center of Hope's Middle Way is triangulated in discussion among faculty occupying Hope's left, right, and center.

The Senior Seminar also marked the limits of the administration's intervention in the curriculum as far as the Christian faith was concerned; every department continued to develop its own program unimpeded by religious mandates from the administration, and each was largely driven by the demands of its particular guild. A striking example of this was the Religion Department (no longer the Religion and Bible Department since 1969), which by 1974 described its own mission as understanding "the role of religion in human culture," a self-description that hardly differed from those penned by religious studies departments at state universities. Though after 1970 the department gave a bit more attention to religions other than Christianity, its focus shifted to the historical, social, and psychological aspects of religion in general. It was in the 1970s in particular that the Religion

27. Elton J. Bruins, "Hope College: Its Origin and Development, 1851-2001," *Origins* 19, no. 1 (2001): 11.

Department — judging by the subject matter of its courses — most closely copied prevailing scholarly trends. By 1983, however, the catalog had added "to understand the Christian faith" to this more general aim. This may have signaled a willingness to give Christian faith pride of place among religions or a willingness to revamp one role the Religion Department had had through the 1960s: as a service department responsible for the Christian education of the college community.[28] In any event, the Religion Department remained throughout the 1970s and 1980s almost entirely a preserve of practicing Protestants who ranged from moderately conservative to moderately progressive in theology. In this respect, the department's ethos itself expressed the college's Middle Way.

Whatever the developments in the Religion Department, it must be stressed that the administration's relatively hands-off approach in the curriculum did not preclude the existence of various courses that were taught from an intentionally Christian point of view. In this respect, Hope's practice remained the same as it had been since very early in its history; the role of the Christian faith in the classroom (or lack thereof) was left to the discretion and convictions of the instructor. This arrangement, in fact, resonated with Van Wylen's own philosophy of education, which specified only that there be a community of Christians at Hope, not that each faculty member's approach to Christianity, inside the classroom or out, follow a prescribed course.

In order to pursue his middle course, Van Wylen not only had to guard against the "secularization" of the college, but had to neutralize criticisms from the college's conservative constituency, many of whom held that Hope College was not (yet) sufficiently Christian. As an evangelical who himself was taking the college in a more conservative direction, Van Wylen engendered a high level of trust among the college's religious constituency. Precisely because of this, he was able to resist suggestions that the college move even further in a "fundamentalistic" direction. Writing in 1982 to a prominent board member asking about Hope's possible participation in the Christian College Coalition (now the Council of Christian Colleges and Universities), Van Wylen argued,

28. *Hope College Catalog, 1974-1975,* 218; *Hope College Catalog, 1983-1984,* 254.

[W]e often have a difficult time articulating to people, including prospective students, the nature of our Christian commitment. On the one hand, we are committed, without reservation, to the historic Christian faith; on the other, we are not fundamentalist. We work very hard to make our position clear in our communications with prospective students, their parents and other persons. Most of the colleges in the Christian College Coalition are fundamentalistic in their orientation. Our concern is that if we joined this group, it might well be more difficult to articulate where we stand in regard to the Christian faith. . . .[29]

Perhaps Van Wylen's commitment to keeping "fundamentalistic" or politically conservative influences at bay is most evident in his correspondence. One of the thickest files of correspondence in Van Wylen's presidential archive pertains to the college's theatre program. The program's commitment to community theatre increased the number of patrons who professed shock to Van Wylen at the profanity and subject matter they saw on stage. Van Wylen (or his Dean of Arts, James Malcolm, and, later, Nyenhuis) would typically respond to such letters citing "committed Christians" who found the play deeply meaningful, or suggesting that "one must judge the Christian commitment of Hope College in its totality and not through one activity."[30]

There were other fires that the president sought to extinguish. They included defending members of the Religion Department against accusations of heresy, deflecting the possibility of bringing "creation scientists" to Hope, and explaining the decision to establish a lectureship in honor of Hope alumnus and renowned pacifist A. J. Muste, condemned as a "pinko" — or worse — in several letters. These letters were not so voluminous as to take up much of Van Wylen's time or energy, but they are indicative of Van Wylen's decision to choose a middle course. This did not mean that Van Wylen refrained from speaking to faculty about decisions that generated controversy outside the college. For example, the president defended to critics the merits of letting a 1983 speaker urge full acceptance of homosexuals within the

29. Gordon Van Wylen, letter to Trustee A, Van Wylen, Office of the President, "Correspondence — General," JAH.

30. Letters in Van Wylen, Office of the President, "Correspondence — Department of Theatre," JAH.

church. At the same time, he permitted himself to share a written "observation" to a faculty supporter of the speaker that he found the speaker's tone too arrogant.[31] But in this instance, as in others, Van Wylen was discreet enough to shape his "observation" in the form of a dialogue rather than a directive. He clearly did not agree with all of the initiatives made by his faculty, and at times he remonstrated with them. But at the same time, Van Wylen protected the programs and faculty of the college from conservative religious intrusions.

Religious Freedom — for Whom?

Hope's campus atmosphere in the 1970s and 1980s also exemplified a spirit that resembled neither that of a mainline Protestant college like Ohio Wesleyan or a conservative one like Wheaton. It would go too far to attribute this to Van Wylen alone. As it had throughout much of its history, Hope remained a mix of conservative, moderate, and progressive religious factions that vied with each other during this period, helping to create the *via media* that characterized the college. At the same time, if there was a spiritual center to the college, it perhaps was populated by faculty and students who attempted to live by a Christian spirit and ethic without (as they would put it) "proselytizing" (others would say without being very committed). One student captured this ideal in the Student Handbook of 1972-73, speaking appreciatively of Hope's "free atmosphere":

> [S]tudents discover that they are under no great social pressure to be Christian. Even more surprising is the fact that Christians discover a greater freedom to practice their faith at Hope than there is in . . . their own homes. This is apparent in the academic life of Hope College where one is not afraid to talk about realistic issues concerning religion and society.[32]

Perhaps this "free atmosphere" was a likely outcome of a faculty that was more religiously diverse than in the 1950s, and a student

31. Letters in Van Wylen, Office of the President, "Correspondence — General," JAH.

32. "What is Hope College?" Student Handbook, 1972-1973.

body that was, at least by church affiliation, more religiously varied than it had been in the 1960s. In the fall of 1972, RCA students constituted around 38 percent of Hope's 2,124 students; by the fall of 1986, that share had fallen to 27 percent in a population of about 2,300 enrolled.[33] The dramatic loss of students from New Jersey and New York in the 1970s, caused in part by new in-state tuition incentives back home, contributed to the decline of RCA numbers, as did declining denominational loyalty. (Students hailing from Michigan rose from 52 percent to 77 percent in the Van Wylen period, leaving less geographical and also less ethnic diversity than had been the case.)[34] At the same time, the number of Catholic students doubled from 5.5 percent to 10.5 percent, while the number of students claiming a non-Christian religion remained tiny (well under one percent). The high percentage of students giving "no report" — from roughly a sixth to a fourth of the total — makes it hard to know how many students claimed no faith tradition as their own.[35] Hope remained predominately Protestant, but with more Catholics and more students with no explicit religious affiliation than ever before.

It is difficult to generalize about something as amorphous and as subjective as "spiritual life," especially at Hope during the 1970s and 1980s, characterized as it was by spiritual crosscurrents. The safest course is to make observations about the religious atmosphere *relative* to eras before or after the Van Wylen years on the basis of *Anchor* articles, a useful if imperfect indicator of student life. The enormous interest in religious issues that dominated the public discussion at Hope in the 1960s was largely over before the decade was out, though an interest in social activism persisted into the early 1970s. *The Anchor* simply

33. Registrar's Enrollment Reports, 1972-1973 and 1986-1987, Office of the Registrar, Hope College.

34. In particular, the number of African American students, who had numbered several dozen in the late 1960s, declined. Many had RCA connections in the South or in the East, and their numerical decline may have stemmed in part from increased educational opportunities closer to home. The number of Latinos was never very great at Hope, a lacuna realized by the administration around 1970, though not very vigorously, or at least not very successfully, addressed. A Chicano Studies program began in the 1970s.

35. Registrar's Enrollment Reports, 1972-1987, Office of the Registrar, Hope College.

devoted less space to spiritual matters in the 1970s and 1980s, and the same was true for political and social issues as well. Chaplain Hillegonds remarked in 1976 that Hope Christians were "turning inward," away from the social issues of the day.[36] And already in 1974, John "Jack" Stewart, historian and Associate Dean for Academic Affairs, cited apathy for political and social concerns as a reason for why he was leaving Hope — and academic life — behind him.[37] Hillegonds's successor to the chaplaincy, Gerard Van Heest, said in an interview shortly before his appointment in 1979 that he hoped that there would be more "excitement" on campus, and he wanted to talk with the many students who just did not care who the new chaplain was.[38] Religion was not a driving force of student life in the 1970s and 1980s in the way it had been in the 1960s and before.

In contrast to other periods in Hope's history, too, the religious tone of the college was less pietistic or evangelical, though there were, to be sure, many Bible studies, an InterVarsity group, and a Fellowship of Christian Students that generally reflected a more evangelical orientation. But the chapel program, first under Hillegonds and then under the low-key but widely loved Van Heest, was generally more interested in a greater social orientation, particularly in themes of liberation movements and social justice. The chapel's Ministry of Christ's People (MOCP), for example, held a lecture series on the changing role of women in society and religion, with one of the lectures entitled: "God: Is He a She?"[39] And in the mid-1980s divestment from South Africa — which Van Wylen and the Board of Trustees for a time resisted, and then conditionally enacted — became another social issue championed by parts of the community. This religiously based social activism was not particularly "radical" by the standards of other schools and other places, but its spirit was clearly in contrast to the religious tone that was predominant in the 1950s. Evangelical students did not, as some recounted later, always feel particularly "free" in Hope's atmosphere

36. Phil Virgen, "Chaplain Views Hope Christians 'Turning Inward,'" *The Anchor,* 16 April 1976.

37. Annette Miller, "Stewart explains resignation," *The Anchor,* 13 September 1974.

38. Nancy Torresen, "New Chaplain Interviewed," *The Anchor,* 8 February 1979.

39. Jill Bowman and Julia Antionetta, "MCOP Women's Lecture Series," *The Anchor,* 6 November 1980.

of this period. A case in point is the InterVarsity chapter, which was sponsored by Nyenhuis in 1977 but approved only after two years of "verbal jousting" with Hillegonds.[40]

Hope's Unsettled Religious Settlement

Whatever one's evaluation of Vander Werf's and Van Wylen's individual administrations, it is evident that their combination resulted in Hope's growing in academic stature and being enriched by genuine ecumenicity between 1965 and 1987. As Van Wylen observed toward the end of his tenure, "One of our strengths is that our faculty members come from a variety of Christian traditions. This provides a rich opportunity for us to learn from each other and to grow together as we seek to be all that God intends for us to be, and fulfill his purposes for us, both individually and corporately."[41] Robert Benne notes that one thing a college needs to retain academic excellence with strong religious connections is a founding tradition that produces adequate numbers of intellectually capable individuals who see how the Christian faith is relevant to higher education, precisely because such production ensures a substantial pool of future faculty and administrators. If the Reformed Church ever was in a position to provide such a pool on its own for Hope College, the RCA's declining numbers made it increasingly unlikely that it could continue to do so.[42] Hope's ecumenical character allowed it to recruit Christian faculty from a much larger pool while maintaining its Christian character. Being itself in a more robust condition than its founding denomination,[43] Hope could be of service not

40. It is unclear whether Hillegonds's main objection to InterVarsity was its evangelical orientation or its parachurch status. Interview with Jacob Nyenhuis, Holland, Michigan, 7 February 2002.

41. Van Wylen, Report to General Synod, 1978, in Van Wylen, Office of the President, "RCA Reports — 1974-1976 [sic]," JAH.

42. See Roger J. Nemeth and Donald A. Luidens, "The RCA in the Larger Picture: Facing Structural Realities," *Reformed Review* 47, no. 2 (Winter 1993-94): 85-112.

43. How does one compare the relative "robustness" of a college and a denomination? Over the last four decades, the Reformed Church has seen a decline in membership, becoming smaller and more fragile; Hope has grown in size while the RCA has shrunk. Yet numbers are crude indicators. More telling is the fact that the RCA has had numerous painful conversations about living within their means that have resulted in

only to the RCA but to other Christian traditions and to the broader world by providing a substantial, diverse, centrist, ecumenical option in the American panoply of church-related liberal arts colleges.

The issue of Hope's religious identity, however, was by no means settled. Controversy over the issue of homosexuality, which generated particularly intense discussion in the mid-1980s, was one indication of unresolved issues, as were the terms of the college's divestment from South Africa. There was also a spate of *Anchor* articles in 1981 that dealt with the Christian nature of the college. Each had a distinctive perspective on the spiritual condition of the college. Sociology professor Donald Luidens, summarizing the observation of one international student, suggested that Hope students had "a very narrow sense of religion" that effectively excluded the validity of "a non-Protestant religious perspective."[44] A Hope student decried the lack of spiritual vigor at the school, "labeling it blatant hypocrisy to call ourselves a Christian college."[45] Another, in contrast, celebrated Hope's religious atmosphere, which was not a "protected Christian environment" but one that challenged students to "re-affirm our own faith."[46] Still another thought the answer to whether Hope was Christian depended on the perspective; the plethora of Christian groups, voluntary chapel three times a week, and a number of Christian faculty who tried "to bring religious dimensions into their teaching" were all evidence that Hope was a Christian place, she wrote. As conflicting evidence she listed "a big emphasis on booze parties," the negative role of fraternities and sororities, and the fact that many students came to Hope for purely academic reasons, some of whom had no interest in religion. She concluded by writing that the character of Hope

---

staff reductions and employee restructuring; these actions have raised concerns among those close to the workings of the denomination about whether its ability to carry out its mission has been compromised. See Roger J. Nemeth and Donald A. Luidens, "Show Me the Money! Funding the Reformed Church in America," *Reformed Review* 53, no. 1 (Autumn 1999): 5-20, as well as "Why Are We Declining?" "Paying the Price," "Insuring Our Future," and "'Witness' Out of Office," *The Church Herald,* July/August 2003. Hope's relatively healthy financial condition has not left its ability to carry out its mission in this kind of doubt.

44. Donald Luidens, "Hope's Foreigners," *The Anchor,* 26 February 1981.

45. Eric J. Sivertson, "Is Hope Christian?" *The Anchor,* 12 March 1981.

46. Meg Biggerstaff, "Hope Has Christian Atmosphere," *The Anchor,* 9 April 1981.

depends on . . . what the individual is looking for. Those looking for a good academic school, those looking for a good academic school that provides Christian activities and those whose fun is in parties and drinking will find [it] all at Hope.[47]

Hope College remained throughout the 1980s — and into the present — a place where judgments about its spiritual character were wildly divergent — too conservative, too liberal, too religious, too secular — or just about right, in part because the school could mean different things to different people. And whether from the 1940s, 1960s, or 1980s, most Hope alumni continued to cherish memories of their alma mater, despite and maybe also because of its complex and contested religious identity.

In his last State of the College Address in August 1986, Gordon Van Wylen expressed satisfaction in what had been achieved during his presidency. Not least, his happiness stemmed from the fact that

> we have clarified, in a real sense, the mission of the College, and . . . we have developed a genuine sense of community around this mission. I am well aware that there continue to be discussions about the mission of the College and that there are some who disagree with the Christian perspective of this mission or the way in which it is implemented. But I believe that overall a very significant, common vision of what we want to be as a college has emerged. This vision has the balance . . . of both informed Christian commitment and a spirit of freedom and openness of inquiry. We also have a healthy diversity in our church affiliations, theological perspectives, and patterns of life, while acknowledging a common faith through Jesus Christ. I am deeply grateful for this rich sense of common purpose.[48]

Van Wylen's speech, like most farewell addresses, doubtless presents us with a rosy gloss on the Hope College community in the mid-1980s. However, though the *via media* that Gordon Van Wylen advocated had never been without its critics (both those who found it too narrow and

---

47. Dannette Matteson, "Hope's Christianity Still Debated," *The Anchor*, 16 April 1981.

48. Gordon Van Wylen, "Retrospect," in *Vision for a Christian College*, 189.

those who found it too broad), the short mission statement articulated during his administration has remained a frequently used self-description that garners widespread loyalty even a decade and a half after his retirement. Moreover, many now speak of Van Wylen's last years as president as the time when the college managed to contain its conflicting impulses and concerns within something approaching a common vision.

In fact, talk of Hope's unique "vital center" that distinguished it from both evangelical and mainline schools seems to be one of the lasting legacies of the Van Wylen years,[49] and one that has persisted to this day. Thus, it might be tempting to end this history in 1987, when Gordon Van Wylen retired as president of Hope College. The conflicts of the 1960s and 1970s seemed to some to have largely — though not wholly — given way to a broader consensus about Hope's Neo-Middle Way. Yet Van Wylen's centrist path was always vulnerable to the suspicion, justified or unjustified, that "informed Christian commitment" — or alternately, "a spirit of freedom and openness of inquiry" — was in danger of being subverted by those exclusively serving the competing ideal. This was in no small part because the new Middle Way's studied ambiguity was rooted in pragmatic compromise rather than in a shared understanding of an overarching, common purpose for Hope. Additionally, by its very nature, a *via media* raises epistemological questions about when one has one's target in one's sights.[50] Though the short mission statement has outlived the Van Wylen administration, the stability of vision that this suggests may be illusory, if subsequent administrations have retained the language but invested the statement with significantly different meaning. If Van Wylen's vision was vulnerable during his administration to the suspicion that it was being subverted by those who valued Christian context more than recognized excellence as a liberal arts college, or alternatively, by those whose quest for academic excellence would relegate Christianity to the margins, how much more vulnerable would it

49. Dennis Voskuil, former professor and chair of Hope's Religion Department and then president of Western Seminary, gave a talk called "Hope's Vital Center" on 23 June 1997, as part of a Provost's-Office-sponsored "Teaching as Faithful Profession" May Term workshop.

50. As Aristotle famously notes, deviation from the "golden mean" brings with it a distorted perception of where the mean lies.

be to such suspicions as time went by? Moreover, even if the nature of Hope's *via media* allowed for widespread consensus concerning its nature in any given present, it remains true that, no matter how balanced one's complexities are, something can always upset the balance. And this in turn meant that, with the transition to a new president and the advent of new challenges and developments in the 1990s, disputes about where Hope's center of gravity should be would reappear, sometimes in new forms, sometimes repeating familiar debates. Indeed, during the last half of the 1990s, Hope College would witness conflicts that, in terms of both passion and ideological intensity, surpassed any that the college had hitherto known.

7 *Testing Hope's Endurance, 1987-1999*

- "A City on a Hill"
- Debate and Irritation: The Hiring Policy
- "Local Morality" Revised in a New Key
- "Uplift" and Crosswinds: The Gathering Storm
- A Full-Scale Tempest
- Anchored or Adrift in the Middle Way?

The decade of the 1990s at Hope College would be one of prosperity, with the college endowment more than quadrupling and the institution advancing on a variety of fronts.[1] Yet it would prove an excruciatingly difficult period in which to successfully follow Gordon Van Wylen's advice: *don't lose the middle*. A number of factors conspired to make this so. In John Jacobson, Hope had a president who was very conscious that his identity — formed as it was more by the East than by the Midwest — necessitated cultivating sensitivity to the concerns of a Midwestern constituency more conservative than himself and most of his faculty. At the same time, vigilant responsiveness toward the Midwestern constituency proved hard to configure with his aim of galvanizing faculty support for his vision for Hope. The 1990s would have been a challenging decade for *any* president to marshal faculty support toward deepening Hope's Christian mission while remaining true to its Middle Way.

For one thing, the debate about the religious composition of the faculty still simmered from the 1960s, 1970s, and 1980s, and in the 1990s it would come to a boil. Jacobson would expend considerable political capital among the faculty by holding fast to his insistence that

---

1. Hope's enrollment in the fall of 1987 was 2710; in the fall of 1997 it was 2911. The college's endowment was $20 million in 1987 and was $91 million in 1998. *News From Hope College*, February 1998, 7.

the college hire only outstanding academics who were also Christians. Moreover, 1990s versions of issues concerning "local morality" would stir the caldron of discontent, in part because they were so divisive within the surrounding culture, but also because they raised questions about the appropriateness of the college's asserting its stake in the character and personal lives of faculty. While in Dimnent's day it had seemed natural to him to seek faculty who do "not dance, play cards, [or] frequent the theater,"[2] the increasing rarity of moral consensus among Christians, together with a growing professionalism that drew sharp distinctions between public and private, had habituated many faculty to assume that the college had no right to concern itself with their behavior beyond the execution of their duties as teachers and scholars. Yet in the 1990s, even in the wider academy, a firm boundary between professional and personal conduct would no longer seem viable. Issues of what constituted sexual harassment, for example, blurred the public/private distinction — and Hope would have to come to terms with these trends. This and other factors brought debate to the fore over what practical consequence the college's "context of the historic Christian faith" should have on college policy — and policy would need to be hammered out and implemented long before disagreements could reach resolution. On deeply felt issues, protagonists often thought in terms of winning and losing, frequently casting their own faction as the losers of the conflict.

But perhaps the largest challenge to Hope College's Middle Way was one that even as late as 1993 would have been difficult to foresee. With no clear intentions of doing so, Hope College hired one man who in hindsight many would see as transforming the college's religious center of gravity, for good or for ill. Whatever one's judgment about that, there were very few students, and probably even fewer faculty, who did not possess strong feelings about President Jacobson's controversial new Dean of the Chapel appointed halfway through his presidency — feelings strong enough for the campus to erupt in anger and recrimination in the last year of Jacobson's presidency. Indeed, the Rev. J. Ben Patterson's opposition to Hope's Middle Way itself[3] — which he

2. See Chapter Three, p. 78.
3. As Ben Patterson would reflect with biting irony toward the end of his ministry at Hope, "The useful vagueness of the word 'centrist' in the culture of diversity. A buzz

regarded as nothing less than the compromising of the Christian faith — helped generate what was the most heated and sustained debate to date within the Hope community over the import of the college's religious identity.

"A City on a Hill"

The new president's initial years did not presage such troubles. John Howard Jacobson Jr. was an outsider to Hope College when tapped for the presidency in late 1986. A philosopher by training, Jacobson had spent most of his years in the academy as an administrator, as dean in a Presbyterian college, and most recently as Academic Vice President of Empire State College in his home state of New York. While serving at Empire State, he joined a Reformed church, becoming again a member of the denomination of his youth. In a small denomination with few experienced administrators, Jacobson quickly became a finalist for the presidency at Hope.[4]

By temperament and habit a mainline Protestant, the invariably formal Jacobson did not wear his faith on his sleeve — though his personal testimony evidently passed muster with search committee members who inquired, as the candidate recalls, about his relationship with Jesus. By his own definition an "orthodox" Christian, Jacobson devel-

---

word in the mainline church for the last two decades. Don't get hung up on differences, hold to the center. The metaphor is revealing, because a center can be an infinitesimally small point, i.e. really a lowest common denominator. . . . *Question:* What can possibly hold so much diversity together, especially if the diversity includes the heretical and apostate? *Answer:* Keep the conversation going, give all outlooks an equal voice at the table." Epaphras Fellowship Prayer Letter, edition 3, December 1999, 2. Personal Archives of J. Ben Patterson.

4. Others would see him as a compromise candidate between one favored more by the Board of Trustees and one favored more by the faculty. The extant documentation available on the subject, which is from Gordon Van Wylen's presidential archives, does not give much direct evidence that various factions were aligning behind one candidate or another on the basis of the college's religious direction. That is not in itself surprising, since it is also part of Hope's polite and moderate culture to avoid putting a strong opinion on paper, certainly in respect to religion. That concerns about the religious direction of the college did play a role we know from a variety of oral sources, including Jacobson; Gordon Van Wylen, "Presidential Search, 1986-1987," Presidential Papers, JAH.

oped a sympathy with evangelicalism in the course of his adult life —
but always at a distance, electing to attend churches with more of a
mainline flavor, such as Hope Church, during his tenure as president.
A natural and confident leader among college administrators, Jacobson's own administrative experience did not always provide a clear
guide for a convinced Democrat making his way in Republican-
dominated West Michigan and among politically conservative trustees. In contrast to Van Wylen, Jacobson came to the college without a
natural constituency, and he never built a large coalition of loyal supporters on whom he could rely in tough times. His polite reticence, understated (some would say passive) leadership style, and amalgam of
liberal and conservative instincts meant that he remained, in the last
analysis, an enigma to those whom he served as president.

There were early signs that Jacobson had done his homework.
He arrived not only with thirty years of successful experience as a
teacher and administrator, but with considerable understanding of
the college he was to lead. His inaugural address was based on a text
from the Gospel of Matthew, "You are the light of the world. A city set
on a hill cannot be hid." He explicitly linked the text to the aspirations
of Holland's founders to emulate the Calvinists who had built the
Massachusetts Bay Colony.[5] Jacobson emphasized his "vision of progressive continuity with the tradition of Hope College" as well as his
duty to provide "Presidential leadership that will understand and
build upon its historic commitment and tradition." For him that
meant that the college must strive for excellence for Christ's sake and
pursue academics in the "robust original sense of the word in which
academic has to do with learning, scholarship, research, personal cultivation, and the commitment to live an informed, examined, and responsible life."[6]

Jacobson has sometimes been criticized for lacking a coherent intellectual vision for the college. It was never very clear to many what
Jacobson himself thought the relationship was between the academic
mission of the college and its Christian commitments. Ironically, this
perceived lack of clarity may have been at least in part a result of his
penchant for a learned theological subtlety that communicated little to

5. See Chapter Two, pp. 62-64.
6. President John Jacobson's Inaugural Speech, 9 October 1987, 6, JAH.

the uninitiated.[7] Jacobson did make attempts to provide leadership in helping Hope think more deeply about a philosophy of education that would articulate what it meant, in Hope's own particular case, to pursue the liberal arts in a way that was profoundly Christian. However, these initiatives had scant impact, being either too low-key or ill-timed, as was the case for the series of departmental visits and dinner meetings focused on the topic in the wake of the painful 1993-94 disagreements over hiring.[8]

Yet another reason that Jacobson, recognized by many as a team builder,[9] was perceived by some as having no particular views on the connection between Christian mission and academics was his tendency to delegate. Though he consulted regularly behind the scenes with his provost, he gave Jacob Nyenhuis, with whom he had an excellent working relationship, the lion's share of the internal public role in addressing how faith should influence teaching and scholarship, along with a large measure of freedom to develop academic programs as he saw fit. Nyenhuis had, during the Van Wylen administration, already

7. Cases in point start with his linking of Hope's symbol, the anchor, to the high priesthood of Christ as described in the Letter to the Hebrews (President John Jacobson's Inaugural Speech, 9 October 1987, 3, JAH), and continue with remarks at faculty meetings like "I do not quiz candidates about such topics as predestination, inerrancy, premillennialism, or the inclusion of the 'filioque' in the Nicene Creed" (Minutes of Faculty Meeting, 26 April 1994, 6, JAH) and the "Dean of the Chapel of Hope College is expected to be, and is, a member of the clergy of the Reformed Church in America and a member of classis. That means that in his theology he is subject to the teaching of the church, not that the church is subject to his teaching. In a Reformed Church context, theology is not made by declaration from the pulpit — rather the declarations of the pulpit are expected to be in conformity with established theology" (Minutes of Faculty Meeting, 23 April 1996, 10-11, JAH). Such responses communicated effectively to faculty whose background included some study of theology and church history, but others felt that he was dodging the question.

8. Minutes of Faculty Meeting, 27 September 1994, JAH.

9. "As a team builder, John Jacobson would never take the credit for himself, but it's no coincidence that his presidency has been marked by significant gains for Hope College," remarked Board of Trustees chair Kermit Campbell upon the announcement of Jacobson's retirement. *News From Hope College*, February 1998, 7. An editorial in *The Anchor* also characterized Jacobson as one prone not to claim credit for accomplishments that resulted from his efforts: "It is easy to assume that his power is all fictitious and his reach extends no further than the Queen of England's. It is always easy to assume that which is inaccurate." *The Anchor*, 28 January 1998.

developed the habit of using part of the annual Provost's Addresses to exhort and educate the faculty concerning the nature of liberal arts education in a Christian context; he continued this practice throughout the Jacobson administration. Moreover, in 1989 Nyenhuis was successful in procuring a Knight Foundation challenge grant, which underwrote Faith and Learning Research Fellowships, on-campus faith and learning conferences, and faculty travel to national conferences on related topics. In 1996 his office sponsored a "Teaching as Faithful Profession" summer workshop for faculty. He, along with Jacobson, was also active in encouraging and supporting Hope's participation in the Rhodes Regional Consultation on the Future of Church-Related Higher Education as well as the Lilly Mentoring Initiative.[10] Through these varied means Nyenhuis, with Jacobson's blessing, initiated a number of significant contributions toward a more conscious and articulate role for the Christian faith in Hope's academic life.

Debate and Irritation: The Hiring Policy

Jacobson's first six years as president (1987-1993) were by his own account happy ones, characterized by a rapidly rising endowment and an amiable atmosphere on campus. However, by 1994, the faculty hiring policy — a policy that Jacobson came to view as crucial to the religious identity of the college — would become a subject of increasingly thorny debate. Jacobson knew prior to becoming president that the issue was important at Hope. He knew, for instance, that in March 1986 Van Wylen and Nyenhuis had, in his words, "come under heavy fire" in defending the hiring policy, both at a regular faculty meeting and at a special evening meeting devoted to the topic.[11] Moreover, a week before members of the Professional Interest Committee (PIC) were scheduled to meet with President-Elect Jacobson, the committee received a memo from the History Department complaining about a lack of guidelines for judging candidates' commitment to the historic

10. Pre-College Conference materials 1985-1999 and "Teaching as Faithful Profession" in Provost's Collection, JAH.
11. Minutes of Faculty Meeting, 4 March 1986; Agenda for Faculty Meeting, 7 March (7-8:30 p.m.), JAH. Simon, notes from Jacobson interview, 14 December 2002.

Christian faith and questioning the equitable application of the policy across divisions.[12] The new president initially did not possess a strong opinion on the matter of whether Hope's hiring policy should be comprehensive or critical-mass,[13] though he pledged himself to uphold the 1984 guidelines. Some faculty hoped that Jacobson's accommodating personality, Swarthmore and Yale education, and mainline religious pedigree heralded a more open hiring policy. But he turned out to be at times a more stringent gatekeeper than his provost Nyenhuis, a Calvin College alumnus.[14] The strong endorsement of the then-current practice that resulted from the year-long PIC investigation into the subject may have influenced his thinking.[15] Even more important was his ex-

12. PIC Minutes, 17 April 1987, JAH. The Professional Interest Committee, as the name implies, exists to protect and promote the faculty's professional interests, which include "such matters as professional ethics, institutional facilities, salaries, fringe benefits, criteria for promotion and tenure, equitable representation, and other items of faculty welfare." Hope College Faculty Handbook, A6d. The PIC is unusual in Hope College's shared governance system (which relegates policy-making capacities not directly held by the president and the Board of Trustees to boards and standing committees usually made up of a mix of faculty, administrators, and students) in being composed exclusively of faculty members. Given that one of the members of the committee was also a member of the History Department, it is likely that the hiring policy was one topic in their conversation. In any case, the PIC's response to the memo was to form a subcommittee, which met throughout Jacobson's first year in office, to inquire into the department's concerns. The subcommittee solicited input from department chairs, convening a faculty-wide forum at the midpoint and end of its work, having multiple conversations with higher administrators, and giving periodic updates to its parent committee. PIC minutes of 24 April, 1 May, and 8 December 1987, and 8 February, 15 March, and 5 May 1988.

13. As we discussed in Chapter One, a critical-mass policy involves intending to allow the hiring of some number of non-Christian faculty, while a comprehensive policy seeks to have all candidates hired be professing Christians. Indeed, one person submitting a question to a faculty meeting seemed to want to use Jacobson's willingness not to hold Central College's hiring policy as counter-evidence of its genuine nature as a Christian institution as evidence that his attitude on Hope's policy was inconsistent. Jacobson's view on Central was quoted in an article called "What Makes a College Christian?" in *The Church Herald* (the RCA denominational magazine). Minutes of 25 April 1995 Faculty Meeting, JAH. At the same meeting, Jacobson asserted that he did not use a creedal criterion in hiring and would not favor doing so.

14. Kennedy and Simon, notes from interview with John Jacobson, 14 December 2003; notes from interview with Jacob Nyenhuis, 16 May 2003.

15. The PIC and the Sub-Committee on Hiring, having canvassed campus opinion and departmental practice and having examined the deans and provost about how

perience during his second year in office when, as he remembers, it seemed to him that every department wanted to hire a non-Christian. By the end of that year he was confirmed in his opinion that "if exceptions were allowed it would be continual and bitter struggle with departments that wanted to make exceptions."[16]

Jacobson refused to hire an anthroposophist[17] recommended by one department; he also withheld his support for the candidacy of a self-professed Roman Catholic nun who could not offer evidence of her identity.[18] There can be little doubt that under Jacobson's presidency the faculty members (if they were not already so inclined) were compelled to increase efforts to "search diligently" for Christian candidates. Jacobson (and Nyenhuis) resisted so many requests for exceptions that by the end of his tenure in the late 1990s candidates reaching his office for review were seldom rejected on religious grounds.

Principled opponents of the 1984 hiring policy were persistent, however, in making their case. Particularly in the mid-1990s many professors continued to insist that Hope's identity required that hiring not be restricted in all cases to Christians only, though others continued to be concerned that the policy as implemented resulted too often in hiring candidates who had only a minimal interest in, knowledge of, or commitment to Christianity.[19] Controversy over administrative veto of a request by the Mathematics Department to be allowed to

---

they inquired into candidates' religious views, endorsed both the policy and its implementation and urged departments to use the same criteria as the administration in conducting searches; 5 May 1988 PIC Memorandum to All Faculty Regarding Report on Hiring Policies, PIC Minutes, JAH. Interestingly, the report also notes that administrators strongly rejected one chair's suggestion that candidates be asked to sign a document like the Apostles' Creed as too rigid a way to assess candidates' religious commitments.

16. John Jacobson, memorandum to James Kennedy and Caroline Simon, 30 October 2002, and Simon, notes on Jacobson interview, 14 December 2002.

17. Anthroposophy is a school of mystical thought calling for the evolution of human spiritual awareness, founded by, among others, German philosopher Rudolf Steiner (1861-1925). Its roots lie in German Romanticism rather than in orthodox Christianity.

18. Kennedy, notes on Jacobson interview, 14 December 2002.

19. An informal e-mail survey conducted by Caroline Simon in the Spring of 1994 indicated that 47 out of 74 respondents were in favor of the policy as written, but had varying opinions about its implementation, while 25 respondents thought that the written policy was too restrictive and two thought it too inclusive. Survey Results on Faculty Hiring, 30 March 1994, Personal Archives of Professor Janet Andersen.

bring one of two attractive non-Christian candidates for on-campus interviews led to discussion at a special faculty forum,[20] and to a subsequent lengthy statement by Jacobson of his views about hiring. He stated, "One thing I am quite sure of is that we will not strive diligently to appoint professing Christians if we regard the appointment of an exception as a legitimate outcome of every search," something he evidently feared would happen in the current atmosphere if *any* exceptions were allowed. He also asserted, "I use a broad definition of Christian community, but it is not indefinitely broad. I regard as disqualifying adherence to or membership in a cult, sect, or other ecclesiastical body that rejects the cardinal points of the historic Christian confessions."[21]

In reaction to Jacobson's position, a "Faculty Recruitment Study Group" of twenty to thirty participants began meeting to hammer out an institutional rationale for including a wider religious range of candidates — producing a document subsequently discussed in faculty meetings in late 1994.[22] Meanwhile, in an act that administrators and almost all faculty deplored, an anonymous person, presumably a faculty member irritated about the situation, leaked a packet of correspondence on the Mathematics Department hire — including a memo by Nyenhuis — to the *Chronicle of Higher Education*. Under the circumstances, few welcomed a national spotlight on the college's hiring policy.[23]

20. Memo from some members of the Mathematics Department to Dean Gentile and Provost Nyenhuis, 3 March 1994, Personal Archives of Professor Janet Andersen.

21. Minutes of the Faculty Meeting, 26 April 1994, JAH.

22. Agenda and Minutes for 25 October 1994 Faculty Meeting, and Minutes of Hope College Faculty Meeting, 29 November 1994, JAH.

23. The packet of materials had been circulated within the Faculty Recruitment discussion group by Janet Andersen, a faculty member then in her third year in the Mathematics Department who had been a member of its search committee that year. She circulated the packet, after seeking the permission of the authors of all the materials, in order to counter misinformation and rumors about the search that were rife. She and a great many of her colleagues were appalled by the leak, by the breach of trust on the part of an anonymous colleague, and by the callous disregard it displayed for her situation as a junior faculty member identified with the materials; she was grateful for the administrative support and reassurances that she received in the aftermath. Notes from Simon conversation with Janet Andersen, 20 June 2003. Thanks to the *Chronicle*'s ham-handed editing, Nyenhuis suffered an additional embarrassment of having his memo quoted in a way that made him seem to be questioning the policy. Simon, notes from interview with Jacob Nyenhuis, 16 May 2003.

Efforts to loosen the policy or its application were to no avail, and one particular attempt to precipitate a more open policy served only to *tighten* resistance to changing either it or its then-current administrative implementation. In the wake of all of this discussion about hiring, at least two trustees expressed sympathy for broadening the hiring policy, and one of them — a faculty member — informed colleagues at the college that the board was open to considering a loosening of the policy.[24] This drew a strong response from Jacobson, who thought this misrepresented the board's view and who had lost patience with continuing this time-consuming debate. He consequently urged the board's Executive Committee to tighten up the vetting of trustee candidates relative to their stance on hiring, requesting that the board reaffirm its commitment to the hiring policy of 1984 along with its current method of implementation.[25] The motion passed by a roll call vote with a large majority.[26] After this, hiring became a much less frequent topic of public debate, though for many the fight would go on.[27] Throughout Jacobson's administration, board members continued to scrutinize the Christian commitment of faculty coming up for tenure, though no candidates reviewed by trustees have ever been denied tenure on any grounds.

None of this meant that the faculty was without discretion in the hiring of candidates. Christians with a variety of backgrounds and

24. Minutes of Faculty Meeting, 22 November 1994, JAH.

25. Jacobson's actions resulted from his view that there would be "sheer chaos" if there was a sizable minority within the board who favored an open hiring policy. Simon, notes on Jacobson interview, 14 December 2002. Donald Cronkite, at the time both a key person in the hiring discussion group and one of two faculty members on the Board of Trustees, remembers being called to Jacobson's office, where Jacobson and then board chairman Max De Pree told him that they expected discussion of the hiring policy to stop. In hindsight, Cronkite thinks that his link to the petition about the hiring matter discussed on pp. 183-85 — he acted as the messenger to deliver the faculty petition — exacerbated negative attitudes among administrators and board members concerning the more general hiring discussion. Simon, conversation with Cronkite, 23 June 2003.

26. Jacobson's report to the faculty in the Minutes of the Faculty Meeting of 31 January 1995, JAH.

27. History professor Earl Curry expressed public thanks to those "with whom I stood side by side in a continuing collective effort to maintain an open hiring policy" at the last faculty meeting before his retirement in 1999. Minutes of the Faculty Meeting, 25 April 2000, JAH.

convictions were hired, some of whom probably possessed only loose ties to institutional Christianity. Jacobson thought that the faculty selection process evidenced a bias against evangelical Protestant candidates, while various faculty members thought the administration favored them too much. Whatever the case, a 1998 survey of the faculty revealed that some 46 percent of faculty were members of some kind of Reformed church (not necessarily RCA) — a high percentage that probably testifies more to the large number of Reformed churches in the area than to the number of Reformed applying for (and getting) jobs at Hope. Twenty-two percent identified with a mainline Protestant church, while 17 percent named Roman Catholicism as their religion, and only 4 percent said they were evangelical — though the last number may be misleadingly low as a result of some evangelicals identifying themselves in the survey as "Reformed." All told, 85 percent of Hope's faculty claimed church membership, and 79 percent identified themselves as "deeply committed" Christians (with an additional 13 percent saying they were "somewhat committed").[28] Hope College was probably closer in practice to the "comprehensive ecumenical" model in 1998 than it had been in 1987, with a tighter hiring policy and with the retirement of professors who had been hired in the more open policy of the late 1960s and early 1970s.

However much discussion of the hiring policy served as "a continual irritant" (to use Jacobson's words) in the 1990s, it was overshadowed by other controversies related to Jacobson's own vision for Hope College. He strongly believed that every Christian college must be a place where Christian character was molded and sustained and where an effective chapel program drew a large number of students to regular worship. Though the resentment that some professors felt over hiring was the beginning of a widening chasm between the president and many of his faculty, it was the implementation of both these aims in the second half of Jacobson's presidency (1993-1999) that generated a great deal of conflict at the college.

28. Charles Green, Barbara Neper, and Jacob Sitati, "Evaluating the Hope College Chapel Programs: Surveys of Students and of Faculty" (Hope College: Frost Center for Social Science Research, 1998), 69-70.

"Local Morality" Revised in a New Key

As we have seen, in earlier parts of its history the issue of how much Hope College should be shaped by "local morality" had forced the college into considering its stance on issues such as dancing, alcohol use, smoking, and the content of plays performed in college facilities. Indeed, the dancing issue had long ago been put to rest — Hope was proud that its Dance Department had one of its four nationally accredited programs in the arts. But alcohol, smoking, and both film and live theatre all received ongoing discussion in the 1990s. The use of "bad language" in the Summer Repertory Theatre still generated — and continues to generate — complaints to the president, as did a showing (abruptly terminated by Jacobson) of what he later characterized as a "marginally pornographic" film in the college-owned movie house.[29] After this episode, the president reemphasized the policy prohibiting the showing of "R" films in the theatre.[30] Alcohol enforcement was tightened by passing a "no empties" regulation and another making it an offense to be in the same on-campus room where alcohol was present (attempts to circumvent students' evading the campus alcohol ban by drinking the evidence or claiming that the contraband belonged to someone else). Smoking was restricted to fewer and fewer campus locations and finally allowed only outdoors, now out of concerns not so much for propriety as for health.[31]

One important difference between "local morality" in the 1890s and "local morality" in the 1980s and 1990s was that part of Hope's locale now included the wider world and the wider academy, most immediately the Great Lakes Colleges Association (GLCA). In the late 1980s, Hope's sense of itself as an institution with global responsibilities led it to struggle over whether its locale within a worldwide Reformed com-

---

29. Jacobson, memorandum to James Kennedy and Caroline Simon, 30 October 2002, 7.

30. This policy was part of the terms of the gift when the theatre was given to the college. The film that Jacobson cancelled was an unrated foreign film that, by his lights, would have earned an "R." Henceforth, he would insist that showings abide by the spirit as well as the letter of the gift agreement. Simon, notes from interview with John Jacobson, 14 December 2002. On-campus showings of "R" films sponsored by the Student Activities Committee in another venue were not prohibited and did in fact occur.

31. Minutes of the Faculty Meeting, 30 January 1996, JAH.

munity with an uneasy conscience over the Dutch Reformed role in the history of South African apartheid conferred particular obligations. By 1988, controversial South African anti-apartheid activist Allan Boesak had been nominated for an honorary degree from Hope College. The Board of Trustees was so split on whether to grant the degree that Jacobson said at a faculty meeting that it was the most difficult question that he had had to face since becoming president.[32]

In addressing personal behavior, college policy-makers were influenced not only by Holland, West Michigan, and the RCA, but by the prevailing concerns of academic policy-makers in the wider locale of the academy. An important example of this was the college's sexual harassment policy, which began to receive sustained attention in 1983 in response to GLCA conversations (though Hope would put its distinctive stamp on these concerns by seeing its policy as an outgrowth of its belief that "God values each person as a unique work of divine creation").[33] While a pilot policy was put in place in 1986-87, the policy received repeated revision and discussion as it was incorporated into the Faculty Handbook. By 1993, the Sexual Harassment Policy Revision Committee was completing its work and finding it necessary to respond to faculty concerns in three areas: due process, verbal offense, and romantic relationships between employees and students or supervisors and employees. The latter two areas were especially sensitive. Sanctions against verbal offense raised concerns about potential restrictions on academic freedom in the classroom.[34] The "unacceptability" of consensual romantic relationships between faculty members and students (an issue not addressed at all in the 1986 policy)[35] was debated by, on the one hand, those who were concerned that the college not extend its domain over faculty lives beyond its physical boundaries[36] and, on

32. Minutes of Faculty Meeting, 22 November 1988, JAH.

33. Minutes of the Sexual Harassment Council Meeting, 17 March 1987; Policy Statement on Sexual Harassment and Grievance Procedure, April 1986; Sexual Harassment Policy Topical File, JAH.

34. Indeed, at one point the Administrative Affairs Board approved removing the whole section regarding generalized sexist remarks; see its Minutes, 21 December 1993.

35. Policy Statement on Sexual Harassment and Grievance Procedure, April 1986, Sexual Harassment Topical File, JAH.

36. Memorandum from Albert Bell to Margaret Kasimatis, 26 January 1993, and Caroline Simon, Statement for Faculty Meeting Panel Discussion, 26 January 1993; Sex-

the other hand, those who thought that power differentials and potential conflicts of interest should preclude such involvements. In characteristic Hope College fashion, panel discussions and forums were held, a sub-committee on Verbal Expression and Sexual Harassment was formed, compromises were reached, and revisions were incorporated into the policy.

The Jacobson era also saw several attempts to reform Greek life at Hope College.[37] Jacobson disliked the deforming influence on student life of a "fraternity culture" of sexual and alcoholic excess that he had witnessed during his time as a professor at Hamilton College. He was alarmed and saddened upon his arrival at Hope to read in the daily Public Safety reports of what he later characterized as the "sad mischances" and unwise behaviors that were occasions of so much pain among some Hope students. A 1995 survey indicated, for instance, that 41 percent of Hope students had engaged in sexual intercourse — far lower than state institutions, but still too high for many Christians concerned with the moral conduct of students.[38] Christians, Jacobson thought, "should try to lead a decent life," and it was clear to him that the Hope College community — primarily the students — did not work at this as hard as they should. He viewed the hazing and parties associated with some of Hope's Greek-letter organizations as a part of this problem.

Among the first task forces to be created under his administration was one on Greek life.[39] That he was always willing to encourage the massive work involved in addressing the problem — and its relative intractability — is evidenced by recurring reports to the faculty on the subject in multiple meetings in 1988, 1990, 1991, and 1996. A full-

---

ual Harassment Topical File, JAH. Simon was reminded by her archival work of what she said on the issue: "Sometimes when we succeed in getting students to fall in love with our subject, they think they have fallen in love with *us*. . . . I think that an explicit policy stating that students should not be exploited [by taking advantage of this] would be a good thing."

37. Such efforts had also occurred in the Van Wylen period; Minutes of Faculty Meetings, 3 March 1987 and 28 April 1987, JAH.

38. "Students Support Condom Distribution in Campus Survey," *The Anchor*, 25 January 1995; 61 percent of students surveyed thought the Hope Health Clinic should provide condoms for free.

39. Minutes of Faculty Meeting, 24 November 1987, JAH.

scale investigation of Greek pledging was launched in 1995; 300 interviews with Greek students over the summer revealed instances of "serious hardcore hazing."[40] In order to address the problem, an ad hoc committee was formed to revise the pledging process.[41] Pledging, now to be called "New Member Education," was to be a more positive, less pointlessly arduous, demeaning, or dangerous process. This was to be monitored by faculty advisors to the fraternities and sororities and vigilant oversight — including random spot checks — by the student development staff and volunteer faculty, with stiff penalties for violations. A mixed report on whether these reforms were effective, and how thoroughly they had been implemented, was given at the last faculty meeting of 1996-97, noting some improvement but many ongoing problems.[42]

Since the mid-1980s, homosexuality had been a polarizing issue on the Hope campus. Throughout the 1990s, *The Anchor* would devote extensive attention to the subject roughly once every two years, with students either expressing Christian opposition to homosexuality or articulating Christian rationales for the support of homosexuals. On both sides, theological arguments dominated the discussion.[43] In the spring of 1994 the issue of homosexuality would manifest itself in the

40. Minutes of Faculty Meetings, 25 April 1995 and 24 August 1995, JAH.

41. Minutes of Faculty Meeting, 26 September 1995, JAH. Jacobson gave effusive thanks to Profs. James Allis and Janet Andersen for their wisdom and sacrificial effort in the attempt at reform at a faculty meeting at the beginning of 1996; Minutes of Faculty Meeting, 30 January 1996, JAH.

42. Faculty members closely involved with attempted reforms felt that the highest levels of administration of student development were less than wholeheartedly supportive of these efforts. Simon, conversation with James Allis and Charles Green, July 2003. Hope's Dean of Students often felt pressure both from faculty and others who thought that there should be more strictures on Greek life and Greek alumni who were often outraged by what they thought were unreasonable restrictions on Greek activity. Simon, interview with Richard Frost, Vice President for Student Development and Dean of Students, Hope College, 4 September 2003. That excesses and problematic behavior among some Greek organizations had not been put permanently to rest by these sustained efforts is evidenced by serious incidents, involving personal injuries and multiple criminal charges, at Greek-sponsored "social events" in 1999-2000 — though the outrage and strength of then-new President Bultman's response seems to have made Greek organizations more nearly, if not cheerfully, compliant with Hope's rules governing their activities in the new millennium. Minutes of Faculty Meeting, 25 January 2000, JAH.

43. See *Anchor* issues in 1992, 1994, 1996, and 1998 for these discussions.

question of whether or not to hire an openly gay faculty member who was also a professing Christian. Jacobson objected to appointing the favored candidate of the department in question, in part because he was concerned about whether a connection between the candidate and a current, pivotal member of the department constituted a conflict of interest. But Jacobson's opposition to the appointment was not restricted to preventing a conflict of interest. He simply did not think it was appropriate for a Christian (or specifically RCA) college to condone what he regarded as moral misconduct, particularly in respect to appointing, as in this case, someone whose role involved a high public profile. Jacobson's position put him on a collision course with one of his deans, with most members of the department in question, and with forty faculty members who signed a petition protesting his decision. Petitioners acted with varied motives. For some it was an act of solidarity with colleagues, for others it was a matter of departmental autonomy to exercise professional judgment in evaluating candidates, for still others it was a matter of social justice. Jacobson, despite these entreaties, stuck to his position, and accepted the resignation of the dean who had backed the candidate (and with whom Jacobson had, by his own account, a relationship he saw as already strained by past disagreements).[44] And Jacobson went further than that: in 1995, in response to a weeklong series of "LesBiGay" events on campus, Jacobson encouraged the Board of Trustees to make an unprecedented moral stand, stating in a declaration that Hope College, like its parent denomination, opposed homosexual behavior as sin.[45] The next aca-

44. Kennedy, notes on interview with John Jacobson, 14 December 2002.

45. Many faculty were disturbed that newspaper articles about the college's position oversimplified both the college's and the RCA's position, summarizing it tersely as "homosexual behavior is sin." Barton Dieters, "Students Rescind Invitation to Gay Christian Speaker," *Holland Sentinel*, 6 March 1999, A5. Hope College's 16 August 1995 statement says this, but also reflects, to the extent a brief statement can, the RCA's complex position on this matter. Both the college's statement and the RCA's 1978 report (still in force) on the subject entitled "Homosexuality: A Biblical and Theological Appraisal" make a careful distinction between homosexuality and homosexual practice; both support the kind and fair treatment of homosexuals. However, the RCA report, which by its nature is more extensive in its treatment of the subject, emphasizes more strongly and in more detail than Hope's statement that "It is one matter to affirm that self-chosen homosexual acts are sinful. It is quite another to reject, defame, and excoriate the humanity of the person who performs them. This distinction has often been missed. It is possible and

demic year, the provost's office offered a series of panel discussions, carefully crafted for ideological balance, on the theological, scientific, civil, and moral issues surrounding homosexuality.[46]

The tensions generated by this incident would undermine Jacobson's attempt (started earlier, and for unrelated reasons) to develop a communal consensus on character. The fall of 1993 would see another instance in which Hope's reference group for "local morality" was the broader academy. Hope's Multicultural Life Committee, along with then-Assistant Provost Alfredo Gonzales, requested that Hope College consider having a policy to address racial and ethnic harassment and offense, and proposed that Hope emulate a document in use at other colleges and universities.[47] Jacobson's concern that liberal arts in a Christian context should encourage people to lead examined and responsible lives led him to broaden the project. He attempted to create a collective document, framed by a committee he chaired of faculty, students, and administrators, on Hope's "Ideals of Character." His hope was that the college could collectively affirm, in broad outline, what kind of community it aspired to be and, consequently, what attributes of character it affirmed in its members.

By October of 1994, Jacobson's Ideals of Character committee reported back to the relevant college board with a draft document, which generated significant controversy. Much of the content of the

---

necessary on biblical grounds to identify homosexuality as a departure from God's intent. However . . . there are no theological grounds on which a homosexual may be singled out for a greater measure of judgment. All persons bear within them the marks of the fall"; and "The denial of human and civil rights to homosexuals is inconsistent with the biblical witness and Reformed theology." *The Church Speaks: Papers of the Commission on Theology, Reformed Church of America, 1959-1984* (Grand Rapids: Eerdmans, 1985), 251, 257. The latter two assertions were the basis for at least some people's questioning the president's claim that it was inappropriate for a college affiliated with the RCA to hire a known practicing homosexual. In October 1994 the Philosophy Department sought clarification of whether sexual orientation and practice were to be treated in the same way as marital status when hiring — not to be inquired into and not to be taken into account (letter of Anthony Perovich to Provost Nyenhuis, 27 October 1994, Personal Archives of Anthony Perovich). Both Jacobson and Nyenhuis gave verbal assurances to them, as well as to other department chairs, that in the future this would be the case under their administration. An important basis for this mutual understanding was that it concerned the future and did not reflect an evaluation of past decisions.

46. Minutes of the Faculty Meeting, 26 September 1995, JAH.

47. Minutes of Administrative Affairs Board, 21 December 1993, JAH.

document seemed unproblematic on the face of it; the stated ideals of concern for justice, intellectual and practical wisdom, loving concern for others, servant leadership, and love of God and neighbor seemed unexceptionable. Yet in the tense atmosphere of 1995, suspicions ran high.

Opponents of the proposed "Ideals of Character" feared that such a document would be used by the institution to judge their personal lives, and that its explicitly Christian preamble and conclusion constituted an indirect attempt to impose a statement of faith on the faculty.[48] More crucially, as had been the case under Van Wylen, many faculty members preferred saying less rather than more about the Christian nature of the college, fearing theological and moral constraints upon themselves and their peers. Unsurprisingly, "a good part of most discussions, in fact, focused on the specifically religious parts of the document," which made some "feel excluded and marginal."[49]

The fallout of the 1994 confrontation over the relevance of sexual orientation in a specific departmental hire, including the exacerbation of suspicions toward the "Ideals of Character," had ongoing ramifications. One of its odd outgrowths seems to have been a tussle over whether offensive remarks aimed at people or groups because of their sexual orientation should be prohibited under the generalized sexist remarks section of the Anti-Sexual Harassment Policy.[50] Those in favor of

48. There were also concerns that the document had become so broad that the original request of the Multicultural Life Committee for a policy to address racist speech had been obscured.

49. Though the document was still deemed useful enough to recommend for trial use in discussion with incoming students during orientation in the fall of 1995, the board permanently tabled its discussion of the matter at its September 1995 meeting. Donald Cronkite, Ideals of Character Retreat Summary of Discussion, 26 April 1995, Ideals of Character Topical File, JAH. According to Don Cronkite, who was Administrative Affairs Board secretary at the time, it was Jacobson who first suggested tabling the issue, having concluded that "it wasn't going to get anywhere." Minutes of the Administrative Affairs Board, 12 September 1995, JAH. Simon, notes from conversation with Don Cronkite, 23 June 2003.

50. The policy (as discussed above — see notes 33-36 of this chapter) was slowly making its way through committees as part of the full-scale revision of the Faculty Handbook. The 1986 version of the policy had defined sexist remarks as demeaning ones "directed at the victims because of their gender or sexual orientation." In its report to the Administrative Affairs Board, the Subcommittee on Sexual Harassment and Ver-

not including homosexual slurs in the policy may have been motivated by concern that this would be interpreted as an endorsement of homosexual practice on the part of the college. However, given the position deploring the defamation of homosexuals in the RCA's own statement on the matter, the outcome of the controversy — which was to explicitly proscribe homosexual slurs along with other sexist remarks — aligned Hope's policy with its parent denomination's study document.[51]

Considerably more important than these short-term effects was the 1994 confrontation's role in sensitizing those on both sides of that issue in ways that affected the tempestuous controversies over homosexuality several years later, in 1999. It probably further alienated a portion of mostly liberal and moderate faculty from Jacobson's leadership, and it certainly alienated Jacobson from key signers of the petition.[52] And it probably made Jacobson less willing to countenance faculty criticism of his newly appointed Dean of the Chapel, the Rev. J. Ben Patterson.

"Uplift" and Crosswinds: The Gathering Storm

"I come from a long line of pugilists," Ben Patterson is supposed to have remarked when introducing himself to people at Hope College.[53]

---

bal Expression, formed in 1994 to address faculty concerns about the relationship of the policy to academic freedom, had recommended a definition of sexist remarks as those "demeaning remarks . . . serving no scholarly, artistic, or educational purpose that are directed at individuals or groups because of their gender or sexual orientation." All the recommendations of the subcommittee were adopted; however, its recommendation was amended by deleting the phrase "or sexual orientation." The board subsequently reinstated this phrase on 13 September 1994. When the Women's Studies and Programs Committee protested the phrase's absence in the policy as published in 1997, the omission was rectified upon President Jacobson's instructions. Minutes of the Administrative Affairs Board, 8 March 1994, and attached report of the Subcommittee on Sexual Harassment and Verbal Expression, 28 February 1994; Minutes of Administrative Affairs Board, 13 September 1994; Minutes of the Women's Studies and Programs Committee, 6 January 1997; all in JAH.

51. See note 45 of this chapter.

52. Kennedy, notes from interview with John Jacobson, 14 December 2002.

53. Kennedy and Simon, notes from interview with John Jacobson, 14 December 2002.

And indeed, Patterson had many quintessential characteristics of "the fighting Fundamentalist," though Patterson was not, strictly speaking, a Fundamentalist at all. For many years, in fact, he had written critiques against the narrow Fundamentalism of his youth in the satirical journal *The Wittenberg Door*.[54] Patterson's ministry at Hope reflected this journey from Fundamentalism: he affirmed Roman Catholics as Christians, and appointed women to important positions in his leadership team, including responsibility for preaching. His appointments also made the chaplain's staff one of the most ethnically diverse on the campus. By the time of his coming to Hope at the end of the 1993, however, Patterson had become more concerned with liberalism within the mainline Presbyterian Church in which he had become an ordained minister. Though he demonstrated flexibility on a range of theological and moral issues, Hope's new chaplain could not, and would not, compromise with people or programs that he believed were at odds with Christian essentials. Gifted intellectually, a good writer, and well-read in theology, Patterson was at the same time uneasy in academic life, whose ethos of free inquiry seemed to him to evince the moral and theological relativism he despised.[55] Loved for his personal warmth and humor by those who knew him best, he was criticized by others for being aloof to their concerns; a powerful communicator in the pulpit, he was chastised for being unable or unwilling to engage with others through the give-and-take of public discussion. As is the case with many strong personalities, his strengths — and his weaknesses — loomed larger than life, and at Hope College he engendered both adulating praise and bitter enmity for what he did, and did not do, as Dean of the Chapel.

Patterson had been hired, in fact, to shake up the chapel program. Jacobson and others on campus were worried and embarrassed by the very low levels of chapel attendance. All acknowledged that the situation was an understandable consequence of a lone chaplain in a less-than-lavishly funded program doing ministry while also fulfilling other demanding roles for the college — such as chairing one of the college's three major boards and serving as the lead sexual harassment

54. Kennedy, interview with J. Ben Patterson, 21 October 2002.

55. Ben Patterson, Epaphras Fellowship Prayer Letter, edition 3, December 1999; Personal Archives of J. Ben Patterson.

counselor.[56] Yet the president's experiences at other colleges had convinced him that ensuring a dynamic chapel program was one of the most important ways for a Christian school to achieve its mission. Since 1991, Jacobson had worked hard not only to secure funding to endow the Dean of the Chapel but also to recruit a large staff to assist the new dean — a challenge enthusiastically met by evangelical stalwart supporters of the college like Max and Connie Boersma, after whom Patterson's endowed chair was named. Patterson now benefited from this money, hiring several full-time assistants and a Christian rock musician with considerable local repute as worship leader. Meanwhile, Patterson assiduously guarded his time from incursions by campus committee work.[57] In terms of worship format, Patterson, after initial theological misgivings, borrowed heavily from Holland's charismatic Vineyard church because of its effective ministry to students.[58] From the very beginning, traditional music (including the chapel organ), hymn singing, and the more "high art" aesthetics of the Music Department were effectively sidelined from the chapel program.

Together, Patterson and his ministry team were phenomenally successful in increasing the appeal of the chapel program for students. According to Patterson himself, some 500-600 students began attending within two weeks of his ministry (a more than tenfold increase over various estimates of the old chapel program), and filled the cha-

---

56. As Dean of Students Richard Frost remembers, under Chaplain Gerard Van Heest the spiritual life of the campus had been closely aligned with the Student Development Office. Van Heest, in addition to all his other responsibilities, took part in resident-director training for the dorms and provided pastoral input to the Counseling Center and Health Center staff. His pastoral presence was pervasive and deeply appreciated by those who benefited from it. Simon, interview with Richard Frost, 4 September 2003.

57. Paul Boersma and Dolores Nasrallah were appointed chaplains and Dwight Beal became the worship leader. Over time, the staff was also supplemented with an administrative assistant, a lighting and sound technician, a gospel choir director, and a coordinator for mission trips and student volunteer work. On the issue of the Dean of the Chapel's guarding his time, it might have been a comfort to some of the faculty who began to suspect that Patterson was using his position as a member of the president's senior staff to influence college policy to know that his absence from senior staff meetings was an ongoing irritant to his vice presidential colleagues. Simon, notes from interview with John Jacobson, 14 December 2002.

58. Kennedy, interview with Patterson, 21 October 2002.

pel to capacity by the end of two years. By 1996, over a third of Hope's student body was voluntarily attending one or more of the weekly services the chapel team offered; by 1998, half of Hope's students claimed to attend chapel at least once a week, and 42 percent attended "The Gathering," the Sunday evening service, at least once a month.[59] Evidence suggests that most of those who attended were underclassmen (opening Patterson to the charge that he appealed chiefly to less mature students), and were, predictably enough, more likely to come from evangelical backgrounds than mainline or Catholic households;[60] yet many of the latter did attend enthusiastically. The services, with their heavy doses of high-volume contemporary praise songs and messages emphasizing discipleship and repentance, were clearly not for everyone, but there is no denying they sparked excitement among large sections of the student population.[61] Similarly, the chapel program launched annual spring break mission trips, in which hundreds of students forewent recreational travel in favor of short-term service trips; many students, in fact, camped out overnight in order to be near the head of the line for the Spring Break mission trip sign-up. In these respects, the arrival of Patterson and his team substantially changed the religious ethos of the school, particularly among students. There was more enthusiasm for missions at Hope College by the end of the 1990s perhaps than at any time since the days of the Student Volunteer Band in the 1920s.

Why did the new chapel program achieve such an early, sustained, and striking measure of success? It is probable that the services received immediate support from hundreds of evangelical students who were already at the college. The campus culture of the 1970s and 1980s, including the classroom, was often cool toward students who seemed too evangelical, and students with this kind of piety often stayed out of the limelight. With Patterson and his staff, they found a

59. Kennedy, interview with Patterson, 21 October 2002; see Seth Dale, "Skyrocketing Chapel Attendance Packs Pews," *The Anchor*, 14 September 1994; Dan Cwik and Carrie Tennant, "Crowds Leave Standing Room Only at Chapel," *The Anchor*, 11 September 1996; Dana Lamers, "Survey Unveiled," *The Anchor*, 30 September 1998.

60. Green, Neper, and Jacob Sitati, "Evaluating the Hope College Chapel Programs," 10-16.

61. The Gathering also engendered a loyal following among religiously conservative citizens of the college's surrounding community.

message and form of religious expression for which they had longed, and they responded in large numbers. Seen this way, Patterson's tenure as chaplain illuminated the fact that Hope students of the 1990s were to a large extent conservative and evangelical in their theological orientation. As President Jacobson would later remember, Patterson remarked that upon his arrival "he found that Hope was not a city set on a hill, but a collection of unrelated villages set on a hill."[62] Clusters of conservative Christian students who had believed that they were (by the standards of their theology) the only Christians on campus now knew that there were many others of like mind.

None of this contradicts the fact that the Patterson ministry generated Christian conversion and renewal among many students — evidenced in a revival in 1995, when for a number of days students publicly confessed their sins in Dimnent Chapel and then at nearby Pillar Church, sometimes into the early morning hours.[63] Trustees, alumni, and some faculty were delighted at the new student enthusiasm for the Christian faith and service. Student life was more strongly characterized by an evangelical ethos than it had been prior to Patterson's arrival.

But for a variety of reasons, the happy marriage of Christian piety and humanitarian progressive impulse that had characterized Hope earlier in the century[64] seemed impossible as Hope moved toward the new millennium. "Uplift," in the revivalist sense, seemed to many to be divorced from "elevation" through the liberal arts — and crosswinds swirled into increasing disquiet.

For one thing, the Dean of the Chapel immediately ran afoul of various members of the campus community, most notably, but not restricted to, faculty. Even before Patterson had fully assumed his duties, he alarmed some professors by announcing at the faculty luncheon in spring 1994 that he hoped that Hope College would move from being known as an academic institution with a religious heritage to being a religious institution with an academic dimension.[65] He criticized Stu-

---

62. Jacobson, memorandum to Kennedy and Simon, 30 October 2002, 5; this view was confirmed in Kennedy, interview with Patterson, 21 October 2002.

63. The first service was on April 9 (Palm Sunday); services at Pillar Church were on the 10th, 11th, and 17th. Minutes of Faculty Meeting, 25 April 1995, JAH.

64. See Chapter Three, pp. 187-93.

65. At the Sept. 27, 1994, Faculty Meeting, Patterson was asked to explain this remark. His response was that he had been "stating in a provocative way" the biblical and

dent Life for its reputed (by him) toleration of events like "Porno Night" in a dormitory and for introducing programs sympathetic to homosexuality.[66] He angered members of the football team after he rebuked them for what he regarded as a tasteless and cruel skit performed at a team party.[67] He offended feminists — both students and faculty — by vigorously defending traditional male language for God in the pulpit and being, at times, prone to gender stereotyping.[68]

His messages — perhaps most especially his highlighting of sin and frequent calls for repentance — struck some as simplistic at best, and traumatizing at worst. Many, though not all, faculty members and a significant minority of students found his message both anti-intellectual and far too theologically conservative and "exclusive." Moreover, many faculty and staff, as well as some students (twenty-

---

Reformed view that all that is, is the Lord's. He had succeeded in provoking — some by his initial remarks, others by faxing in his response instead of coming to the faculty meeting. Minutes of Faculty Meeting, 27 September 1994. JAH.

66. Kennedy, interview with Patterson, 21 October 2002. Dean of Students Richard Frost remembered the relationship between Student Development and Patterson as distant. "You were either in complete agreement with him or there was no contact," Frost recalled. He and his staff often felt themselves handicapped in helping students because of a lack of prior communication about Chapel Office events (for example, in the case of the April 1995 "revival" services) that were likely to affect student life. While he remembered no direct conversations with Patterson about the purported "Porno Night" and knew of no formal organized events that could fit that description, he was aware that some individual male students accessed pornography on the Internet in their rooms and would not be surprised to find that informal viewing groups happened from time to time. He did have a direct conversation with Patterson about Patterson's desire that Student Development more explicitly articulate what Patterson took to be the biblical view of homosexuality. In both sorts of cases, Frost described Student Development's approach as striving to help individual students consider how their own faith should inform their attitudes and behavior and to help students mature as independent decision-makers. Simon, interview with Richard Frost, 4 September 2003.

67. Kennedy, interview with Patterson, 21 October 2002. Kennedy and Simon, notes of interview with John Jacobson, 14 December 2002.

68. Though the Women's Studies and Programs Committee seems to have made no official response to Patterson's controversial sermon "Why God Is Father and Not Mother" (audio tape, January 1996, Campus Ministry Collection, JAH), they did send the chapel staff a memorandum, in response to a student complaint, expressing concerns about gender stereotyping in chapel talks. Minutes of Women's Studies and Programs Committee, 14 October 1996, JAH. See also Jenn Dorn, "'Genderless God' Spirits Individual Faith," *The Anchor*, 31 January 1996.

three of whom circulated a letter of concern), viewed the "revival" in the spring of 1995 as a reckless encouragement of emotional and disclosive excess.[69] In addition, among some of his critics there was a tendency to assume, on scant evidence, that he was responsible for all of the views of their students that struck them as benighted, and for any public event of a conservative Christian sort that they found embarrassing.[70] Some of them feared that Patterson's approach was encouraging students to become less religiously tolerant — evidenced, in their view, by anecdotes of students collectively praying over the dorm room doors of non-Christians and refusing to do selected assignments on religious grounds.[71] Other faculty began to spend many hours in informal counseling sessions with students offended, alienated, or bruised in one way or another by the chapel program.

One vivid instance of student distress, late in Patterson's ministry, generated a question at a faculty meeting regarding the exclusion of some students from a regular Sunday communion service in the chapel. Though Patterson himself had not presided over the communion service where he had preached, he gave a carefully researched and couched response to concerns about how the "invitation" was given, contrasting having discouraged those who did not agree with the sermon from coming forward with turning away any who did; "humbly repenting of anything we might have done . . . to erect barriers . . . where no genuine barriers exist" but also asserting their duty to "issue words of caution to those whose theology is a conscious turning

---

69. In response to a question at a faculty meeting, Patterson said of the events, in the words of the faculty secretary's summary, "all such activities are messy and ambiguous but that overall it was good and positive." Some faculty — notably Robin Klay — tried to allay others' concerns about excess. Minutes of the Faculty Meeting, 25 April 1995, JAH. Dean of Students Richard Frost would later recall having to counsel students who felt as if their best alternative was to leave Hope rather than live with public disgrace when public sexual confessions implicated not only the confessor but also his or her partner. Simon, interview with Richard Frost, 4 September 2003.

70. See Minutes of the Faculty, 23 April 1996, JAH. Minutes of the Faculty Meeting, 25 March 1997, indicate that at least one faculty member was irked by a "Biblical archeologist" who "had no academic credentials and spoke about his adventures seeking Mt. Sinai while violating the laws of his host country," though the questioner did not imply that Patterson was responsible for setting up this speaking engagement.

71. See Question 2 during Question Time at Faculty Meeting, 23 November 1999, JAH.

away from the faith entrusted by Jesus to His apostles."[72] Patterson's tenure both confirmed and deepened the wide theological chasm between adherents (students, faculty, and staff) of a more conservative and evangelical Christian faith, and a more variegated group of people who wanted the college to become (or remain) more open religiously. "Please don't take away my God," one student wrote plaintively in response to the chaplain's insistence on traditional masculine language for the Almighty.[73]

Yet even some of Patterson's vociferous critics were heard saying during his tenure at the college, "God worked through Ben Patterson" — if not a sentiment that they would own in every instance where he saw himself as God's instrument, certainly one they expressed about some of them. Moreover, despite his actively warning students to beware of the theology of several members of the Religion Department, numbers of religion majors grew during this period — a growth probably fueled, at least in part, by the high profile of religious discussion gained from the very controversy his ministry generated.[74] In a comment similar to scores of others addressed to Patterson, one appreciative student wrote upon graduating from Hope in 1999, "I am overwhelmed thinking about how God will change the world through the students graduating from Hope. He is calling so many to missions and service."[75]

Perhaps Patterson's unpardonable sin at Hope College was that

72. Minutes of the Faculty Meeting, 21 April and 29 September 1998, JAH. The sermon that preceded the perceived-to-be-unwelcoming invitation to the Lord's Table denounced religious pluralism, and the offended students felt they had been told that if they disagreed with the sermon they should not partake. Though Patterson indicated in his response that strong warnings were sometimes obligatory, the authors never saw or heard about any subsequent communion service where the presiding minister did not make every effort to convey that all Christians were welcome at the Table.

73. Tracy Bednarick, "Student to Patterson[:] Please Don't Take Away My God," *The Anchor*, 14 February 1996.

74. Jeffrey Tyler, memorandum to Kennedy and Simon, 22 July 2003, 27-28. Statistics kept by the Religion Department indicate an increase from thirteen Religion majors in 1993 to twenty-three in 1995. Moreover, this growth was sustained; in 1996, Religion had twenty-five majors and ten minors, figures almost identical to the numbers in 2001, a year after Patterson's departure.

75. From Personal Archives, Ben Patterson, File 840 "Hope College Letters — Positive '99."

he showed no great compunction to operate according to the school's irenic "culture of nice," as he himself termed it.[76] Despite urgent appeals to make the chapel program more "inclusive" in tone and message, he had no intention of opening up chapel services to those with a substantially alternate point of view. "A pulpit," he maintained, "is not a roundtable," in explaining that the Word of God could not countenance other, competing claims.[77] Nor did he have much interest in spending time with people who opposed his views, thinking his day better spent on those who were interested in the Christian faith than with those set against his ministry. He refused to work together with the Religion Department, for example, because it included faculty who held views he regarded as unorthodox.[78] It was this stance in particular that frustrated and sometimes infuriated his faculty critics, who believed that collegiality, a spirit of academic give-and-take, and the mild Christian ethos of Hope College demanded that Patterson listen more and compromise more. "You don't understand Hope," he was often told.[79] Jacobson — in one of the few pointed suggestions he made to Patterson in his annual evaluation — wrote in 1997,

> While I recognize that what you do is bound to make some people mad, I would like to invite you to come and talk with me before you make statements or take actions that will predictably have that effect. In the controversies around feminist theology and the football team skit, my experience of college life might have been of some use to you in making a forceful response without generating as much antagonism.[80]

It was not advice that Patterson would heed, at least not to the extent that Jacobson had hoped.

76. Kennedy, interview with Patterson, 21 October 2002.

77. Kennedy, interview with Patterson, 21 October 2002.

78. A cooperative effort to plan and execute a "Certificate of Ministry" Program involving the Religion Department, Western Seminary, and Hope's Campus Ministries began in the fall of 1995 but was permanently — at least during Patterson's tenure — put on hold for this reason. Minutes of the Faculty Meeting, 27 February 1996, JAH, and Kennedy and Simon, notes from interview with Jacob Nyenhuis, 16 May 2003.

79. Kennedy, interview with Patterson, 21 October 2002.

80. Letter of John Jacobson to Ben Patterson, 8 April 1997, Personal Archives of J. Ben Patterson.

Meanwhile, there was no campus consensus about what lay at the root of the problem. Patterson and many of his supporters, on and off campus, regarded his conflict with his critics as essentially theological in substance — between "Christian orthodoxy" and "heterodoxy, the work of theological revisionists," as the "Chapel Program Self Study" put it in 1998.[81] Seen in this light, Patterson was a prophet calling Van Raalte's "school of the prophets"[82] back to its true self. Many of Patterson's critics also saw the issue as theological — but construed it as pitting what they took to be Patterson's "sectarianism" against a spirit of Christian unity that deplored the elevation of passing social controversies, however heated, to the level of Christian essentials. Indeed, one might argue that some of Patterson's critics stood in Hope's long "nonsectarian" tradition; just as Hope's early leadership had labeled the Christian Reformed "seceders," Patterson's contemporary critics saw him as pulling away from fellow Christians over matters that were not central to the gospel. Others of Patterson's critics contended that the conflict had more to do with Patterson's uncompromising personality, which had a less-than-pastoral effect on those with whom he disagreed. His critics considered all members of Hope's student body, faculty, or staff to be part of Patterson's flock; his ability to make those with whom he differed feel like "goats" among the sheep made him, in their eyes, anything but a good shepherd.

A Full-Scale Tempest

In the spring of 1998, these tensions reached new heights when it became known that a Bible study leader for the chaplain's office had been dismissed from her position after telling the staff that she was a lesbian. After some discussion, her dismissal was made permanent because she refused to regard her orientation as a condition to be resisted — and ideally overcome — rather than embraced.[83] Predictably, homosexuality had again become the most divisive issue at the college,

81. "Hope College Chapel Program Self Study," August 1998, Personal Archives of J. Ben Patterson.

82. See Chapter Two, pp. 33, 37.

83. Glyn Williams, "Homosexual Bible Study Leader Dismissed," *The Anchor*, 15 April 1998.

though Patterson's pulpit attacks on religious pluralism[84] and a not-so-veiled critique of a religion faculty member who held this view were other reasons for increased tensions that spring. In response to a call by faculty members for a review of the chapel program,[85] a motion originating from the Student Life Committee of the Board of Trustees was passed — after heated debate — by the full board in May 1998 urging, among other things, that Jacobson and the Board of Trustees authorize such a review. They soon did so.

By now, Jacobson was having his own doubts about Patterson's continued service at the college. Whatever the misgivings of others, the president had staunchly backed Patterson, admiring his evangelical faith (Jacobson, Nyenhuis, and James Bekkering were in a Bible study with Patterson during the 1994-95 academic year) and the fact that he had made the chapel program so remarkably popular. Perhaps above all, he deeply resonated with Patterson's no-nonsense stance against un-Christian conduct at the college, whether in the fraternities, on the football team, or elsewhere. Until mid-1998, he had regarded the problems raised by Patterson's presence as serial and thus manageable, but by mid-1998 Jacobson began to regard them as cumulative and increasingly unmanageable.[86] Moreover, the effectiveness of Jacobson's attempts at defending his Dean of the Chapel had been seriously undermined by the still-simmering resentments over presidential actions and initiatives in the mid-1990s. Beginning to reach the end

---

84. "Religious pluralism" in this context refers to a theological view — the view (roughly) that non-Christian religions are all paths to God on a par with Christianity. Patterson not only preached against religious pluralism but felt obliged to help Hope guard itself from any appearance of practicing or endorsing pluralism. As Dean of Students Richard Frost remembers, Patterson protested Frost's having provided a room for a Muslim student to use for prayers. Frost had provided the room because the student reported being persecuted when he tried to pray in his own dorm room. Simon, interview with Richard Frost, 4 September 2003.

85. Memorandum from David Myers to John Jacobson, 22 April 1998, copied to Chris Barney, Robin Klay, and Elton Bruins; Memorandum from Chuck Green to Robin Klay, 28 April 1998, copied to Chris Barney, John Jacobson, Jack Nyenhuis, and Ben Patterson; Personal Archives of Professor Christopher Barney.

86. In April of 1996 Jacobson still held on to the "dream that we can continue to discuss important issues, and even improve the quality of our discussions, and that our conversations about these matters will become less divisive." Minutes of Faculty Meeting, 23 April 1996, JAH.

of his patience not only with faculty critics but with Patterson, Jacobson now distanced himself from Patterson — a fact that Patterson himself was not slow to perceive.[87]

After flirting with the idea of firing Patterson, Jacobson decided that he could not do so.[88] The Dean of the Chapel enjoyed overwhelming support from regional RCA (and other) churches, and the Board of Trustees, Jacobson reckoned, "was 95 percent in support" of Patterson, at least before receiving the report of the external reviewers.[89] Firing a popular and evangelistic chaplain would be hard to explain to key, financially generous constituencies. Nor in the end, in all likelihood, did Jacobson really want to part with someone who was the instrument of the president's signal achievement at the college: the revitalization of the chapel program.

In the meantime, the review process designed to detail strengths and weaknesses of the chapel program, as well as to outline ways to improve, had been set in motion. If the process had been initiated as an institutional way to manage tensions on Hope's campus, it was an unmitigated failure. The "Chapel Program Self Study" of August 1998 clearly indicated why the chaplain thought that a more friendly posture would do little to improve the situation:

> Can we work with people whose beliefs are inimical to our own?
> We think we can when our differences don't come to bear directly on the things we are doing together. But we are honestly confused over how this can be done effectively . . . we want to be as irenic as possible. But how?
> . . . [T]he bigger picture of the problem is the fissure that runs through mainline Protestantism. Hope's struggle is very similar to the turmoil within the Reformed Church. . . . It will not do to

87. Kennedy, interview with Patterson, 21 October 2002.

88. Kennedy and Simon, notes from interview with John Jacobson, 14 December 2002.

89. Evidence that Patterson saw the Report of the External Review team as a threat is provided by his carefully prepared rebuttal to it, which he intended to present to the Board of Trustees but was blocked by Jacobson. In lieu of presenting his rebuttal, Patterson gave a devotion that put the board on notice of the spiritual danger they would be in if they sided with the "revisionists" — remarks that Patterson later remembered made many board members quite angry; Kennedy, interview with Patterson, 21 October 2002.

preach that we can somehow "rise above" these differences, and peacefully coexist. That is the revisionist's sermon, and a self-serving one at that. Some hard choices must be made. That, we believe, is the difficulty before the trustees and administration of the college.[90]

Patterson was in effect throwing down the gauntlet, challenging the president and trustees to move forcefully against "revisionist" faculty at the college — a point not lost on many Hope professors. In turn, the survey of faculty opinion taken in September 1998 in conjunction with the review indicated "an astonishingly low" rating in particular areas of performance — especially Patterson's ability to "participate in college life" and "establish relationships with others."[91] A substantial minority of faculty strongly supported the Dean of the Chapel, and others were willing to admit strengths to the program. But hostility to Patterson personally and perception of his message as "intolerant," "immature," and "fundamentalistic" set the tone of the survey. Students tended to be much more positive about both Patterson and the chapel program, though their reactions varied somewhat according to religious affiliation, gender, and number of years in college.[92]

In this context, internal and external reviewers inviting public testimony over the chapel program heard strongly emotional responses by students, staff, and faculty either in strident support or rejection of the program. There were those, too, who were more mixed in their assessment, but their comments did not set the tone in a climate where many faculty and students, regardless of their views, felt angry and beleaguered. The reviewers, "moved by the distress that they observed" but also by "the love of Hope College that everyone expressed," did not, according to Jacobson, discount anything that they heard, nor did they pick winners or losers.[93] In the climate of "distress and perplexity" into which their report came, the admonition of the reviewers, the president himself, and the Board of Trustees to seek reconciliation proved

90. "Hope College Chapel Program Self Study," August 1998.

91. Green, Neper, and Sitati, "Evaluating the Hope College Chapel Programs," esp. 78-116.

92. See p. 190 above.

93. Jacobson, remarks on the chapel review, Minutes of the Faculty Meeting, 29 September 1998.

impossible to enact. Jacobson's invitation to faculty to attend special dinners with Patterson in late 1998 in hopes of facilitating such reconciliation were widely panned as completely ineffectual.

Exacerbating these tensions still further was the fact that Jacobson, reaching retirement age, was to step down as president by mid-1999. The two finalists to succeed him seemed to embody the polarization that had come to characterize a large portion of campus life. The first, James Bultman, was president of Northwestern College, a more conservative and evangelical institution than Hope. Bultman, with his doctorate in education, was at once an alumnus of Hope College and a former Hope professor and Dean of the Social Sciences. From West Michigan himself, he possessed strong ties to influential evangelicals in the Midwestern RCA. His rival for the job, James Muyskens, had been raised in the RCA and had attended another of its schools, Central College. A chancellor in the University of Georgia system, Muyskens was a Presbyterian who had been away from the Midwestern RCA for a long time. With longer and deeper ties to Hope, Bultman was clearly on the inside track for Hope's presidency, and Muyskens's equivocation on the existing hiring policy (in contrast to Bultman's strong endorsement of it) reduced whatever chances the chancellor may have had for the job — at least with key members of Hope's board, if not among a majority of the faculty. The emotional debate over the merits of Patterson's ministry intensified partisanship over the candidates and over the older conflict concerning the direction of Hope College. Would the new president consolidate or undermine recent progress of the college toward a deeper Christian commitment? Or, alternately, would the new president advance or retard the growing sectarian and religiously narrow vision of the college? Larger questions about the college's direction, then, reemerged with new urgency and intensity in the waning months of the Jacobson presidency, even after Bultman was declared president-elect.

But the most dramatic episode of Hope's recent religious conflict would not wait for the new president to take office. In the spring of 1999 Patterson launched a new preaching series on sexuality — called "Setting Love in Order" — that would include homosexuality as a topic. The dean himself had never systematically addressed biblical objections to homosexuality from the pulpit, and felt led to do so in part to respond to opposing views that had already gained common currency on campus.[94] Jacobson and other senior staff thought Patterson's course imprudent, given that his critics would regard his choice of topic as a provocation. They did, and many perceived the event as additional strong evidence that Patterson had no real interest in reconciliation, helping to explain why by April 1999, 82 percent of faculty surveyed thought that the "process of reconciliation" between faculty and the Dean of the Chapel had gone poorly or very poorly.[95]

The chapel staff's decision to bring in Mario Bergner to speak in early March 1999 invited particular fury. Bergner's claim that, like himself, homosexuals could be freed from their desires and choose to become heterosexual generated anger at Patterson for using "unscientific" evidence to push his moral agenda. Prominent faculty quickly reacted, helping students to invite gay Christian activist Mel White to speak at Hope within days of Bergner's departure. Gay and lesbian students and sympathizers organized a demonstration outside Dimnent during Bergner's presentation, and the campus was full of animated, and sometimes heated, discussions about the merits of Bergner's and White's presentations.

All this intellectual debate might seem just what any place of higher learning ought to desire. But for many of the protagonists, the

94. Kennedy, interview with Patterson, 21 October 2002. Indeed, in response to a talk by Episcopal bishop the Right Rev. Edward L. Lee Jr. on Hope's campus earlier in the same semester, a 1998 Hope graduate was depicted as asserting that all the speakers he had heard at Hope were "praising homosexuality." Bishop Lee advocated that Christian churches take homosexuality as a "natural given." "I'd like to see an opposing view. I don't see that happening on this issue. I see one viewpoint expounded over and over," the graduate lamented; "Bishop Says Church Must Be Open to Homosexuals," *Holland Sentinel,* 22 January 1999.

95. Memorandum to Board of Trustees, "Faculty Survey on the Process of Reconciliation," April 1999, Personal Archives of Professor Christopher Barney. An independent letter, signed by twenty-three faculty members strongly supportive of Patterson, was submitted to the board as a rebuttal to the survey done by Barney and Simon. It stated, "We have been discouraged by the resentment evident among many of our faculty colleagues, who seem unwilling to extend tolerance toward students and faculty who espouse evangelical Protestant and traditional Catholic views." Letter to Board of Trustees, 3 May 1999, Personal Archives of J. Ben Patterson. It is unclear that that letter added information not already contained in the survey, since the survey itself showed that a minority of faculty members thought that efforts at reconciliation had been successful — though unlike the survey it did attempt to assign blame for the failure of reconciliation.

presence of either White or Bergner was viewed as irrefutable evidence of the other side's ill intentions — and a monstrous portent of what was to come if the other side should prevail.

Anchored or Adrift in the Middle Way?

Our saga has reached the place where we began — the atmosphere that led several dozen Hope College faculty, staff, and administrators to gather and wait in silent openness and expectation — some might say, hoping against hope for better days.[96] But large as the drama surrounding Patterson loomed in the late 1990s, it would be a mistake to end an overview of the Jacobson administration on this note. For despite all the tensions and, at times, notoriety of the 1990s, controversy was not the only thing — or even the main thing — that went on at Hope College during this period. Students were educated, research was pursued, books and articles were written, and Hope College was reflecting on how to improve its understanding and execution of its mission as a liberal arts college in the context of the historic Christian faith.

In the academic arena, a restructuring of the general education requirements was enacted in the mid-1990s after several years of planning and at times acrimonious debate. Though the restructuring was largely motivated by pragmatic concerns, it generated several years of faculty-wide discussion about Hope's educational vision and priorities. The foundational importance of the academic study of religion was reaffirmed as the Religion Department retained its two-course requirement in the turf wars that are a common feature of all curricular reform efforts. The importance of having seniors reflect on how Christianity can inform a philosophy of life was also reaffirmed in Hope's decision to keep its interdisciplinary Senior Seminar program. Among the eight cross-curricular themes in the characteristics of the general education curriculum is integration of faith and learning — its description is given over twice as much space as that of others such as cultural diversity, critical thinking, and oral and written communication.[97]

---

96. See Chapter One, pp. 1-3.
97. *Hope College Catalog*, 2003-2004, 99.

Hope College also undertook to transform the vague, progressive sentiments that had long made it voice a desire to become a more diverse community, ethnically and racially, into effective action. Here was one place that all elements of Hope seemed to pull together in the same direction: Hope's "locale" in the Christian tradition seemed to demand it, as did its "locale" in the broader academy (where such initiatives had become *de rigeur*) and even more insistently, its literal locale in the city of Holland, with its 25 percent Hispanic population. For all these reasons, Hope found the potential of its appearing to be a white enclave in an increasingly multicultural local and national environment an embarrassment — not least to its sense that it had a religious obligation to do better. A Comprehensive Plan to Improve Minority Participation at Hope College was developed and pursued starting in 1998. In addition, the Phelps Scholars Program (a residential and curricular concentration option for students who are interested in exploring cultural diversity) was inaugurated. Faculty joined in the efforts by passing a resolution promising to more rigorously seek minority candidates in faculty searches and by starting faculty-funded minority scholarships.[98] As the vision statement for the Office of Multicultural Life acknowledges, these efforts are motivated by recognition that "all people, regardless of ethnic and/or cultural background, are full participants in God's global society."

In his Inaugural Address in 1997, John Jacobson remarked, "We Reformed Christians do not believe that ours is the only way of being Christian, but we do believe that our tradition and our faith have an important and essential part to play in the ecumenical concert that is the Christian Church."[99] Under his leadership a process for formulating a Vision of Hope statement was begun and was approved by the Board of Trustees in 1997; the most often quoted phrase from the "Vision of Hope" document re-expressed this sentiment: Hope is "a Christian college, ecumenical in character while rooted in the Reformed tradition." Though the earliest drafts of the document made Hope sound more exclusively Reformed,[100] the linkage between

---

98. Minutes of Faculty Meeting, 22 April 1997, JAH.

99. John Jacobson's Presidential Speech, 9 October 1987, 2.

100. An October 1993 draft of the statement read, "Anchored in the tradition of Reformed Christianity. . . ." Draft of Vision Statement, Personal Archives of Janet Andersen.

Hope's Reformed and ecumenical impulses became an important guiding vision for many. In its less constructive uses, the phrase "Reformed and ecumenical" was wielded as a rhetorical weapon against the perceived narrowness of the chapel program. More constructively, this self-conception made it natural for the college to extend an invitation to St. Francis de Sales Catholic Church to use Dimnent Chapel for their masses after a fire destroyed the parish's sanctuary.[101]

As we have seen, perhaps the most pressing question about Hope's religious identity raised by the travails of the 1990s is whether Hope, or any institution, can sustain a "middle way" or instead must choose either a denominational *or* ecumenical *or* evangelical direction. Jacobson tried, in his own subtle way, to signal that Hope could indeed pursue the Middle Way by rotating his choice of Convocation speakers among Catholic, mainline, and evangelical faculty members.[102]

What some might deem another significant attempt at living out the Middle Way (albeit from a left-of-center orientation) arose among Hope students in the late 1990s in the Refuge In Spiritual Expression (RISE) group. As its name implies, RISE was formed in response to a feeling of exclusion on the part of some students. At its core were liberal Christians and those with an amorphous spiritual interest who felt disenfranchised. Yet despite the group's reactive agenda, RISE's leadership responded to Ben Patterson's refusal to see "the pulpit as a roundtable" by going out of their way to create a roundtable that included Patterson and his staff. While their rotating schedule of topics and faculty speakers leaned, both socially and religiously, in a decidedly liberal direction, they repeatedly invited Patterson, along with his chaplains and worship leader, to speak, listening politely and engag-

---

101. Faculty Minutes, 27 January 1998, JAH; see also Jane Bast, "Being Catholic at Hope," *The Anchor,* 12 April 2000, in which ignorance of Catholicism among Hope students was highlighted as a continuing problem.

102. Simon, notes on interview with John Jacobson, 14 December 2002. Jacobson's enactment of his sincerely held belief that Hope should be both Reformed and ecumenical was, as in so many cases, nuanced. His sense that Hope's Reformed tradition should be of paramount importance in Religion Department hires would draw criticism from some in the early 1990s (Minutes of Faculty Meeting, 18 February 1992, JAH), yet his sense that Catholics were full contributors to Hope's mission made him happy, beginning in 1994, to have Catholics as two of his three deans.

ing in civil discussion.[103] However, while the RISE students did better than many Hope faculty in living out a vision of ecumenical exchange that did not shut out evangelicals, RISE could never fully transcend its role as co-belligerent in the campus conflict, and it probably never felt like a refuge to the relatively small number of conservative evangelical students who came from time to time.

In April 1999, Hope College was a house divided. Christian conservatives lived out their faith with the support of the chapel program, while more liberal Christians and others held religious discussions mostly among themselves, under the aegis of sympathetic faculty members, including some in the Religion Department. The silence of Winants Auditorium during the waiting sessions on three April afternoons seemed, for many who came, the only common place that they could be fully present without hostility among those who disagreed. And, of course, considerable numbers of people did not (perhaps could not) seek peace even there — including Ben Patterson, who, though invited repeatedly and much to Donald Cronkite's disappointment, never came. Over the silences and barbed speech of Hope College in 1999 hung a pressing question: Was Hope's Middle Way a grand illusion that had been unmasked or could it, through grappling with the shortcomings revealed by Hope's time of testing, endure?

103. See Katie Paarlberg, "New Group On the R.I.S.E.," *The Anchor,* 28 October 1998.

8 Calling, Creativity, and the Future of Christian Higher Education

- Calling and Creativity
- The Challenges of Genuine Ecumenicity
- "All Excellent Things Are Difficult"
- Identity, Faithfulness, and Enduring Hope

While John Jacobson's holding his "finger in the dike"[1] on the hiring policy continued a course that his predecessor Gordon Van Wylen had begun, there is no doubt that Hope College changed during the Jacobson administration. In fact, inaugurating a high-profile, high-energy chapel program transformed Hope's religious ethos. Admissions Director James Bekkering noted that whereas he worried in the early 1990s whether conservative Christian students would find a place at Hope, by 2001 he worried that a range of other students might struggle to call Hope home.[2] That transformation was more than temporary, despite the fact that by early 2000 Ben Patterson, as he later remembered, "just had the feeling that my work was finished at Hope."[3] Accepting an offer as the chaplain at Westmont College in Santa Barbara, he left Hope late in the fall of 2000, after an emotional farewell service in Dimnent Chapel in which hundreds of his supporters — students, faculty, alumni, and townspeople — offered tearful goodbyes to their spiritual mentor.[4]

---

1. John Jacobson, memorandum to James Kennedy and Caroline Simon, 30 October 2002, 11. As we have seen, some think that Jacobson had his finger even more tightly in the dike than did his predecessor.

2. James Kennedy, interview with James Bekkering, 26 December 2001.

3. Kennedy, interview with Ben Patterson, 21 October 2002.

4. Patterson remembered his last year at Hope (also President James Bultman's first year) as his toughest; as he recalled, "I was miserable. Jim did what he had to do. I

As long as the memory of Patterson remains vivid, Hope will remain divided over whether he was a prophet and pastor for whom it should be grateful or a source of dissension who in the end did the college more harm than good. "You've ruined the college and it will take us years to get back where we were," said one critic to Patterson toward the end of his tenure at Hope. But others looked at the very same changes this critic deplored as signs of hope that the college was — again or finally — taking its Christian mission seriously. As Hope College moves into the third millennium, tensions have lessened — resolved or suppressed — and in many ways the college has reverted to its "centrist" character in the wake of Patterson's departure. Yet the chapel program, now shaped by the two-year interim ministry of the deeply evangelical but more irenic Rev. Dr. Timothy Brown,[5] continued to thrive after Patterson's departure.

Though tensions on campus declined, homosexuality — still — would remain an issue that could excite public passions at the college. Faculty and students continued to discuss in what ways Hope ought — and ought not — be a church-related college. And it was a discussion that often, at least on the part of the faculty, focused on how to stay on the Middle Way. They sensed that Hope was, or had been, different, and they, for the most part, wanted to keep it that way — a school with strong commitments to the Christian faith, and at the same time more open and ecumenical than most other strongly Christian schools. But the way to get there, or to stay there, remained as challenging as ever — a challenge which Hope, or any college so conceived and so dedicated, would be better equipped to face if lessons from its past could be carried into its future.

---

just didn't like it." While the new president differed very little in his theology from Ben Patterson, Bultman (a former coach) had a strong preference for team players — people who would not plunge the college into controversy and conflict. In a variety of ways Bultman made it clear that he expected the Dean of the Chapel to serve the entire campus community. Though Patterson had no objections to being a team player, he chafed under the close administrative scrutiny Bultman gave his day-to-day operations. Bultman was willing to retain Patterson as chaplain — he declined the dean's offer to resign late in 1999 — but only on the president's own terms. Kennedy, interview with Ben Patterson, 21 October 2002.

5. Brown, unlike Patterson, is a Hope and RCA insider. A Hope College alumnus, he had a very successful ministry in a local RCA congregation before becoming a professor of preaching at Western Theological Seminary.

Calling and Creativity

Some of the lessons that Hope College's particular history can teach about the durability of Christian higher education are prosaic commonplaces; others are more distinctively its own. As we have seen, Hope was hardly immune to the impulses that (as George Marsden argues) led many Christian colleges toward secularism: a commitment to "nonsectarian" religion, to an increased specialization and professionalism among its faculty, and to economic pressures. Hope has also evidenced its share of pietism which, if it reduces faith to a matter of emotions or to a handful of "simple truths" (as Burtchaell fears it too often does), inhibits an institution's ability to grapple with the complex challenges facing Christian higher education.[6] Yet in the late twentieth century and into the twenty-first, Hope College continues to attempt to carry out a shared mission — whether described as liberal arts education in the context of the Christian faith, being a Christian college, or being Reformed while ecumenical — all the while remaining of service to its founding denomination. And in doing so, it has continued to be more demonstrably faithful to the Christian faith and the church than the many church-related schools where a Christian presence on campus is but vaguely discernible.

Hope's continuing commitment to its church-relatedness can be partly explained by structural and self-interested factors — factors exemplified or replicable elsewhere. Seats reserved on the Board of Trustees for Reformed church clergy and denominationally appointed lay people provided (and still provide) the RCA an ongoing voice in shaping Hope's mission.[7] And though by the late twentieth century RCA congregants represented a shrinking "market" for Hope's educational services, the absence of the RCA students it does recruit would

---

6. Since we do not equate pietism with simple-mindedness in the way that James Burtchaell does, we are less convinced than he is that pietism *per se* is a threat to the health of a Christian liberal arts college. Hope College has always had a mix of pietistic and more intellectualist Christian resources in its makeup (sometimes embodied in the very same person); here as elsewhere Hope has — sometimes more successfully than others — pulled off a balancing act between disparate elements.

7. Candidates for these slots are proposed by the Trustee Affairs Committee of the board, passed on to the full board for approval as nominees, and forwarded to the General Synod where they receive denominational approval.

still cripple the college financially. This gives Hope College a self-interested stake in maintaining good repute within its founding de-nomination as well as within the other denominations increasingly represented among its students.

But structural and self-interested factors are not the whole story; conviction, gratitude, and loyalty have also strengthened Hope's church-relatedness. After the 1950s, the RCA became less and less able — and willing — to treat its colleges as children who could be kept in line by the threat of a withheld allowance, though individual donors and congregations will, no doubt, continue to attempt this strategy.[8] Historically, as financial and governance linkages between founding de-nominations and colleges weakened, colleges have often moved toward pluralism and secularism. These patterns are depicted to some extent within the small sample of RCA-related colleges, but countervailing ten-dencies are also evident. The three colleges affiliated with the RCA have exercised their freedom from direct denominational oversight in varied ways: Central College (Pella, Iowa) taking a critical-mass, perhaps even pluralist approach; Northwestern (Orange City, Iowa) seeking to remain a comprehensive evangelical/Reformed institution; Hope veering to-ward pluralism in the 1960s but pursuing a critical-mass Reformed/comprehensive ecumenical trajectory through the 1990s.[9]

That Hope College has not by this time become, on the one hand, formerly church-related or unintentionally pluralist or, on the other hand, comprehensively evangelical, stems from any number of histori-cal factors — factors that illuminate the situation of other church-related institutions, both those who find themselves with analogous historical circumstances and those for whom Hope provides an in-structive contrast. Location mattered; Hope probably remains closer to the RCA than does Central College because it has been surrounded by

8. In Chapter Five, we noted that changes in attitudes toward rules governing stu-dent behavior could be illuminated by David A. Hoekema's observation that *in loco pa-rentis* has been replaced with, in some cases, a permissive stance that he dubs *non sum mater tua* ("I'm not your mother") and, in other cases, by replacing requirements with ex-hortation and education, a stance that he calls *in loco avunculi* ("in the place of the un-cle"). See Chapter Five, note 39. Hoekema's categories can be usefully extended to illu-minate the change in the relationship between the RCA and its colleges, which have shifted from *in loco parentis* to *in loco avunculi*.

9. See Chapter One, pp. 17-20, for definitions of these categories.

a much denser network of Reformed churches than is the case in Pella, Iowa. And the college's early history mattered; as the first chapters of this book make clear, if Hope College had not been habituated early in its history to walk a middle course between, as Dimnent put it, Iowa and New Jersey, the college might have gone in either a more pluralist or evangelical direction quite some time ago. And unexpected and unpredictable circumstances mattered in all kinds of ways, too: some think that if Vander Werf's presidency (and hence the hiring policy that he was pursuing) had not come to the early end precipitated by his illness, Hope might have become unintentionally pluralist or even formerly church-related by now.

Similarly, a different relationship between faculty and administration from the 1970s onward might have made for a different history. Conceivably, Hope, for example, might have been able to successfully execute a critical-mass hiring policy without that sending it down the proverbial slippery slope to secularization[10] if dialogue and cooperation between its faculty and administration had been more effective. If a critical-mass approach to hiring is to work anywhere, there must be a high degree of cooperation and trust between administrators and departmental faculty. Those at all levels need to be actively assessing the religious commitments of faculty and taking seriously that Christian commitment, though not decisive in every case, is a weighty positive consideration. Moreover, non-Christians who are hired need to be genuinely happy to be at a Christian critical-mass college and not seeking to make it shed its Christianity as a purported rite of passage into full "maturity."[11] In contrast, at Hope during the Van Wylen and Jacobson administrations there were (indeed, perhaps still are) a significant number of faculty with principled objections to, or deep discomfort with, taking faith commitments into account at all in evaluating candidates. Under these circumstances, upper administrators who cared about the religious identity of the college felt as if they had to be gatekeepers — and as they perceived increases in faculty protest or lack of cooperation, their gatekeeping became concomitantly less flexible.

10. See Chapter One, pp. 4-6, 10-11, 14.

11. As noted in Chapter One (pp. 6-7), Roberts and Turner think that it is a natural and good thing for "knowledge to shed its Christian chrysalis" — that is that colleges and universities become less and less distinctively Christian over time as they "mature."

Hope College's more or less comprehensive ecumenical nature is thus a product of the interplay of self-conscious faithfulness to its Christian calling, creative response to surprising circumstances, and shaping — at times unperceived or unacknowledged — by vicissitudes of its history. Has this interplay resulted in Hope College becoming its "true self," or led it to wander from its institutional vocation?[12] As the 1990s show at Hope, the answer to that question is not likely to be drained of controversy any time soon. Yet, by our lights, the interplay of forces that has produced Hope's particular ecumenical mix has had salutary effects — not the least of which is making Hope distinctive among other sorts of Christian colleges. Yet the path it has trod has exacted considerable personal and institutional costs at crucial junctures.[13] Moreover, Hope's very ecumenicity also presents many challenges. If Hope College perceives its calling to be living out a comprehensively ecumenical Middle Way, then faithfulness will necessitate squarely facing those challenges.

The Challenges of Genuine Ecumenicity

As we have seen, even before World War II, Hope thought of itself as not only Reformed but also both evangelical and ecumenical. During the Vander Werf, Van Wylen, and Jacobson administrations, when "ecumenical" was for the first time defined more widely than "exclusivist Protestant," the college actually became a mix of all three. The result has been that theologically informed conversations, when they go well at the college, are enriched by a wide variety of perspectives within the historic Christian faith — Protestant (including mainline, evangelical,

---

12. Caroline Simon has written in various books and essays about a concept of being faithful to one's individual destiny — becoming a self that conforms to God's intentions. See, for example, "On Seeing What Does Not Yet Appear: Reflections on Love and Imagination," *Faith and Philosophy* 10 (1993): 311-29; and *The Disciplined Heart: Love, Destiny, and Imagination* (Grand Rapids: Eerdmans, 1997). Do institutions, like persons, have destinies or callings to fulfill? Whatever the answer to that question is at the metaphysical level, it is natural for an institution shaped by the Reformed tradition, with that tradition's strong view of divine providence, to think of itself as having a calling that it is obliged to strive to discern and live out.

13. See note 28 below.

Pentecostal, and independent), Roman Catholic, and Eastern Orthodox. Some who advocate a pluralist or at least critical-mass approach to hiring at Hope are concerned that without the breadth provided by significant numbers of non-Christians on the faculty, Hope will be too homogeneous or complacent. Yet, if the late 1990s showed anything about Hope College, it is that there is plenty of room for vivid disagreement about important matters within its comprehensive ecumenical mix. Ben Patterson's impact also served to show how much every Hope constituency cared in some way — or could be challenged to do so — about the religious identity of the college.

Indeed, the 1990s highlight three challenges with which many church-related colleges need to grapple in seeking genuine Christian ecumenicity. The first large challenge is the difficulty of understanding one another. Different Christian traditions have their own insider vocabulary, set of iconic figures, heroes and heroines, and passion-infusing issues. A look back over the course of Hope College's history reveals that protagonists often, unbeknownst to them, were talking at cross-purposes. Ecumenical breadth in a liberal arts setting is a resource if faculty are willing to become theologically poly-lingual, in contrast to being theologically indifferent, as is too often the *modus vivendi* in theologically diverse communities. At Hope that would mean that faculty should learn the salient features not just of Hope's founding Reformed tradition but of the Catholic, Methodist, Baptist, Episcopal, Lutheran, Pentecostal, and other traditions represented at the college. This would take considerable work and effort — more work and effort than has been widely evident at Hope College to this point.

The second large ecumenical challenge is to make sagacious decisions about what, in a polymorphic religious environment, the college as a unified community can say univocally. Again and again in the latter part of the twentieth century, attempts — however mild — to frame a jointly held statement with any theological content at all ran afoul of suspicions about their intended use and intended or unintended abuse. Whether this is a problem or just a condition is itself a matter of internal disagreement, some holding ineffability as one of Hope's defining charms, some fearing that without being more articulate Hope will too easily be held hostage by happenstance and wander from its Middle Way in one direction or the other.

The third challenge presented by ecumenicity is perhaps the

most serious — the one that became not just evident but painful in the late 1990s at Hope, though it had been present for quite some time. When John Jacobson set out to hire someone who could ratchet up Hope College's chapel program, he had hoped, as he remembers, for a "charismatic New Englander" — someone similar to the chaplain he fondly remembered from Hamilton. The search instead produced Ben Patterson — a Californian who identified with the hero in the movie "Braveheart,"[14] and who was, both critics and loyalists must grant, a master at program building. The "isolated villages on a hill" that Ben Patterson found at Hope College in 1994 were clusters of evangelical students who felt marginalized by Hope's ecumenicity. These students perceived — accurately or inaccurately — that conservative Christian opinions and practices were not welcome within Hope's vaunted openness and niceness. When those villages consolidated and filled Hope's chapel, the volume of their newfound voice had the effect of making more liberal Christians among Hope's student body, faculty and staff, as well as Hope's relatively few non-Christian students, feel alienated. The question still hanging over Hope in the new millennium is whether it can create genuine dialogue, understanding, and appreciation across the wide gap between the evangelical and progressive elements it has long seen itself as encompassing.

Unless Hope — and by analogy any church-related college with a mix of religious traditions among its constituents — faces into these challenges, its ecumenism will all too easily become a least-common-denominator affair that renders all theological conversation at the college vapid. In contrast, what is needed in an academic institution is a robust ecumenism in which everyone is willing to speak from their particular Christian perspective, ask for clarification when others' ways of speaking need translation, and work at genuine understanding — which may include informed disagreement. In the process, Hope's community will need to cultivate dialogue among conversation partners, some of whom have largely incompatible definitions of "ecumenical." Some at Hope are shaped by non-denominational evangelicalism, which has abandoned the old confessional dividing lines (on issues, for example, like baptism) but discounts anything that looks "liberal" as sub-Christian, or worse. Others resonate with a lib-

14. Simon, notes from interview with Jacobson, 14 December 2002.

eral religious ecumenism that finds dialogue easier with like-minded people of other faiths (or no faith) than with conservative Christians. All too often, these forms of ecumenism stand with their backs toward each other. Striving to remain in Christian fellowship — and academic colleagueship — with someone who frankly tells you that you are mistaken in thinking yourself a faithful Christian calls for significant forbearance. Yet this is nothing new. Boundary issues have, since the time of Christ, always been among the knottiest ones for Christ's followers. However, as the spiraling vitriol of the disagreements at Hope in the late 1990s illustrates, discussion of such boundary issues will be greatly facilitated if they do not become linked with *institutional* issues of who belongs. This is one reason why clear statements — and frequent reaffirmation — about academic freedom on the part of Hope's Board of Trustees and upper administration are absolutely vital to Hope's future as a Reformed *and* ecumenical liberal arts college.[15] It is also why faculty, no matter what their views, need to be cheerful — or at least philosophical — when the administration grants an analog of academic freedom to Hope's chapel program staff.

We think that Hope College needs to retain (or finally find) a third kind of ecumenism that transcends the polarizing opposition between evangelicals and more liberal Christians and encompasses the range of Christian conviction at Hope. In fact, this is a pressing need not only at ecumenically-oriented church-related colleges but within and between many major Christian denominations.[16] It is no accident that this third form of ecumenism is rarely enacted,[17] for it is

15. Indeed, one part of the explanation for why Hope College has maintained a close filial relationship with the RCA even after structural ties have loosened may be that the denomination did not frequently or heavy-handedly exercise denominational oversight of the college in a way that limited academic freedom. The college was not made to feel that it had to distance itself from its founding denomination in order to escape the kind of rigidity that Richard Hughes notes as a hindrance to Christian colleges becoming "serious colleges and universities of the highest order." See Chapter One, p. 14.

16. See, for example, an insightful pair of articles on why liberals and conservatives need one another and why continuing dialogue between them is so difficult: Barbara G. Wheeler, "Strange Company," and Richard J. Mouw, "Hanging in There," *Christian Century*, 13 January 2004, 18-25.

17. See Robert Benne's account of how difficult Baylor University has found this to be in "Crisis of Identity," *Christian Century*, 27 January 2004, 22-26.

far easier to insist that people ought to forget all their theological convictions for the sake of rapprochement or to assume that the only point of speaking with those who do not hold one's cherished convictions is their potential conversion to one's point of view. Yet Hope's history illustrates that the interplay between liberals and conservatives can be a saving grace. Roberts and Turner spoke of the "chrysalis of Christianity" that universities and colleges need to shed in order to reach maturity as intellectual institutions. As committed Christians, we do not view Christianity itself as a chrysalis. However, Christianity is always and everywhere incarnated in particular human cultures. Human cultures, while exhibiting the splendor conferred by the *imago Dei*, also evidence human fallenness and finitude. The particular cultural accoutrements to Christianity in a given time and place are, from the standpoint of faith, always dispensable and sometimes downright pernicious. While it would probably be too strong to say that rules against only women smoking are pernicious (to take an example from Hope's particular history), the sexism of which such rules were part and parcel was not just innocently silly. The vigorous, sometimes heated, conversations that have been endemic at Hope over the last half-century have helped it shed more than one cultural chrysalis. That certainly has not made Hope's religious ethos the embodiment of some pure form of Christianity that transcends culture; yet some of these changes have been for the better and arguably have made Hope more faithful to its calling.

Identifying when change constitutes progress rather than regress in Christian faithfulness is, of course, a knotty issue with which Christians have lived since the first days of the church. Hope thus needs to be grateful not just to its internal and external progressive critics, who have called it to discard unhelpful cultural baggage, but to conservatives both within and without, who have exhorted it not to "throw out the babe with the bath water." Contrary to what this metaphor implies, there is no easy or foolproof way to tell "babe" from "bath water," but what more suitable place to debate such issues than a Christian liberal arts college? Indeed, if Christian liberal arts colleges can succeed in living out an ecumenism that encompasses evangelicals and liberals, they can provide additional models and resources for the health of the Church at large.

"All Excellent Things Are Difficult"

Hope College serves as a case study for assessing the desirability, challenges, and feasibility of genuine ecumenism. As we have seen, Hope's Reformed *cum* evangelical *cum* ecumenical hybrid has often been a resource for durability, though at many junctures it has looked as if the college's disparate elements could not live out a life together. The question Hope College must face is whether its strands can be braided into a strong, flexible, and mutually correcting whole — whether a life-enhancing balance can be forged and retained among those elements. Hope's history shows that this cannot be done without difficulty and controversy. But as Aristotle famously observed, "All excellent things are difficult." As we have seen, periods in which there was no controversy about Hope College's religious identity have been few indeed. Nor have the quiet periods necessarily been among the college's best, either academically or religiously (though the college's president probably slept better during quiet times). Controversy is not a canker on the soul of an ecumenical college, though complacency, indifference, and rancor are. Controversy all too easily generates rancor, yet a studied attempt to avoid controversy too easily breeds complacency and indifference. As long as those who disagree can respect and value one another (and seek one another's forgiveness when they do not), controversy is safer than attempting its avoidance.

Rancor is one potential danger in Hope College's penchant for self-examination and intramural debate; spending so much time discussing its mission that people neglect to carry it out is another. During the years of Hope's contested past it has been educating men and women, nurturing faith, producing books, articles, works of art, and scientific results. Have its constant conversations about its mission at times prevented it from getting on with its mission? Could it have accomplished more if it had had fewer controversies and taken a "let's just do it" attitude? Though some bemoan the "waste" of time that such discussions entail, it has been through controversy that Hope's mission and vision statements have been held at the forefront of its awareness.

For in contrast to James Burtchaell's evaluations of other colleges, Hope College's and the Reformed Church in America's position papers, covenants, mission statements, reports of Blue Ribbon committees, etc., cannot be dismissed as "bilious prose" that have "be-fogged" its sense of self and served as self-deluding window dressing for a process of secularization. Rather these documents and the conversations that produced them often have been intelligent, balanced, and sincere attempts to bring a diverse constituency together around a shared purpose. While these documents have not all succeeded in their purposes, many of them have not only been taken seriously when they were being produced but have also served as touchstones for later conversations about institutional identity — sometimes after having been "forgotten" for decades. This was nowhere more obvious than in the 1990s, when such statements informed debates among faculty and administrators.

Two important cases in point are the RCA's study documents on homosexuality and the "Covenant of Mutual Responsibilities" between the RCA and its three affiliated colleges. Controversies at Hope College about homosexuality, especially in the 1990s, sent faculty and administrators (whether RCA or not) back to the 1978 "Homosexuality: A Biblical and Theological Appraisal" document. While the empirical research upon which this document was based is obviously outdated, its willingness to face squarely the theological complexities of the issue of homosexuality and homosexual practice makes it a resource for common conversation — not just among those who are in fundamental theological agreement with it but also among those who would wish it took a firmer stand or a more latitudinarian view.

Renewed interest at Hope College in the "Covenant of Mutual Responsibilities" goes back at least to the unfinished working paper produced by the Faculty Recruitment Study Group in 1994. Since then the Covenant has received periodic attention in various discussions of Hope's nature and mission.[18] Moreover, in 2000, changes in college catalog copy incorporated quotations from the Covenant into the "Hope's Reason for Being" and "Philosophy of Education" sections.[19] The intent of these changes — which are still extant in Hope's *Catalog* — was to inform members and prospective members of Hope's community that its church affiliation and Christian context were fully compatible with open inquiry. At the same time, these changes in the

18. See, for example, PIC Minutes, 4 September, 1 and 8 October 1998.
19. Minutes of Administrative Affairs Board, 7 March 2000, JAH.

Catalog have built an additional explicit linkage between Hope and its founding denomination.

In each of these cases, the documents in question were put to a polemical use in debates perceived to be directly relevant to the religious identity of Hope. "Homosexuality: A Biblical and Theological Appraisal" was the basis of the statement issued by the president's office linking Hope's connection with the RCA with the administration's stance that any appearance of endorsing homosexuality must be avoided. While one might say that in that case conversation over that document started from its use by (to speak crudely), those on the theological "right," the "Covenant of Mutual Responsibilities" first came to the fore when cited by those on Hope College's "left." Yet, in both cases, these documents were substantively and rhetorically complex enough to allow for countermoves based on their content by those on the other side of the controversy as well. This allowed discussion of central issues of institutional identity to take place on the basis of some common ground — importantly, a denominationally linked common ground. Irwin Lubbers, when explaining why Hope took the "middle lane," linked this to deep features of its denominational affiliation: "The innate Dutch antipathy to extremism in any form has enabled the church to hold together the most liberal and most conservative elements throughout three centuries of history. Tensions constantly arise but differences are resolved and practical *modus vivendi* achieved."[20] Hope's Middle Way has thus been rooted in lessons learned from its founding denomination — lessons gleaned from observing characteristic habits of interaction within institutional life that in turn produced documents that are resources for carrying out debate that holds relative extremes together. When placed under pressure in the 1990s, both these habits and the documents they produced were resources for continuing — if heated — engagement.

In the new millennium Hope has continued to craft documents that stand in this long tradition. Hope's desire to do better at having frank, non-polarizing, and constructive discussion of the role of scripture in campus morality and of homosexuality led, early in the Bultman administration, to the development and official recognition

20. Lubbers, "Hope College as a Factor in the Assimilation of Netherlanders in American Life," "Addresses, 1953-59," JAH.

of the "Virtues of Public Discourse" statement. This document has not, of course, magically caused all discussions at Hope to rise to its standards. However, its explicit expectations about the nature of discussion have at least made it possible for events like "Homosexuality: Two Christian Views" to generate civil debate in a single packed auditorium[21] — a step in the right direction from 1999, when Bergner's and White's monologues occurred on separate nights amidst demonstrations and acrimony.

Hope's Middle Way is indeed a difficult path, but Hope's past gives some basis for optimism about the college's ability to pursue it. As Hope's trajectories have varied from exclusivist Protestant to pluralist, to critical-mass, to comprehensive ecumenical, it seems always to have been blessed with a significant number of people who cared deeply for Hope, saw Hope differently from one another, and took the time to speak with and listen to those with varying senses of what was best for the college. This is still true.

Yet it is prudent not to be overly sanguine. Hope College could easily lapse back into a too-blithe assumption that its "niceness" will make everyone feel equally welcome — or, alternatively, let its fear of offending keep it from talking through real, important disagreements. Moreover, in the current scramble for resources and students in American higher education Hope could also easily become even more market-driven than it is at present, thus risking selling its spiritual and academic soul to the latest and highest bidder.

Perhaps the greatest danger that Hope's Middle Way faces is widespread internal suspicion of becoming too articulate about its religious identity. As this historical case study has illustrated, concepts and self-conceptions shift over time. Hope's Middle Way has been variously construed as triangulating between Iowa and New Jersey, as being willing to pull out into the passing lane, as being "not-Oberlin-not-Calvin," and most recently, being vibrantly Christian without being prescriptive or parochial. These metaphors and terse formulations can easily turn into clichés — and it is here perhaps that Burtchaell's warning about not having one's self-understanding "befogged" with words

21. Hope's Interim Dean of the Chapel, the Rev. Dr. Timothy Brown, was one presenter; he took a more conservative view than did professor of psychology David G. Myers, who argued for Christian acceptance of monogamous gay and lesbian unions.

needs to be heeded. At some point, Hope College may have to risk saying more rather than less about its religious identity. In doing so, Hope's strain of Reformed-and-always-reforming in its DNA can guard it from a hubristic assumption that it speaks for all future heirs of its mission in doing so. Articulating a more vivid philosophy of education that fits Hope's particular and complex nature — not losing the middle while holding together its most liberal and conservative elements — would be no easy feat. Yet one of our hopes is that venturing our own historical articulation of Hope's religious identity might be a fresh beginning, rather than an end to, conversations on these matters.

Identity, Faithfulness, and Enduring Hope

Yet another of our hopes is that reflection on Hope College's particular history can help inform the broader conversation about church-related higher education. While we do not want to cheapen the richness of the historical narrative we have constructed by drawing simplistic "morals" from it, broad observations about transferable lessons are appropriate. Indeed, two of those lessons have been articulated in the preceding sections: the challenges and benefits of genuine ecumenicity and the resource embodied in well-crafted, theologically-informed statements as a basis of public debate related to institutional mission. Additional lessons concern how shifts in institutional identity affect student life and faculty culture.

While many of the specifics of Hope College's shifts in mission over the course of its history are particular to it, the structural questions raised by these shifts are of general relevance to all church-related colleges and universities. As we saw in Chapter Three, Hope's early educational vision was to shape young men and women into activist Christians who would transform the world through service in the public sphere, through ministry and through missionary endeavors. Perhaps the easiest way to analyze shifts from this vision is in terms of a distinction made by many Christian traditions (including the Reformed) between *special (or particular) grace* and *common grace*. Special grace is a gift from God, conferred on the basis of Christ's saving sacrifice and through the mediation of the Holy Spirit — a gift that transforms those who are alienated from God into those whose eternal happiness will be intimate fellowship with God. Common grace is also a gift from God, conferred out of longsuffering compassion for God's infinitely valuable but broken creation. Common grace ameliorates the effects of sin and the Fall and keeps things from going even more badly than they do. Reformed Christians, and others who recognize this distinction, see all excellence within human accomplishments as having its ultimate source in special and common grace.

Hope's early educational vision can be restated in terms of this distinction. Hope College, at least up to World War II, sought to produce graduates shaped by special grace who would in turn transform the world as agents of both special grace and common grace. Call this, for ease of reference, the Initial Vision. Between the world wars this educational vision began to change. Though for most at the college — at least for a long time — the fundamental motivation for providing an excellent education remained a Christian one, Hope as an institution came to see itself as primarily an agent of common grace. The college now sought to send out Christian and non-Christian graduates who would be agents of common grace; if students encountered and grew in special grace in the course of their time at Hope that was also a welcome outcome. Yet the latter was no longer as central a focus of the educational mission of the college; to a degree that varied over time and from person to person, it became an optional, extracurricular matter.[22] Call this the Subsequent Vision.[23] Notice that both the Initial Vision and the Subsequent Vision are theologically informed and fueled by

22. The dual meaning of "extracurricular" here is intended. For some, the Subsequent Vision kept Christian nurture at the center of Hope's mission, though it was mainly carried on outside the classroom and curriculum; for others, Christian nurture came to be seen as peripheral to the mission — an optional background context.

23. The terms "Initial Vision" and "Subsequent Vision" are designed to be rhetorically neutral, and for this reason they are likely to seem humdrum. These visions are meant to adumbrate very general structures that can be embodied in a variety of ways; they also mark points on a spectrum (see below). In Hope's particular case, the tussle between those who envisioned Hope as a "School of the Prophets" and those who saw it as a Christian liberal arts college engaged Hope at its inception in a debate about what the college's center of gravity should be regarding special grace and common grace. So in Hope's particular case it might be tempting to dub these the Prophetic Vision and the Christian Collegiate Vision. Our choice of less descriptive, more generic, terms helps to illustrate that the particular shifts that have affected Hope have structural analogs with which many Christian colleges must grapple.

Christian motives. The most crucial differences between them are the degree to which special grace is emphasized and the extent to which producing mature agents of special grace (i.e. providing specifically Christian nurture) is seen as everyone's business — not just that of a particular sector of the college.

The shift from the Initial Vision to the Subsequent Vision is subtle; moreover, it is gradual enough that each Hope generation saw itself as engaging in fundamentally the same educational mission as its predecessors. Official denominational blessing was bestowed on the Subsequent Vision by the preamble to the "Covenant of Mutual Responsibilities," which goes out of its way to say that RCA colleges are not churches, and, more specifically, "The colleges as such are not primarily institutions for evangelism or places to prepare men for the ministry."[24] Hope College, of course, never conceived of itself as a church, but under its Initial Vision it did see itself as a community of Christians undertaking an educational project for Christian reasons — an educational project that included evangelism, nurturing students' faith, and producing future ministers and missionaries among its central purposes.

Given our narrative's treatment of the 1980s and 1990s at Hope, it might be natural to wonder whether Hope College has moved toward reclaiming its Initial Vision. Here it is important to emphasize that the Subsequent Vision is a very general structure that can be embodied in a variety of ways, some closer to the Initial Vision than others. If the Initial Vision were one pole on a spectrum, different embodiments of the Subsequent Vision would mark points at relative distances from that pole. A midpoint might be where Hope College appears to have been in the 1950s — a college where most faculty were assumed not only to be Christians but also interested in the spiritual lives of those in their charge, yet a few people whose most evident connection with Christianity was an appreciation of Milton could be tolerated. At the pole most distant from the Initial Vision would be a college or university that still retained self-consciously Christian motivations for pursuing its educational endeavors, and perhaps still retained a college chaplain, but which was otherwise indistinguishable from a secular university. Hope College has indeed

24. Minutes of the Reformed Church General Synod, June 1969, 66.

moved within that spectrum from a point more distant from the Initial Vision in the course of the 1960s — though, it must be emphasized, not even then very far toward the most distant pole — and then to points closer to the Initial Vision in the 1980s and 1990s. However, because at no point since the 1950s has there been a shift back to seeing every student's coming-of-age as a believer as a goal of Hope's academic enterprise, all Hope's institutional ways of being a Christian college in the Van Wylen, Jacobson, and Bultman eras have been instances of the Subsequent Vision.

We are not interested here in adjudicating whether Hope's transformation in educational vision from the Initial Vision to the Subsequent Vision was an advance or a decline, though we think that this is an important conversation for the Hope College community to have. Suffice it to say that it is a fairly predictable shift concomitant with welcoming a more religiously diverse student population within the context of an increasingly professionalized academic world. Many church-related colleges in the course of their history have made transitions from their own analogues of an initial vision to a subsequent vision. Change is not a threat to enduring hope for Christian higher education, but unreflective change has the potential to be. All church-related colleges would benefit from reflecting on their particular histories so that such shifts can be noted and subjected to reflective evaluation, for these shifts are not without implications for either the academic mission or the Christian mission of a college, or for the degree to which those missions coincide. Reflecting on Hope's particular changes can stimulate reflection about shifts that have taken place elsewhere.

Consider first the question: what rules governing student life should be promulgated? Within the Initial Vision, rules governing student life sought to inculcate Christian character by mandating participation in certain Christian practices — for example, daily worship and Sabbath observance — and prohibiting behaviors that were thought to undermine Christian character. Controversies over what the rules should be were framed within the common assumption of this context. For example, does dancing undermine Christian character or not? Within the Subsequent Vision, rules governing student life have a different point: protecting student safety, preventing disruptions of other people's sleep and privacy, or discouraging criminal behavior — sometimes on Christian grounds, sometimes not. Controversies over what the rules should be are now debated in the context of what fosters the kind of civil society in which education can take place,[25] though at Hope there are some anachronistic holdovers, such as rules prohibiting organized athletic competition on Sundays. Shifts in Hope College's rules for student life, then, have occurred against the background of a deeper shift in the rationale for such rules. In the 1960s, arguments for the cessation of mandatory chapel were disputed on a horizon that straddled the Initial and Subsequent Vision — some advancing arguments that participating in worship could not contribute to the shaping of Christian character unless it was voluntary; others arguing that the college, especially given that it had no religious requirements for admissions, had no business trying to turn people into good Christians once enrolled.

One challenge that Hope, and many church-related colleges, are now facing is a dilemma for those who do care about shaping students through Christian practices. Now that chapel and other Christian practices have ceased to be mandatory, they often feel the need to cater to student tastes in order to gain an audience. The large and important question hanging over many campus ministry programs is whether they can "market" themselves to a student population *and* provide the kind of significant exposure to the depth of the Christian tradition that will make progress toward Christian maturity more likely.

In Hope's case, the shift toward the Subsequent Vision also raised the question about one of the most perennial grounds of debate at the college in the last several decades: why would Hope College, or any college, seek to have a comprehensively Christian hiring policy for faculty? There are several ways of answering this question, none of which are mutually exclusive. One sort of answer to this question is an intellectualist one: a college might want all its classes taught from a particular point of view or by people who had a certain knowledge-base related to the Christian tradition. This answer, as we have seen, has seldom — perhaps never — been in ascendancy at Hope. Another

---

25. The faculty debate over the Sexual Harassment Policy in the 1990s is an interesting echo of this structural shift. The role of faculty had become so different from that of the Initial Vision in some people's minds that they could argue that the college could have no appropriate concern over whether they were romantically or sexually involved with their students as long as the relationships were consensual and sexual activities happened off campus.

sort of answer is a communitarian one: a college might want to foster special grace and think that this was much more likely within a certain sort of community — a community led by Christian teacher/scholars who could nurture the faith of students, not primarily or always through overt instruction, but by shaping a certain ethos. This answer seems to have been paramount under Hope's Initial Vision. But does this answer make sense against the background of the Subsequent Vision? Did the shift in Hope's educational vision rob the comprehensive hiring policy of its rationale? Certainly Calvin Vander Werf was not the only person to think so.

But there are other answers to "Why hire only Christian faculty?" For example, consider a different sort of communitarian answer: a college might want to be a certain sort of scholarly community — a community of Christian scholar/teachers. Why? Because it is a valuable and not very common thing to be; moreover, such a community can be a rich setting in which Christians confer, produce scholarship, and carry out the Subsequent Vision. This answer can plausibly be taken to reflect Van Wylen's philosophy of education. Mixed with this philosophy, even in Van Wylen's mind, and seeming more dominant during the Jacobson administration, were pragmatic and strategic answers aimed at keeping Hope from moving so far toward the distant pole of the Subsequent Vision as to be de facto secular in the execution of its mission.

These pragmatic questions can best be addressed against the backdrop of yet another question: what makes a college with the Subsequent Vision different from a secular institution of higher learning? The latter are, after all, from a Christian point of view, vehicles of common grace. Moreover, frequently there are faculty and administrators at such institutions who have Christian motivations for pursuing academic excellence and would rejoice were some of their students to encounter special grace and grow in that grace. It would seem that the difference between a Christian institution with the Subsequent Vision and a secular institution must reside in how central Christian motivations are to the educational enterprise and how many key people care about the spiritual health of their students. The Christian identity of an institution with the Subsequent Vision is thus tied to having a significant number of Christians among its administrators and faculty members. This in itself does not dictate a preference for hiring only Christians over hiring them in critical mass. But institutional realities in American higher education and Hope's specific dynamics make it hard to see how a critical-mass policy would be a stable alternative for maintaining Hope's Christian vision.

In the first place, faculty members, as they will frequently remind administrators, are not just employees of the institution; a college's faculty *is* the college. To the extent that this is not just a noble sentiment left over from the days when European universities were guilds of scholars who banned together and set student fees, it is embodied in the fact that faculty members have significant say in shaping a college's mission and curriculum. Moreover, they either comprise hiring committees or represent a large voice in hiring decisions. Gordon Van Wylen maintained that it is these faculty roles, not primarily their roles as teacher/scholars, that raised pertinent questions about the appropriateness of hiring non-Christian faculty at a Christian institution: "All faculty members have a stake in discussions on the mission of the college. However, how can persons who have no interest in, or simply dismiss the Christian faith as irrelevant, effectively participate in defining the mission of Hope College?"[26]

Non-Christian faculty at Hope College have been fully able to make excellent contributions to its execution of the Subsequent Vision. Moreover, in many cases they have helped the college understand when its ways of speaking about itself have sounded smug and self-righteous.[27] More than that, they have sometimes demonstrated a deep understanding of the Christian mission of the school that put many of their Christian colleagues to shame. But their presence — together with concerns on the part of others not to make them feel

26. Gordon Van Wylen, letter to Kennedy and Simon, 21 February 2002, 2.

27. President Van Wylen made this very point to history professor Bill Cohen in responding to Cohen's suspicion that if Hope headed in a comprehensive ecumenical direction there would be no appropriate role for a Jewish faculty member. Van Wylen, letter to Cohen, 23 November 1986, Personal Archives of Bill Cohen. Cohen, though he naturally gravitated toward making trenchant observations in campus debate, was uncomfortable with Van Wylen's endorsing this role for him while at the same time implying that the hiring issues over which they differed were settled. On later reflection, he came to realize that his discomfort stemmed from a sense that Van Wylen was asking him to become an "assistant Christian." Cohen, conversation with Simon, 16 January 2004.

marginalized — has presented a roadblock to articulating Hope's mission in ways that are theologically explicit enough to make its distinctiveness over against a secular college or university apparent. Hope's Subsequent Vision *does* differ from a secular vision, but Hope has been hard-pressed to say much about what makes it different beyond getting the word "Christian" into self-descriptions somewhere.[28] Having non-Christians on the faculty is, of course, not the only obstacle here — Hope's very ecumenicity makes the issue of what all can say together complex, if not problematic, as does suspicion about potential misuse of such statements. Because of its ecumenical Christian character, the Hope community will continue to find articulating a collective identity and purpose a challenge. A critical-mass approach would likely only further inhibit such discussions — not as a *logical* consequence of a more open policy, but as the *sociological* consequence of well-meaning, open-minded Christians seeking to create a climate as non-offensive as possible for those who believe differently.

And there are other, more practical problems with the critical-mass approach. John Jacobson himself noted two problems with this more inclusive approach. Faculty would be less likely to "strive diligently" to find Christian faculty, and fight with each other over which departments would receive the exceptions. And ultimately the very idea of making religious distinctions at all would come to seem arbi-

---

28. Hope College's particular history illustrates a dilemma facing all colleges that strive to take their Christian identity seriously. As institutions shaped by the Christian tradition, they cannot be indifferent to collateral costs to individuals caused by shifts in institutional vision or the policies that implement them, even when those changes are viewed as necessary to carrying out the college's mission. Many faculty hired at Hope during the Vander Werf era thought that the Subsequent Vision would be enacted at Hope through a critical-mass or pluralist hiring policy. Some of them even thought that the Subsequent Vision was on its way to becoming a Successor Vision that would be almost indiscernible from that of a secular institution. Though the Subsequent Vision did not fundamentally change under Van Wylen and Jacobson, administrative opinions did change about the sort of hiring policy that was needed to carry it out. This resulted in some people whom the institution valued and who were making excellent contributions to the Subsequent Vision feeling marginalized. Yet if sensitivity to such concerns leads to minimalist articulations of Christian identity or policies that put that identity at risk, this is also an untoward result. All church-related colleges will need to come to terms with the costs that their decisions — to change or not to change — exact on those to whom the institutions owe debts of gratitude for their service. Key individuals will need to prayerfully consider how to repair human relations that are bruised by institutional policy.

trary and unjust — that is, many might conclude that non-Christians already serving on campus could only be made fully welcome if the selective hiring policy were scaled back or eliminated altogether.[29] Either the Christian faith of a faculty member is of central importance for the college's educational mission, or it is not. Critical-mass or pluralist church-related institutions are highly vulnerable to hiring policies that, in practice if not in intent, have in fact said that it is not.

Hope College's choice over the last several decades to strive for a comprehensive ecumenical hiring policy has not in the first instance been rooted in a deeply held principle that its mission can only be executed by a faculty consisting exclusively of Christians, let alone Christians with a strong sense of how their faith impinges on their academic work. Rather, it has arisen from a quest for a practical means to maintain an identifiable Christian motivation for its mission. Critical-mass and pluralist hiring policies all too often inhibit the quest for more than minimal consensus regarding articulation of basic mission. Hope's comprehensive ecumenical policy is a natural outgrowth of the college's hard-to-maintain Middle Way and may very well be a necessary means to preserving it.

But policies such as the hiring of Christian faculty form only the necessary conditions for an ecumenically Christian college; alone, they are not sufficient to offer a vision of incisive Christian academic community. That requires above all a vision that seeks, collectively as a school steeped in the Christian faith, to engage students in a deep and broad sense of human vocation.[30] In Hope's case, the continuing dynamism of the chapel program and popularity of the religion offerings, facilitated in part by an unusually strong teaching faculty, are impor-

29. Jacobson, memorandum to Kennedy and Simon, 30 October 2002, 3.

30. In a Christian liberal arts setting, it is possible to seek to help all students, whether or not they identify with the Christian tradition, to discern their human vocation. From a Christian point of view, all human beings, Christian or not, are created in the image of God and as such have unique combinations of valuable potentials that should be cultivated and lived out. For Christians, the love of God must order all our other loves; yet God's creation is filled with good things that God loves and blesses as fitting objects of our love. Throughout the years, many students — whether professing Christians or not — have been helped by Hope College's curriculum and ethos to grow in love for what God loves and discern their vocation in the broad sense of recognizing a life path suitable for utilizing their (from a Christian point of view) God-given abilities in fulfilling ways that serve humanity.

tant parts of fulfilling this mission. Nor is the promise of Hope College restricted to the "religious" sectors of campus — the strikingly universal commitment of Hope faculty to their students, illustrated in the impressive extent and quality of student-faculty research and in the Pew Scholars Program,[31] is another part of the story. The recent implementation of a program for the exploration of vocation at the college is another sign of Hope's continuing commitment to stimulate Christian conviction and service in the world.[32]

Still, enduring hope for a unique vision of Christian education is not a destination at which Hope — or any college — can arrive and rest, but a journey to be undertaken by each of its generations. What Hope's Middle Way will look like far into the twenty-first century — and whether it endures — crucially depends on present endeavors steeped in faithfulness, creativity, and discernment.

31. The purpose of Hope's Pew Society Program (which is connected with the national Pew Younger Scholars Program) is to challenge some of Hope's most academically successful students with a vision of college and especially university teaching careers as avenues to Christian service, and to help these students gain admission to Ph.D. programs at major universities. It pairs each student member with a faculty mentor, provides guidance in the graduate school application process, and stimulates discussion of the relationship of Christianity to scholarship.

32. In 2002, Hope College joined the scores of church-related colleges and universities across America who have benefited from the generosity of the Lilly Foundation by receiving a two-million-dollar Lilly Theological Exploration of Vocation Grant. Hope's grant funds a wide variety of curricular and co-curricular initiatives aimed at helping students consider the place of service to humanity and the possibility of church-related occupations in their future.

APPENDIX I

Chronology of Hope College Presidents

Philip Phelps, Jr.	1866-1878
Charles Scott	1885-1893*
Gerrit J. Kollen	1893-1911
Ame Vennema	1911-1918
Edward D. Dimnent	1918-1931
Wynand Wichers	1931-1945
Irwin J. Lubbers	1945-1963
Calvin A. Vander Werf	1963-1970
Gordon J. Van Wylen	1972-1987†
John H. Jacobson, Jr.	1987-1999
James E. Bultman	1999-

*Scott functioned as provisional president from 1878 to 1885.
†Dr. William Vander Lugt was named chancellor and functioned as interim president from 1970 to 1972.

Biographical Notes on Selected Figures in Hope College's History

Compiled by Dr. Elton Bruins

Bast, Henry. b. Zaltbommel, the Netherlands, May 6, 1906. A.B., Hope College, 1930; B.D., Western Theological Seminary, 1933; D.D., Hope C., 1956. Minister, Reformed Church in America; prof., Hope C., 1939-44; prof., W.T.S., 1956-63; Reformed Church in America radio minister on *Temple Time*, 1952-72. President of the General Synod, R.C.A., 1960-61. d. Grand Rapids, Michigan, March 29, 1983. A prominent pastor, preacher, and professor in the R.C.A.

Blekkink, Evert John. b. Oostburg, Wisconsin, May 26, 1858. A.B., Hope College, 1883; New Brunswick Theological Seminary, 1886; D.D., Hope C., 1909; D.D., Rutgers C., 1920. Minister, Reformed Church in America; prof., Western Theological Seminary, 1913-28; pres., W.T.S., 1923-24. Pres., General Synod, R.C.A., 1918-19. d. Holland, Michigan, July 17, 1948. Author of many articles in the denominational press.

Bultman, James Eldon. b. Fremont, Michigan, October 5, 1941. A.B., Hope College, 1963; M.A., Western Michigan University, 1966; Ed.D., Western Michigan U., 1971. Teacher, Portage Public Schools, 1963-66; assistant principal, Portage Northern High School, Portage, Mich., 1966-68; professor, Hope C., 1968-85; dean, social sciences, Hope C., 1982-85; president, Northwestern College, Orange City, Iowa, 1985-99; president, Hope C., 1999-.

Brown, Timothy L. b. Kalamazoo, Michigan, April 22, 1951. A.B., Hope College, 1973; M.Div, Western Theological Seminary, 1976; D.Min. W.T.S., 1992. Minister, Reformed Church in America; prof., W.T.S., 1995-; interim dean of the chapel, Hope C., 2001-3.

De Jong, Nettie R. b. Greenleaften, Minnesota; graduate of Hope College, 1906. Missionary at Changteh, Hunan Province, China, under the auspices of the American Presbyterian Mission Board, 1919-40.

Demarest, William Henry Steele. b. Hudson, New York, May 12, 1863. A.B., Rutgers College, 1883; A.M., Rutgers C., 1886; New Brunswick Theological Seminary, 1888; D.D., Rutgers C., 1901; LL.D., Columbia University, 1910; LL.D., Union College, 1911; LL.D., University of Pittsburgh, 1912; D.D., New York University, 1916; LL.D., Rutgers University, 1942. Minister, Reformed Church in America; prof., N.B.T.S., 1901-6; pres., Rutgers C., 1906-24; pres., N.B.T.S., 1925-35; pres., General Synod, R.C.A., 1909. d. New Brunswick, New Jersey, June 23, 1956. He gave many years of distinguished service in the pastorate and educational institutions of the R.C.A.

Diekema, Gerrit John. b. Holland, Michigan, March 29, 1859. A.B., Hope College, 1881; LL.B., University of Michigan, 1883; LL.D., Hope C., 1913. State of Michigan representative, 1885-91; member, board of trustees, Hope C., 1893-1930; mayor, City of Holland, 1895-96; chairman, Republican State Committee, 1900-1910; United States Representative, Fifth Michigan District, 1907-11; U.S. minister plenipotentiary to the Netherlands, 1929-30. d. the Hague, the Netherlands, December 20, 1930. A popular public speaker and a well-known Republican Party leader in the state, he was also known as "Holland's Leading Citizen." President Herbert Hoover rewarded his services to the Republican Party by appointing him a minister to the Netherlands, the equivalency of an ambassadorship.

Dimnent, Edward Daniel. b. Chicago, Illinois, August 14, 1876. A.B., Hope College, 1896; Western Theological Seminary; A.M., Hope C., 1899; L.H.D., Hope C., 1919; LL.D., Central C., 1919; Litt.D., Rutgers C., 1919. Prof., Hope C., 1898-1946; pres., Hope C., 1918-31. d. Holland, Mich., July 4, 1959. The building of the Memorial Chapel, dedicated in

1929, was a major accomplishment of his presidency. The chapel was re-named in his honor in 1959.

Dosker, Henry Elias. b. Bunschoten, the Netherlands, February 5, 1855. A.B., Hope College, 1876; New Brunswick Theological Seminary, 1877-78; McCormick Theological Seminary, 1878-79; D.D., Rutgers College, 1894; LL.D., Central University, Kentucky, 1905. Minister in the Reformed Church in America; lector, Western Theological Seminary, 1884-88; pastor, Third Reformed Church, Holland, Mich., 1889-94; prof., W.T.S., 1894-1903; prof., Louisville Theological Seminary, Louisville, Kentucky, 1903-26. d. Louisville, Kentucky, December 23, 1926. Author of the first published biography of Dr. Albertus C. Van Raalte, founder of Holland, Mich., 1893, and author of many articles in the church press.

Granberg-Michaelson, Wesley. b. Chicago, Illinois, June 14, 1945. A.B., Hope College, 1967; Princeton Theological Seminary, 1967-68; M.Div., Western Theological Seminary, 1984. Congressional aide to Sen. Mark Hatfield, 1967-76; managing editor of *Sojourner Magazine*, 1976-80; pres., New Creation Institute, Missoula, Montana, 1984-88; director, Church & Society, World Council of Churches, 1988-94; general secretary, Reformed Church in America, 1994-.

Hillegonds, William C. b. Chicago, Illinois, February 11, 1922. A.B., Hope College, 1949; B.D., Western Theological Seminary, 1951. Minister, Reformed Church in America; pastor, Hope Church, Holland, Mich., 1960-65; chaplain, Hope C., 1965-78; pastor, Second Reformed Church, Pella, Iowa, 1978-80; pastor, First Presbyterian Church, Ann Arbor, Mich., 1980-90. His work as chaplain at Hope College guided the student body's response to the Vietnam War crisis.

Hollenbach, John William. b. Allentown, Pennsylvania, February 10, 1913. A.B., Muhlenberg College, 1934; M.A., Columbia University, 1935; Ph.D., University of Wisconsin, 1941. Asst. prof., Northeastern Missouri State Teachers College, 1941-45; prof., Hope College, 1945-78; academic dean, Hope C., 1946-67. He was instrumental in the curriculum revision at Hope College in the 1960s. After his retirement from Hope, he established the Hope Academy for Senior Professionals, 1988. d. Holland, Mich., April 19, 1998.

Jacobson, John H. b. Evanston, Illinois, November 6, 1933. A.B., Swarthmore College, 1954; M.A., Yale University, 1956; Ph.D., Yale U., 1957; Litt.D., Hope College, 1987; L.H.D., State University of New York, 1996. Prof., Hamilton College, New York, 1957-63; prof. and administrator, Eckerd College, St. Petersburg, Florida, 1963-72; dean, vice pres., and provost, Empire State College, State University of New York, 1972-87; pres., Hope C., 1987-99. In addition to overseeing the restructuring of Hope's chapel program, Jacobson dramatically increased the college's endowment in the prosperous 1990s, enabling the expansion of the college's physical plant and increasing the number of endowed chairs for faculty as well as scholarships for students. Under his leadership the college's traditional emphasis on student research was encouraged both in the sciences, with the appointment of James Gentile as dean, and, with the establishment of the Frost Center for Social Science Research, within the social sciences.

Kollen, Gerrit John. b. Notter, the Netherlands, August 9, 1843. A.B., Hope College, 1868; A.M., Hope C., 1871; LL.D., Rutgers College, 1894. Teacher, Overisel, Michigan, district school, 1868-71; instr., Holland Academy, 1871-78; prof., Hope C., 1878-93; pres., Hope C., 1893-1911. d. Holland, Mich., September 5, 1915. He was instrumental in strengthening the academic program of Hope College and in adding many new buildings to the campus during his administration.

Kuizenga, John E. b. Muskegon, Michigan, December 20, 1876. A.B., Hope College, 1899; Western Theological Seminary, 1904; A.M., University of Michigan, 1915; D.D., Hope C., 1916. Minister, Reformed Church in America; instructor, Northwestern Classical Academy, Orange City, Iowa, 1900-1903; pastor, Graafschap Reformed Church (now Central Park Reformed Church), Holland, Mich., 1904-6; prof., Hope C., 1906-15; prof., W.T.S., 1915-30; pres., W.T.S., 1924-30; prof., Princeton Theological Seminary, 1930-47. d. Holland, Mich., July 8, 1949.

Lubbers, Irwin Jacob. b. Cedar Grove, Wisconsin, November 15, 1895. A.B., Hope College, 1917; M.A., Columbia University, 1927; Ph.D., Northwestern University, 1931; Litt.D., Hope C., 1945; LL.D., Central C., 1945 ; Litt.D., Rutgers C., 1945. Instr., Voorhees C., India, 1919-22; instr., Hope C., 1923-24; prof., Hope C., 1924-28; instr., Northwestern

U., 1929-30; prof. and assistant to the pres., Carroll C., 1930-34; pres., Central College, Pella, Iowa, 1934-45; pres., Hope C., 1945-63. d. Grand Rapids, Mich., September 3, 1985. Hope College expanded rapidly in the number of students enrolled and in the number of new buildings constructed during his presidency.

Mast, Samuel Ottmar. b. Washtenaw County, Michigan, October 5, 1871. A.B., University of Michigan, 1899; Ph.D., Harvard University, 1906; Sc.D., U. of Mich., 1941. Instr., Hope College, 1899; prof., Hope College, 1902-8. d. February 3, 1947. He was influential in setting the standard for science education during his tenure at Hope College.

Mott, John Raleigh. b. Livingston Manor, New York, 1865. Ph.B., Cornell University, 1888. Founder and chair, Student Volunteer Movement, 1888-1920, and the World's Student Christian Federation, 1895-1920; convened the Edinburgh Missionary Conference, 1910; director of student and foreign work departments, Y.M.C.A., and general secretary, 1915-28; chair, International Missionary Council, 1921-41; a founder of the World Council of Churches, 1948. He received the Nobel Peace Prize in 1946. d. 1955. He was a world leader in the ecumenical movement.

Muilenberg, James. b. Orange City, Iowa, June 1, 1896. A.B., Hope College, 1920; M.A., University of Nebraska, 1923; Ph.D., Yale U., 1926; L.H.D., U. of Maine, 1936; D.D., Hope C., 1955. Instr., U. of Nebraska, 1920-23; prof., Mount Holyoke C., 1926-32; dean, College of Arts and Sciences, U. of Maine, 1932-36; prof., Pacific School of Religion, 1936-45; prof., Union Theological Seminary, New York City, 1945-63; visiting prof., Hope C., 1967. d. Claremont, Calif., May 10, 1974. An Old Testament scholar, he was also known for his skill in classroom teaching at Union Seminary. He was one of the translators of the Old Testament for the Revised Standard Version of the Bible, published in 1952. Ordained Congregational Church minister.

Mulder, Arnold. b. Holland, Michigan, November 12, 1885. A.B., Hope College, 1907; Litt.D., Hope C., 1947. Local newspaper publisher, Holland, Mich.; prof., Kalamazoo College, 1929-53. d. Kalamazoo, Mich., March 27, 1959. Published *Americans From Holland*, 1947, as well as several novels in which he lampooned his Dutch heritage. His brand of Christianity emphasized the Social Gospel.

Mulder, John Mark. b. Chicago, Illinois, March 20, 1946. A.B., Hope College, 1967; M.Div., Princeton Theological Seminary, 1970; Ph.D., Princeton University, 1974; L.H.D., Centre College, 1984; D.D., Rhodes College, 1984; L.H.D., Bellarmine University, 1990; D.Th., Institut de Protestant Theologie, Montpellier, France, 1996; D.D., Hanover College, 1996. Prof., Princeton T. S., 1974-81; editorial assistant and associate editor, *Theology Today*, 1969-81; pres., Louisville T. S., 1981-2002.

Muste, Abraham John. b. Zierikzee, the Netherlands, January 8, 1885. A.B., Hope College, 1905; New Brunswick Theological Seminary, 1909; M.A., Hope C., 1909; B.D., Union T. S., New York, 1913. Minister in the Reformed Church in America; pastor of the Fort Washington Collegiate Church, Manhattan, New York City, 1900-14; pastor, Central Congregational Church, Newton, Mass., 1914-18; director, Presbyterian Labor Temple, N.Y.C., 1937-40; director, Fellowship of Reconciliation, 1940-53. d. New York City, February 11, 1967. A strong advocate for peace, he visited Hanoi during the Vietnam War. His ideological and spiritual pilgrimage went from his conservative Dutch Reformed roots to Liberalism, then to Communism, and back to deep Christian spirituality. He is regarded as one of the most famous and influential graduates of Hope College and is memorialized by the annual Muste lecture at his alma mater.

Patterson, J. Ben. b. Los Angeles, California, December 22, 1942. A.B., LaVerne University, 1966; M.Div., American Baptist Theological Seminary, 1972. Minister in the United Presbyterian USA and the Reformed Church in America; chaplain, Hope College, 1993-2000. During his tenure as chaplain at Hope College, the chaplain's staff was enlarged and the program changed significantly.

Phelps, Philip Jr. b. Albany, New York, July 12, 1826. A.B., Union College, 1844; New Brunswick Theological Seminary, 1849; D.D., New York University, 1864; LL.D., Hope College, 1894. Minister, Reformed Church in America; pastor, Elmsford Reformed Church, 1850-51, and First Reformed Church, Hastings-on-Hudson, N.Y., 1850-59; principal,

Holland Academy, Holland, Mich., 1859-66; first pres., Hope College, 1866-78; pres., General Synod, R.C.A., 1864. d. Albany, N.Y., September 4, 1896. His dedication to the cause of Christian higher education led him to begin teaching college courses in 1862. He obtained the incorporation of the college in 1866 when the first college class graduated and when he became the first president. He, with Van Raalte, founded the program of theological education at Hope in 1866, ultimately leading to the founding of Western Theological Seminary.

Pieters, Albertus. b. Alto, Wisconsin, February 5, 1869. A.B., Hope College, 1887; M.A., Hope C., 1890; Western Theological Seminary, 1891; D.D., Hope C., 1924. Minister, Reformed Church in America; missionary to Japan, 1891-1923; prof., Hope C., 1923-26; prof., W.T.S., 1926-39; pres., General Synod, R.C.A., 1920. d. Holland, Mich., December 24, 1955. A revered teacher and scholar, he was a champion of the Reformed faith. He was also the leading opponent of Fundamentalism in the R.C.A. during the 1930s while affirming the historic Reformed position on the interpretation of the Bible. His articles in the church press and many books and pamphlets had a wide circulation in the denomination.

Prins, Jacob. b. Fulton, Illinois, November 21, 1898. A.B., Hope College, 1924; Th.M., Western Theological Seminary, 1927; D.D., Hope C., 1943. Minister, Reformed Church in America; minister of evangelism, R.C.A., 1945-59; director of church relations, Hope C., seven months, 1945; pres., General Synod, R.C.A., 1943-44. d. Holland, Mich., January 6, 1975.

Romeyn, James. b. Greenbush, New York, 1797, A.B., Columbia College, 1816; New Brunswick Theological Seminary, 1819; S.T.D., Columbia C., 1838. Minister, Reformed Church in America; pres., General Synod, R.C.A., 1841. d. September 7, 1859. He was a prime proponent in getting the denomination to extend the church in the Midwest during the 1840s.

Scott, Charles. b. Little Britain, New York, December 18, 1822. A.B., Rutgers College, 1844; New Brunswick Theological Seminary, 1851; D.D., New York University, 1875. Minister, Reformed Church in America; prof., Hope College, 1866-92; vice-pres., Hope College, 1878-81;

provisional pres., 1878-85; pres., 1885-92; pres., General Synod, 1875. Scott guided the college through the difficult years following the resignation of Pres. Phelps. He put the college on a solid financial footing. He obtained the funding for the building of Graves Hall and Winants Chapel that was constructed in 1893-94. He and fellow faculty members disagreed strongly with Pres. Phelps at the time Phelps wished to develop Hope College into a university.

Van Heest, Gerard John. b. Amsterdam, the Netherlands, April 9, 1929. A.B., Hope College, 1949; M.Div., Western Theological Seminary, 1952. Minister in three Reformed Church in America congregations in New York State, 1952-79; chaplain at Hope C., 1979-94.

Van Raalte, Albertus Christiaan. b. Wanneperveen, the Netherlands, October 17, 1811. Leiden University, 1834; D.D., Rutgers College, 1858; D.D., New York University, 1858. Pastor of the Genemuiden and Mastenbroek Separatist Reformed congregations, the Netherlands, 1836-38; Ommen Separatist Ref. Ch., 1838-44; Arnhem Separatist Ref. Ch., 1844-46; First Reformed Church, Holland, Mich., 1847-67; d. Holland, Mich., November 7, 1876. In addition to being the founder of the Holland Colony in Western Michigan, 1847, he founded the Pioneer School in 1851 that became the Holland Academy in 1857 and later under the leadership of Philip Phelps, Jr., became Hope College in 1866.

Van Wylen, Gordon John. b. Grant, Michigan, February 6, 1920. A.B., Calvin College, 1942; B.S.E., University of Michigan, 1942; M.S., U. of Mich., 1947; Sc.D., Massachusetts Institute of Technology, 1952; Litt.D., Hope College, 1972; L.H.D., Meiji Gakuin University, 1987. Prof., Pennsylvania State U., 1946-48; prof., School of Engineering, U. of Mich., 1951-72; dean, School of Engineering, U. of Mich., 1965-72; pres., Hope C., 1972-1987. He authored a widely accepted textbook in the field of thermodynamics and was a skilled academic administrator.

Vander Werf, Calvin Anthony. b. Friesland, Wisconsin, January 2, 1917. A.B., Hope College, 1937; Ph.D., Ohio State University, 1941. Prof., U. of Kansas, 1941-63; pres., Hope C., 1963-70. d. Alachua, Florida, July 18, 1988. An author of chemistry textbooks, he was also a prominent researcher, consultant, and lecturer.

Vennema, Ame. b. Holland, Michigan, May 25, 1857. A.B., Hope College, 1879; New Brunswick Theological Seminary, 1882; D.D., Hope College, 1904; D.D., Rutgers College, 1916. Minister, Reformed Church in America; pres., Hope C., 1911-18; pres., General Synod, R.C.A., 1907. d. Passaic, New Jersey, April 26, 1925. He guided the college through the difficult years of World War I. During his tenure, the 50th anniversary of the college was celebrated. He gave leadership to the recognition of intercollegiate sports.

Wichers, Willard Chester. b. Zeeland, Michigan, March 20, 1909. A.B., Hope College, 1932. L.H.D., Hope C., 1979. Director of the Netherlands Information Service, Holland, Michigan, 1942-74; co-founder of the Netherlands [Holland] Museum, 1937; director, 1937-86; member and secretary of the Hope C. Board of Trustees, 1949-82; member and chair, Michigan Historical Commission, 1950-90. d. Holland, Mich., May 19, 1991. Not only was he a prominent civic leader and active in state and local history organizations, he was also well known in the Netherlands for his wide knowledge of Dutch-American communities.

Wichers, Wynand. b. Zeeland, Michigan, February 15, 1886. A.B., Hope College, 1909; M.A., University of Michigan; LL.D., Hope C., 1931; L.H.D., Central College, 1931; Litt.D., Rutgers University, 1931. Instr., Hope Preparatory School, 1909-13; prof., Hope C., 1913-25; cashier, First National Bank, Holland, Mich., 1925-31; pres., Hope C., 1931-45; vice pres., Western Michigan U., 1945-56. He was the first layperson to be elected president of the General Synod of the Reformed Church in America, 1937; cofounder of the Netherlands [Holland] Museum, 1937; author of the centennial history of Hope C., *A Century of Hope.* d. Kalamazoo, Mich., March 28, 1971.

Yntema, Hessel. b. Holland, Michigan, 1891. A.B., Hope College, 1912; M.A., Hope C., 1915; Ph.D., University of Michigan; J.D., Harvard U., 1921. Instr., U. of Michigan, 1917-20; prof., Columbia U., 1921-28; prof., Johns Hopkins U., 1928-33; prof., U. of Michigan, 1933-66. Rhodes Scholar, 1914. d. Ann Arbor, Mich., February 21, 1966. Son of Douwe B. Yntema, prof., Hope C., 1893-1916; brother of Dwight, prof., Hope C., 1946-67. He specialized in international law.

Selected Bibliography

Benne, Robert. *Quality with Soul: How Six Premier Colleges and Universities Keep Faith with Their Religious Traditions.* Grand Rapids: Eerdmans, 2001.

Burtchaell, James Tunstead. *The Dying of the Light: The Disengagement of Colleges and Universities from Their Christian Churches.* Grand Rapids: Eerdmans, 1998.

De Jong, Arthur J. *Reclaiming and Mission: New Directions for Church-Related Colleges.* Grand Rapids: Eerdmans, 1990.

Hoekema, David A. *Campus Rules and Moral Community: In Place of In Loco Parentis.* Lanham, Md.: Rowman & Littlefield, 1994.

Holmes, Arthur F. *The Idea of a Christian College.* Grand Rapids: Eerdmans, 1975, 1987.

Hughes, Richard T., and William B. Adrian, eds. *Models for Christian Higher Education.* Grand Rapids: Eerdmans, 1997.

Kilgore, W. J. "Report of the Special Committee on Academic Freedom in Church-Related Colleges and Universities." *AAUP Bulletin,* Winter 1967, 369.

Luidens, Donald A. "Between Myth and Hard Data: A Denomination Struggles with Its Identity." In *Beyond Establishment: Denominational Cultures in Transition.* Louisville: Westminster John Knox, 1989, pp. 248-69.

Marsden, George M. "The Soul of the American University." In *The Secularization of the Academy.* New York: Oxford, 1992, pp. 9-45.

Marsden, George. *The Soul of the American University: From Protestant Establishment to Established Nonbelief.* New York: Oxford University Press, 1994.

McCormick, Richard P. *Rutgers: A Bicentennial History.* New Brunswick, N.J.: Rutgers University Press, 1966.

Ramm, Bernard. *The Christian College in the Twentieth Century.* Grand Rapids: Eerdmans, 1963.

Roberts, Jon H., and James Turner. *The Sacred and the Secular University.* Princeton, N.J.: Princeton University Press, 2000.

Ryskamp, Henry J. "The Dutch in Western Michigan." Ph.D. dissertation, University of Michigan, 1930.

Simon, Caroline J., et al. *Mentoring for Mission: Nurturing New Faculty at Church-Related Colleges.* Grand Rapids: Eerdmans, 2003.

Sloan, Douglas. *Faith and Knowledge: Mainline Protestantism and American Higher Education.* Louisville: Westminster John Knox Press, 1994.

Smith, Page. *Killing the Spirit: Higher Education in America.* New York: Viking, 1990.

Stegenga, Preston J. *Anchor of Hope: The History of an American Denominational Institution, Hope College.* Grand Rapids: Eerdmans, 1954.

Van Wylen, Gordon J. *Vision for a Christian College.* Ed. by Henry Boonstra. Grand Rapids: Eerdmans, 1988.

Wichers, Wynand. *A Century of Hope: 1866-1966.* Grand Rapids: Eerdmans, 1968.

Index of Topics

Index of Names